THE POPULIST
TEMPTATION

THE
POPULIST
TEMPTATION

Economic Grievance and Political
Reaction in the Modern Era

BARRY EICHENGREEN

OXFORD
UNIVERSITY PRESS

OXFORD
UNIVERSITY PRESS

Oxford University Press is a department of the University of Oxford.
It furthers the University's objective of excellence in research, scholarship,
and education by publishing worldwide. Oxford is a registered trade mark of
Oxford University Press in the UK and certain other countries.

Published in the United States of America by Oxford University Press
198 Madison Avenue, New York, NY 10016, United States of America

© Oxford University Press 2018

First issued as an Oxford University Press paperback, 2020

Names: Eichengreen, Barry J., author.
Title: The populist temptation : economic grievance and political reaction in
the modern era / Barry Eichengreen.
Description: New York, NY : Oxford University Press, 2018. |
Includes bibliographical references and index.
Identifiers: LCCN 2017054216 | ISBN 9780190866280 (hardback) |
ISBN 9780190866297 (updf) | ISBN 9780190866303 (epub) |
ISBN 9780190058821 (paperback)
Subjects: LCSH: Populism—History. | Populism—Economic aspects. | Welfare
state. | BISAC: POLITICAL SCIENCE / General. | POLITICAL SCIENCE /
Political Process / General. | POLITICAL SCIENCE / Political Process /
Political Parties.
Classification: LCC JC423 .E348 2018 | DDC 320.56/62—dc23
LC record available at https://lccn.loc.gov/2017054216

1 3 5 7 9 8 6 4 2
Printed by Sheridan in the United States of America

TABLE OF CONTENTS

LIST OF FIGURES

———◆◆———

PREFACE

Populism is a new phenomenon but also a very old one. This is most visibly true in the United States, where what is referred to as the Populist Revolt occurred in the nineteenth century. But it is also true of Europe, where charismatic leaders with anti-establishment, authoritarian, and nationalist tendencies, from Benito Mussolini to Ioannis Metaxas, captured the popular imagination, or at least the levers of power, in the 1920s and 1930s. Whether these specific individuals should be identified as populist is debatable. Charisma, for one thing, is in the eye of the beholder (as Max Weber reminded us).[1] More fundamentally there is the question of whether populism as a concept is well defined. But to the extent that there is something afoot in the United States, the United Kingdom, and Europe that involves the reaction of voters against the political establishment, nationalist and racialist sentiment directed against foreigners and minorities, and a yearning for forceful, charismatic leadership, this something, whatever we call it, is not new.

By looking back at the history of the United States and Europe I hope to identify the economic, social, and political circumstances under which populism takes hold and the policies that most effectively combat it. I seek to determine why radical political movements with anti-elite, authoritarian, and nativist tendencies succeed at some times but not others. I hope to understand why in some cases the center held, while in others political extremists carried the day.

Historical comparisons are powerful but perilous. A focus on extreme cases lends itself to exaggeration, and parallels can be overdrawn. Today is not the 1930s. By acknowledging differences and considering instances where a populist reaction was contained as well as those where populist leaders and movements usurped power, I hope to avoid the worst pitfalls.

The answers matter. The characteristic economic policies of populist leaders are damaging and destructive, and the impact of populists on political institutions is corrosive. The attitudes they animate bring out the worst in their followers. Populism arrays the people against the intelligentsia, natives against foreigners, and dominant ethnic, religious, and racial groups against minorities. It is divisive by nature. It can be dangerously conducive to bellicose nationalism.

The history recounted here suggests that populism is activated by the combination of economic insecurity, threats to national identity, and an unresponsive political system, but that it can be quelled by economic and political reforms that address the concerns of the disaffected. A first step is for policymakers to do what they can to reinvigorate economic growth, giving young people hope that their lives will be as good as those of their parents and older people a sense that their lifetime of labor is respected and rewarded. Populist revolts rarely arise in good economic times, in other words.

Equally important is that the fruits of that growth be widely shared and that individuals displaced by technological progress and international competition are assured that they have social support and assistance on which to fall back. Assuring them starts with acknowledging that there are losers as well as winners from market competition, globalization, and technical change, something that economists are taught at an early age but which they have a peculiar tendency to forget. It continues with acknowledging that economic misfortune is not always the fault of the unfortunate. It concludes by putting in place programs that compensate the displaced and by providing education, training, and social services to help individuals adjust to new circumstances. This is not a novel formula. But if its elements are commonplace, they are no less important for that.

Commonplace, however, is not the same as straightforward. Modern societies show disturbingly little capacity to respond in this way. They struggle to develop a political consensus around the desirability of implementing and, no less important, adequately financing programs that compensate the displaced and help them adjust to new circumstances. In turn this points to a second source of populist disaffection, namely, the dysfunctionality of the political system. Here the relevant institutions include the electoral system, the legislature, the civil service, and the courts, but also civil society and the Fourth Estate. Their structure shapes the responsiveness of government, which is the ultimate measure of whether the citizenry has a voice. Political institutions are also a key ingredient of political stability and hence of the capacity of society to pursue policies making for growth and an equitable distribution of its fruits. Suitably designed, they give voters and candidates for office an incentive to move to the political middle. They help cultivate a social and political consensus for prevailing policies, which in turn makes for stability, economic and political both. But those institutions can also provoke dissatisfaction and incite a political reaction when they fail to deliver the goods.

The problem is that political institutions are not malleable. By design, they are hard to alter, precisely in order to prevent the players from changing the rules in the middle of the game. The institutional inheritance will therefore reflect the imperatives of the past. For instance, the peculiar history of the United States, notably the historical division between free and slave states, bequeathed an Electoral College and a bicameral legislature whose upper chamber gives disproportionate voice to rural interests, accentuating the rural-urban divide that figured prominently in Donald Trump's election in 2016. By delegating to state legislatures the power to draw congressional district lines, this legacy has encouraged the creation of safe districts whose occupants have little incentive to move to the middle. A history of institutionalized racism—institutionalized by political means—has bequeathed a legacy that continues to limit trust, complicating efforts to agree on the provision of public goods. This inheritance is one reason the United States has a less elaborate social insurance state than other advanced economies, rendering it particularly susceptible to a backlash from individuals displaced by changes in technology and globalization.

Reform of these institutions, while easy to imagine, is hard to accomplish. Hard, though, is not the same as impossible. In the early twentieth century, the Populist Revolt was quieted by political reforms, including the direct election of senators and referendum processes that allowed voters to bypass captured and corrupt state legislatures. More recently, states have sought to address gerrymandering by delegating the drawing of congressional district lines to independent commissions. But given the country's history and, consequently, its current political configuration, more fundamental reforms, such as of the Electoral College, are beyond the pale.

If the challenge facing the United States stems from America's distinctive national identity, then the challenge for Europe is the absence of a European identity. The European Union (EU) was Europe's response to three wars in less than a century. It was most visibly an economic project, a framework for fostering stability and growth that, by preventing economic disasters like those of the 1930s, would remove the basis for an anti-establishment, authoritarian, nationalist revolt. But at a deeper level it was a political project, since it was necessary to provide for the accountability of those making decisions for the continent as a whole. Creating a single market, the argument went, would highlight the need for shared oversight and governance of that common European space. A true single market would require an anti-trust (or competition) authority to prevent the abuse of monopoly power. It would require an anti-subsidy (or anti-state-aid) authority to prevent favoritism of national champions and ensure a level playing field. Carrying out those tasks would require the creation of European institutions. And through the creation of European institutions and the day-to-day process of shared governance, deeper integration and, ultimately, a common European identity would emerge.

But that European identity, in practice, has been slow to develop, national identities being deeply rooted. In its absence there has been a hesitancy to cede significant prerogatives to European institutions. There has been reluctance to delegate meaningful powers to the European Parliament, the body of EU-wide elected representatives. Key decisions are taken in intergovernmental negotiations by European heads of state, meeting as the European Council or Eurogroup, in a process that highlights differences between countries instead of moderating them.

Accentuating those differences makes it hard for EU members to agree on policies that foster growth with equity, giving populist politicians an economic platform on which to stand. And where there has been a willingness in practice to delegate powers to entities like the European Commission, the EU's proto–executive branch, its members are perceived, not unreasonably, as unaccountable technocrats, given the absence of a European polity to hold the bureaucrats in question fully accountable for their actions.

One can imagine modifying these political arrangements—for example, strengthening the powers of the European Parliament and directly electing the president of the Commission. But even if the history of the EU is shorter than the history of the United States, the institutional inheritance again stands in the way. Not just are the EU's institutions a product of the continent's peculiar history, but they are embedded in a set of international treaties whose modification requires unanimous consent, something that is even less likely than getting three-quarters of U.S. states to agree on a constitutional amendment changing the Electoral College. And the absence of those reforms, whose proponents struggle to overcome the shadow of history, renders the EU a prime populist target.

The present book, which elaborates these themes, is prompted by the rise of European populism, by the victory of Leave in the UK referendum on EU membership, and by the election of Donald Trump. But many of the ideas it elaborates arose already in my earlier writing. In *Golden Fetters: The Gold Standard and the Great Depression* (1992), I described the policy choices that led to economic and social breakdown in the 1930s and traced their roots to political institutions that gave rise to unstable governments, perverse and inconsistent policies, and political reaction. A subsequent book, *The European Economy Since 1945: Coordinated Capitalism and Beyond* (2007), was an attempt to describe the historical origins of the European Union, the nature and limits of European identity, and the rise and fall of the mixed economy. My recent book, *Hall of Mirrors: The Great Depression, the Great Recession, and the Uses—and Misuses—of History* (2015), was an effort to show how politics sets the stage for financial crises, how those crises fuel political extremism, and how history shapes the response for better and worse.

But this book differs from that earlier work in that the questions are more fundamentally political, although the answers remain heavily economic. Those answers are also fundamentally historical. Viewing developments in a historical light directs an author's attention not just to deep economic and political structures but also to historical contingency— to chance events, personalities, and human agency. I am conscious that a historical perspective also conduces to a kind of fatalism: to the sense that inherited political arrangements, social structures, and economic institutions render some countries more susceptible to populist reactions and leave them less scope for mounting a constructive response. As someone who likes to think of himself as reasonably optimistic, I do my best to resist that kind of fatalism, concluding this volume with some ideas for how the United States and Europe should respond to the populist threat.

Thanks go to Joshua Lustig, who commissioned for *Current History*, the journal that he edits, an essay on the history of populism in the United States. That essay provided the spark for the rest of the book. I acknowledge the permission of *Current History* to reprint material from that earlier piece. Along the way, I have received helpful comments and learned much from collaborators and friends (many of whom are of course one and the same), among them Tam Bayoumi, Seth Ditchik, Christian Dustmann, Michael Haines, Matthew Jaremski, David Leblang, Ashoka Mody, André Sapir, Guido Tabellini, and Gylfi Zeoga. I thank Gianni Toniolo and Nicholas Dimsdale for help with country-specific information. Asha Sekhar Bharadwaj assisted with data and graphics. My editor, David McBride, and two anonymous referees for Oxford University Press provided invaluable comments. Andrew Wylie made placing the book as painless as possible. Alison Rice-Swiss helped with preparing the index and, more generally, kept my office and life running smoothly. Seminar audiences provided spirited feedback, notably at the American Academy in Berlin, the University of California at Davis, the Belgian Consulate in Washington, D.C., and the European Central Bank. I am grateful to them all.

This book is dedicated, once more, to Michelle, for all her love and support.

THE POPULIST
TEMPTATION

I

The Populist Archetype

EFFORTS TO DEFINE populism remind one of Justice Potter Stewart's definition of pornography: "I know it when I see it." The awkward fact is that there is no agreed definition. Populism is a multidimensional phenomenon, with multiple perspectives on each dimension. "To each his own definition... according to the academic axe he grinds," wrote the political economist Peter Wiles half a century ago.[1]

Here I define populism as a political movement with anti-elite, authoritarian, and nativist tendencies. Since populist movements combine these tendencies in different ways, there are different variants of the phenomenon. In particular, there are populist movements of the Left, which emphasize the anti-elite element, and of the Right, which emphasize hostility toward foreigners and minorities.[2]

At the most basic level, populists divide society into the elites and the people.[3] The elites control government, business, and banking, reproducing themselves through favored access to education, the executive suite, and higher echelons of the public sector. Superficial differences notwithstanding, they form a united front. There is little difference, for example, in the backgrounds and interests of the families and networks controlling the major political parties. It follows that there is little difference, in the populist conception, in the policies they espouse. Populists invoke these notions to advance the idea that mainstream politics is an elite conspiracy that produces results inimical to the interests of the people. "Politicians prospered but the jobs left and the factories closed. The establishment protected itself, but not the citizens of our country. Their victories have not been your victories. Their triumphs have not been your triumphs," was how President Donald Trump put it in his inaugural address.

The people may lack the education of the elite, but they possess a basic common sense, passed down through collective traditions, religion, and community, to which populist politicians can appeal. "Virtue resides in the simple people, who are the overwhelming majority, and in their collective traditions," to again quote Peter Wiles.[4] Populist politics is then the process by which the general will, informed by this common sense, is translated into policy.

But who, exactly, constitute the people is easier said in theory than in practice. In nineteenth-century America, members of the agrarian movement, comprising midwestern wheat farmers and southern cotton growers, faced the dilemma of whether to ally with disaffected factory workers, and vice versa.[5] In Donald Trump's America, the candidate sought to broaden his base by appealing not just to blue-collar workers left behind by technological change and globalization but also to a middle class concerned about the decline of traditional American values.

One way of resolving these ambiguities is by defining the people in opposition to the other. In nineteenth-century America, the other was identified as financiers, railroad barons, and industrialists who gained great wealth by exploiting honest, hardworking farm and factory workers. The unity and homogeneity of the people were further defined by the exclusion of visible minorities like indentured Chinese labor and so-called new immigrants from southern and eastern Europe. This same definition by opposition is prevalent in other populist movements. The hostility of populist politicians to not just concentrated economic power but also immigrants and racial and religious minorities thus is intrinsic to the movement.

Viewing society this way breeds an instinctual antagonism to technocrats and governmental agencies. Technocrats are members of the elite, by definition.[6] They use privileged information and preferential access to achieve their objectives. Agencies of government staffed by technocrats, by virtue of their statutory independence and the complexity of their procedures, are remote from the people. Populist politicians regularly impugn the integrity of central bankers, those most technocratic of technocrats, and question the independence of their institution. The Federal Reserve System, together with its early American progenitor, the Bank of the United States, has been a favorite target of politicians with populist leanings, from Andrew Jackson in the nineteenth century to Huey Long in the twentieth and Donald Trump in the twenty-first. In the run-up to the 2016 referendum on whether the United Kingdom should leave the European Union, UK Independence Party leaders like Nigel Farage similarly appealed to voters by criticizing the integrity and competence of EU technocrats and demanding that decision-making power be restored to the British people.

Populism thus favors direct over representative democracy insofar as elites are disproportionately influential in the selection of representatives. It favors referenda over delegating power to office holders who can't be counted on to respect the will of the people. The pioneering referendum processes adopted in Oregon, California, and other western states at the turn of the twentieth century, in which citizens could petition to place questions on the ballot and pass them by simple majority vote, were part of a populist revolt against corruption and a political establishment dominated by large corporations and other powerful interests. The Oregon referendum and initiative movement championed by William Simon U'Ren, for example, was immediately informed by these concerns. Referendum U'Ren, as he was known, mobilized the Farmers' Alliance and trade unions, the two principal sources of support for the Populist Party, of which he was Oregon state secretary, in support of the referendum law adopted in 1902 as a way of making an end run around what he and his followers saw as corrupt politicians, unresponsive elites, and self-aggrandizing railroad monopolies—classic populist tropes all.[7] This value imputed to the will of the people is also a way of understanding why Donald Trump attached such importance to the idea that he would have won the popular vote for the presidency in 2016 but for "pervasive and widespread" voter fraud.[8]

In the case of the Brexit referendum, supporters of Leave defended the outcome on analogous grounds: the result reflected the will of the people.[9] The Brexit campaign was visibly tinged by anti-elite, anti-expert rhetoric, with supporters seeking to discredit the view of professional economists and others that leaving the EU would have significant costs.[10] As

Michael Gove, justice secretary in the soon-to-be-former Cameron government and leading supporter of Leave, put it in a television debate, "People have had enough of experts."[11]

Populism is also a political style. Candidates portray themselves as no-nonsense leaders prepared to knock sense into establishment figures unwilling to address society's urgent needs, an intention they communicate using harsh, unconventional words and tactics. Disregarding the niceties of political convention is a way of demonstrating independence and force of personality. Political incorrectness and off-color language are ways of signaling seriousness of purpose and speaking directly to the people. In the extreme, forcefulness is conveyed by the assertive dismissal of inconvenient facts and a menacing undercurrent of violence.[12]

Populist politicians regularly rely on new technologies to circumvent channels of communication controlled by mainstream parties and convey their views directly to their followers. As Michael Conniff wrote of Latin American populism two decades ago, "Skillful use of…new media [is] an important attribute of…populists."[13] In Latin America in the 1920s and the United States in the 1930s, radio played an important role in disseminating populist views, bypassing the establishment press.[14] Decades earlier, in his 1896 campaign for the U.S. presidency, William Jennings Bryan, the candidate of the Democratic and Populist Parties, made unprecedented use of the railway, a revolutionary transportation and communications technology if there ever was one, delivering more than six hundred speeches directly to the people. Bryan raised few funds, made little use of pamphlets and other conventional political media, and leaned only lightly on the Democratic National Committee for campaign support. There was no little irony in Bryan's reliance on the railway, since he consistently criticized it as exemplifying corporate abuse of monopoly power. But no matter. Bryan's campaign similarly made unprecedented use of the telegraph to schedule and publicize his appearances. His "Cross of Gold" speech at the 1896 Democratic National Convention made such a splash partly because the telegraph was used to transmit his message nationally, rather than relying on reports by newspaper correspondents and their publishers, many of whom were hostile to his candidacy.[15]

Bryan's strategy was in contrast to that of William McKinley, the candidate of the Republican Party establishment, who remained firmly planted on his front porch. McKinley drew—successfully, in the event—on the ample financial and organizational resources of the National Republican Party and its chairman, "Dollar" Mark Hanna. The mainstream Republican newspapers were also firmly in McKinley's camp. For an outsider like Bryan, competing with a generously financed establishment candidate, new technology was the only option. If McKinley triumphed in the end, Bryan's approach exemplified populist tactics.

Later, in the mid-twentieth century, populists in Latin America and elsewhere used small planes to bring their message directly to the people, again circumventing established media channels. The twenty-first-century variant is of course Donald Trump's use of Twitter for bypassing traditional print media and communicating directly with voters. (In his reliance on Twitter, Trump was unwittingly following the precedent of another exemplar of the populist temperament, Venezuela's Hugo Chávez.) Meanwhile, cable television channels, satellite radio talk shows, and alt-right Internet websites undermined control by the political mainstream and party establishment of news flow and political narrative. Resort to these new technologies and outlets enabled Trump, like his populist predecessors, to disintermediate the establishment media and disable its interpretative influence.

A further dimension of populism is its characteristic economic policies. Rudiger Dornbusch and Sebastian Edwards, drawing on Latin American experience, define populism as an approach to economics that emphasizes distribution while deemphasizing the risks to economic stability from sharp increases in government spending, inflationary finance, and government interventions overriding the operation of the market.[16] While mainstream politicians have also been known to run on platforms promising faster growth with greater equity, populists differ in the ambition of their claims. They are distinctive in the directness with which they speak to popular concerns about growth and distribution, their denial of constraints, and their disregard of expert opinion about limits. Populist politicians dismiss objections that ambitious policies intended to spur growth will only fan inflation, create worries about indebtedness, and aggravate balance-of-payments deficits. They deny the existence of trade-offs between restricting immigration and redistributing income toward their working-class supporters, on the one hand, and doubling the rate of economic growth, on the other. The existence of such constraints, as they see it, is falsely promoted by forces hostile to their economic and political agenda.

But pro-growth is not the same as pro-market. Populists, whether of the Left or the Right, are more than willing to see government intervene in markets in order to advance their policy agenda and personal position. This helps to explain the association of populist rule with favoritism toward companies and individuals allied with the regime and its charismatic leader.

Here comparisons of the populist tradition in Latin America and President Trump speak for themselves. In both cases one sees the ambitious goal of significantly boosting economic growth. One sees a similar denial of constraints. If the feasibility of that goal is questioned, then in both cases the doubters are technocrats and entrenched members of the political establishment hostile to the leader and his followers. If its achievement is frustrated, then in both cases the villain is outside forces, the International Monetary Fund in one case and unfair competition from China and Mexico in the other. One sees similar readiness to forswear economic purity and intervene in markets, something that has been common to Latin American governments of the populist Left (Dilma Rousseff in Brazil) and Right (Cristina Fernández de Kirchner in Argentina) and equally in Trump's use of the leverage attached to his office to criticize manufacturers moving jobs abroad and renegotiate the price of government-purchased aircraft.

Against this background, my goal in this volume is to understand the wellsprings of populist movements. Specifically, I seek to identify the economic and political circumstances under which populism takes hold, and the economic and political responses that most effectively combat it.

I do so by enlisting the history of populist and proto-populist movements and parties in the nineteenth and twentieth centuries. My focus is on populism in the advanced Western democracies, although no discussion of the question can be entirely uninfluenced by the large literature on Latin American populism. But whereas Latin American populism is of long standing, the upsurge of populist sentiment in the advanced countries, evident in the election of Donald Trump, the Brexit referendum, and support for populist parties across Europe, is more recent.[17] It is this phenomenon in the advanced countries that motivates what follows. For that reason I concentrate on the United States and Europe, starting with the Populist Revolt in the United States at the end of the nineteenth century, arguably the first populist movement of the modern era, before moving on to its twentieth-century successors.

I exclude another case sometimes cited as a pioneering populist movement: the Narodniks, who sought to organize a revolt of Russian farmers in the 1870s and 1880s. Google Translate, which, conveniently for present purposes, utilizes crowdsourcing, translates *narod* as "people" and *narodniki* as "populists," echoing the contemporary presumption that this abortive agrarian revolt had elements in common with its American counterpart.[18] But Narodnik leaders were in fact urban intellectuals without roots in the countryside. They rejected religion, which is dear to the people, and embraced modern science, of which populists are skeptical because it empowers technocrats and legitimizes experts. I therefore see the Narodniks as a fundamentally different phenomenon.[19]

More generally, there is the challenge of whom to classify as populist. Disagreement about the definition of populism means, inevitably, that there is disagreement about any such classification. Even the definition here, of populism as a political movement with anti-elite, authoritarian, and nativist tendencies, implies uncertainty about specific cases, since politicians may display some of these tendencies but not others. Whether William Jennings Bryan is properly viewed as a populist is disputed, for example, since Bryan, while positioning himself as anti-elite, did not prominently exhibit the authoritarian and nativist tendencies of classic populism.[20]

As the above should make clear, not every political figure described in these pages is necessarily a populist. In some cases my concern is to understand why members of the political establishment responded effectively to popular grievances, preventing a more violent anti-establishment reaction. Franklin Delano Roosevelt is an example of such a figure. FDR and his political allies responded to popular discontent with economic and financial reforms visibly intended to get the economy moving again. He advanced unemployment insurance and Social Security to address popular concerns with economic insecurity. But FDR was nothing if not a member of the elite. He was the son of a wealthy country gentleman, graduated from Groton and Harvard, and had been the Democratic nominee for vice president in 1920 on a ticket with the media mogul and governor of Ohio, James Cox. FDR was neither authoritarian nor nativist.[21] But because he addressed popular concerns with economic hardship and insecurity, sometimes using harsh anti-business rhetoric, there is a tendency to think of him as a populist.[22] Nothing could be less accurate. Whether Donald Trump is a populist politician or simply a pro-business president is similarly open to question.[23]

Nor are populist and anti-system movements necessarily the same. Anti-system movements and leaders seek to subvert the operation of prevailing political institutions. They are opposed to pluralist democracy and the territorial unity of the state.[24] Examples include Nazi, fascist, authoritarian, and Communist parties seeking to replace pluralist democracy with an authoritarian regime where power is concentrated in the hands of an entity or group not directly accountable to the people. Other examples include secessionist and irredentist parties that seek to replace the existing political system with one in which a subset of the people, defined by region, religion, or ethnicity, is represented separately or exclusively.

Conceived this way, populism is not anti-system. Populist politicians and their followers can work through prevailing political institutions to advance the interests of the people as they define them. They can voice their support for the courts, their regard for permanent civil servants, and their respect for freedom of the press. Like William Jennings Bryan, they can attempt to harness existing parties and processes to advance their political agenda. As Charles Postel wrote of Bryan and his followers, most "sought economic and political reform, not the overthrow of the existing systems."[25]

But while nothing prevents populists from working through the political system, populism in practice can be conducive to anti-system tendencies. Because populism as a social theory defines the people as unitary and their interests as homogeneous, populists are temperamentally impatient with the deliberations of pluralistic democracy, insofar as this gives voice to diverse viewpoints and seeks to balance the interests of different groups. Since the people are defined in opposition to racial, religious, and ethnic minorities, populists are intolerant of representative institutions that protect minority rights.[26] To the extent that populism as a political style emphasizes forceful leadership, it comes with a natural inclination toward autocratic, even authoritarian rule. And the longer popular grievances are allowed to fester, the more willing are followers to embrace leaders with this inclination.

Thus, even when there is no intent on the part of members of a populist movement to subvert the prevailing pluralistic system, there may be a tendency for its leaders to do so by weakening or circumventing checks on executive power. Seeing political institutions as captured and irredeemably corrupt, they will seek to advance the interests of their followers by weakening the system. Even when they take office through legitimate means, as a result of electoral support or by being asked to form a government, they may advance legislation or issue emergency decrees that abrogate the operation of representative institutions, as in the cases of Benito Mussolini in Italy or, more recently, Nicolás Maduro in Venezuela. They may use force and violence, or at least fail to reject them, while curtailing the rights of minorities and denying the legitimacy of rival politicians and governments.[27] When I describe in Chapter 6 how in Weimar Germany the popular reaction against economic instability and a succession of ineffectual governments set the stage for the rise of the Nazis, this is not because I see National Socialism as populist, but rather because I wish to show how populist grievances, if left unaddressed, can descend into something worse.

In explaining why populist movements gain traction in some cases but not others, an obvious starting point is economic factors. Poor economic performance, which manifests itself in slow or no growth, feeds dissatisfaction with the status quo. It fosters support for populist alternatives when that poor performance occurs on the watch of mainstream parties. Rising inequality augments the ranks of those left behind, fanning dissatisfaction with economic management. Declining social mobility and an absence of alternatives reinforce the sense of hopelessness and exclusion. Rapid economic change heightens insecurity—the sense that even if there is no lack of opportunity now, there will be a lack of opportunity in the future—when the political establishment fails to buffer the effects.[28]

Such economic grievances are not equally likely, however, to give rise to populist reactions in all circumstances. Rather, economic hardship, exclusion, and insecurity are most likely to do so when they result from, or at least are closely associated with, developments that highlight the divergent interests of the people and the elite. Banking and financial crises are an example, combining as they do the classic ingredients of a populist reaction. Not only are the financiers and plutocrats who are the precipitating agents of such crises indisputably members of the elite, but they are seen as profiting at the expense of taxpayers—that is to say, at the expense of the people. Hence financial crises and bailouts regularly induce political swings to the extremes and popular reactions against the political establishment.[29] The banking crises of the 1930s had this effect, as have banking crises in other times, including our own.

Populist politicians, moreover, are best able to capitalize on these economic circumstances in polarized, low-trust societies where unfavorable conditions are readily attributed to outside forces, either elites or immigrants and foreigners—the antipodes with reference to which the people are defined.[30] In such circumstances, populist leaders can more easily capitalize on anti-immigrant, anti-foreigner, and anti-elite sentiment to drain mainstream parties of popular support.

Non-economists will object that populism is about more than economics—it is also about identity. "It's no longer the economy, stupid: our identity politics are polarizing us" is how Fareed Zakaria put it in describing the Trump phenomenon.[31] Populism is about the challenge to the majority from immigrants and racial, religious, and ethnic minorities. It is a protest against the declining influence of the traditions, beliefs, and community of the once-dominant group. It is a reaction against the challenge posed by immigrants and minorities to the people as a homogeneous, well-defined entity. Populists seeking to capitalize on these feelings appeal to a glorious, mythologized past grounded in the collective traditions of that once-dominant majority. They invoke nationalism as intrinsic to that vision and criticize mainstream politicians who embrace diversity, open borders, and equal rights as out of touch with the people.

Those emphasizing identity politics have a point. But identity politics is most powerful against an unfavorable economic backdrop. Once-dominant groups can blame their economic plight on immigrants, foreigners, and minorities, and populists seeking to make hay from their economic dissatisfaction can play up those identity politics. In this way economic grievances and identity politics feed on each other.

The question ultimately is why the populist alternative is marginalized at some times but not others. It is why some campaigns, like Donald Trump's, succeed, while others, like William Jennings Bryan's, fail to loosen the grip of mainstream politicians on power. In answering this question, it is again tempting to start with economic factors. In the same way deteriorating economic conditions breed support for populist movements, improving conditions limit that support. Bryan campaigned against the gold standard, an arrangement dear to the political establishment, painting it as an engine of deflation injurious to the people. But by the time he rose to national prominence in 1896, deflation had given way to inflation. This change may have been fortuitous, or it may have been intrinsic to the operation of the monetary system. The discoveries of gold in the Klondike and Western Australia that ended the deflation of the 1870s and 1880s can be interpreted either way.[32] But whatever the interpretation, the end of deflation meant lower borrowing costs for farmers, more investment, and faster employment growth, which together took the wind out of the Populists' sails.[33]

Similarly, when Huey Long broke with Franklin Delano Roosevelt in 1934, preparing to launch a left-wing populist campaign for the presidency, the U.S. economy, after suffering through four years of depression, was firmly on the road to recovery. The low point was in March and April 1933, coincident with FDR's bank holiday and just preceding his decision to take the United States off the gold standard. In 1934, the first full year of recovery, U.S. GDP jumped by an impressive 10.9 percent. Unemployment was still painfully high, and the worst Dust Bowl year, 1935, was yet to come. But there was no question that the economy was improving dramatically, 10.9 percent growth being nothing if not dramatic. Whether this improvement was due to better policies or because even dead cats bounce is beside the point. The economic upturn is reason to think that the incipient populist movement of the 1930s would have failed to prevent the reelection of a sitting president even had its charismatic leader, Long, not fallen to an assassin's bullet in 1935.

Admittedly, Donald Trump's success rests uneasily against this backdrop. By the time of his election in 2016, the U.S. economy had been expanding for seven straight years. Real GDP was 15 percent higher than at the apex of the 2008 financial crisis. One can object that Barack Obama's achievement in raising GDP by 15 percent in seven years was less impressive than FDR's feat of raising it by 11 percent in one. It can be argued that income gains under FDR were more widely shared. Average per capita weekly earnings in manufacturing, deflated by the cost of living, rose by 4 percent between 1933 and 1934, while employment in manufacturing rose by 14 percent.[34] In 2016, in contrast, there was much discussion of how real hourly earnings had stagnated or even fallen for workers at all wage levels, not just since the financial crisis but for decades. There was anger over how economic gains accrued exclusively to those at the top of the income distribution. In 2015, real median household income as measured by the U.S. Census Bureau was still nearly 2 percent below its 2007 peak and nearly 3 percent below its level at the end of the twentieth century.

This is a reminder that the economic argument about the success or failure of populist insurgencies is as much an argument about distribution as about aggregates. It is less about past economic performance than it is about expectations of the future and the response—or lack thereof—of the political establishment. In the late nineteenth and early twentieth centuries, mainstream politicians and parties responded to the complaints of the Populists with railroad regulation, interest rate regulation, and, eventually, a federal income tax and monetary reforms culminating in the Federal Reserve Act, a crowning achievement that William Jennings Bryan, no less, described as "a triumph for the people."[35] All this gave disaffected voters grounds for hoping that the future would be better than the past. In the 1930s, Roosevelt and the Congress responded to popular discontent and working-class insecurity with legislation creating unemployment insurance and Social Security, as noted above. It wasn't called the Social *Security* Act for nothing, in other words.

The gridlock between President Obama and the Republicans in Congress in the wake of the 2008 financial crisis was not conducive to this kind of activist response. As a result, recovery from the crisis was underwhelming, regulatory reform more limited.[36] The ultimate irony is that the principal measures addressing economic insecurity under Obama, the Affordable Care Act and the Dodd-Frank Wall Street Reform and Consumer Protection Act—the first of which was designed to address insecurity about health care access, the second intended to address the risk of future financial crises—were vigorously attacked by candidate Trump, an attack for which he was generously rewarded in November 2016.

Trump's attacks and the electorate's response point to a fundamental contradiction between the economics and politics of populism, most visible in the case of the United States but also seen more generally. Economic progress creates risks. This includes progress resulting from globalization and technical change. Progress that entails creative destruction poses the risk that some industries and individuals will be left behind. Such displaced people rely on government to provide them with social insurance, since they are poorly placed on their own to insure themselves against these contingencies.[37] Displaced workers lacking the resources to invest in new skills similarly rely on government to provide them with vocational training and adjustment assistance.

But the United States has long invested less in such programs than other advanced countries, while at the same time doing less to limit creative destruction. The result is an obvious tension. Populist hostility to the agencies and functions of government, rather than helping resolve this tension, militates against the public provision of social insurance and adjustment assistance. The identity politics aspect of populism makes it still harder for government to provide these public goods. Communities riven by ethnic divisions spend less on collective goods because each cash-strapped group resists paying taxes to finance programs that also benefit others.[38] This is specifically the case in communities where immigration is an issue and in countries with a history of racial and ethnic division, such as the United States.[39] Populist movements and politicians, for their part, only serve to further accentuate these inter-group differences.

Ironically, then, the populist turn in twenty-first-century American politics, by highlighting these divisions, moved the country further away from the kind of constructive policy responses to the problem of economic insecurity whose absence gave rise to that populist tendency in the first place. This leaves us with the troubling question of where disaffected voters, seeing no solution to their problems, will turn next in search of one.

2

American Panorama

ECONOMIC INEQUALITY AND exclusion dominated electoral politics in 2016 and no doubt will do so again in the not too distant future. The context and country may change, from the Brexit referendum in the United Kingdom and Donald Trump's presidential campaign in the United States, to support for Geert Wilders's anti-immigrant Party for Freedom in the March 2017 Dutch elections, and Marine Le Pen of the far-right National Front making it to the second round of France's 2017 presidential election. But the taproot of support for these anti-system, anti-globalization, anti-immigrant movements and parties is in each case fundamentally the same.

The common denominator is the sense on the part of a growing segment of society of having been left behind. People see their wages stagnating and their jobs growing less secure. Rising inequality suggests that this is not just an economic problem, in that GDP and productivity are growing less rapidly, but also a political problem, insofar as those income gains as occur accrue mainly to the wealthy. Whether technology, trade, or immigration is to blame is uncertain. Hence the tendency to blame all three and to vent one's anger by voting against establishment politicians and parties.

Relatedly, there is the feeling that society and the government through which its members translate their preferences into policy have lost control of these processes. They have lost control of the nation's borders, allowing immigration to run wild. They have lost the ability to guarantee national and personal security, where fear of terrorism merges in popular and political discourse with fear of immigration. They have lost the capacity to create good manufacturing jobs, permitting China to capture them by striking unfair trade deals and manipulating its currency.

Finally there is the feeling that those in charge have allowed the erosion of the collective institutions through which earlier economic and social challenges were met. The decline in trade union membership, which in the United States dates from President Ronald Reagan's efforts to break the air traffic controllers union, weakened an institution through which workers were able to advance their case for security of employment and a fair share of corporate earnings. Deregulation, espoused by politicians receiving campaign contributions from large corporations, allowed pharmaceutical firms, health insurers, and hospital chains to charge their customers what they wished. Local communities that have grown more heterogeneous, whether because of immigration or other reasons, have lost their collective solidarity. They therefore provide less support, both financial and psychological, to their disadvantaged members. All this leaves voters with a helpless sense that their fate is being decided not by their local communities and governments but by forces, some anonymous and others all too identifiable, beyond their borders and beyond their control.

This new populism bears more than a passing resemblance to the old populism of the nineteenth century. The Populist Revolt in nineteenth-century America was a complex phenomenon motivated by a range of economic grievances and social concerns.[1] Much Populist rhetoric singled out rapacious moneylenders and monopolistic railways for exploiting hardworking midwestern farmers powerless in the face of high interest rates and ruinous shipping costs. But there were also others, including the Greenbackers—farmers and miners who focused on the monetary system as the source of their problems and who advocated replacing the gold standard with a paper currency system designed to deliver higher prices. If there was a common factor uniting these disparate groups, it was commercialization, which created a heightened sense of insecurity by exposing farmers and others to market forces beyond their control.[2] Produce sold locally was now priced globally, subjecting farmers to international market forces of which they lacked understanding, much less an ability to cope. A farmer's income from raising wheat in Nebraska now depended on yields in the barley fields of Ukraine. The price of Sea Island cotton was affected by rainfall in the

Nile Basin. Although the telegraph, like the Internet recently, helped farmers obtain more up-to-date information about prices and yields in these far-flung places, that information didn't help them do much about the consequences. Interest rates and freight charges may have played only a subsidiary role in the farmers' difficulties, but it was still easier to blame the railway and the bank, which had a physical presence, than invisible Egyptian cotton and Ukrainian grain growers. And it was easier to blame a government seemingly unable to do anything about these problems.

The Populist Revolt involved more than just agrarian unrest, as famously depicted by C. Frank Baum in *The Wizard of Oz*.[3] The Scarecrow, embodying the beleaguered farmer, had as his steadfast companion the Tin Woodman, the factory worker struggling to cope with an industrial environment dominated by large firms with monopsony power and arbitrary labor-management practices. The Knights of Labor, the first American workers' organization of consequence, may have been founded in 1869, but it was fundamentally a creature of the 1880s. Its growth reflected the sense on the part of workers that their fate was being determined by anonymous market forces that they were incapable of influencing when acting alone.[4]

Earlier efforts at organization had been based on the republican outlook of skilled workers who saw themselves as "partners at the workbench" with their employers, in the words of Samuel Gompers.[5] The Knights, in contrast, spoke for unskilled workers who had little in common with either skilled mechanics or factory owners, and to whom neither those skilled workers nor factory owners felt much obligation. The 1880s, when this labor agitation peaked, was a decade of exceptional industrial "violence and turbulence," in the words of John Commons in his seminal *History of Labor in the United States*.[6] It was a decade when workers engaged in strikes, boycotts, and even sabotage as they sought to regain control of their destinies, or at least their immediate economic circumstances.[7]

This was also a period when the share of income going to the top 1 percent rose sharply. Peter Lindert and Jeffrey Williamson, in their book *Unequal Gains*, document a rise in the top 1 percent share in the United States in the final quarter of the nineteenth century and again after the turn of the century.[8] In 1851 Alexis de Tocqueville had famously described the United States as "more equal...than...any other country of the world...in any age of which history has preserved remembrance."[9] Now, less than fifty years later, the economy was dominated by Carnegies, Vanderbilts, Morgans, and Rockefellers, robber barons who accumulated vast fortunes through new technologies utilized by mega-corporations that operated unrestrained by anti-trust law or other regulation.

The robber barons were resented for their wealth but also their political influence—for how "they held sway over a helpless democracy," in the words of the historian T. J. Stiles.[10] In these circumstances, the policy platform of neither principal political party reassured. The Democrats concentrated on limiting the role of government, while the Republicans focused on extending tariff protection to manufacturing firms. Their policy agendas did not adequately address labor's concerns with wages and factory conditions. Farmers complained that neither party responded adequately to their complaints about railroad rates, interest charges, and deflation.

In response, the People's Party, informally known as the Populists, was formed in 1891. Supported by southern cotton growers and midwestern wheat farmers, and uneasily allied with labor unions and the advocates of the free coinage of silver from western mining states, the Populists attracted 9 percent of the presidential vote in 1892. In 1896, the Populists fused with the Democrats, nominating William Jennings Bryan, who ran on a platform of "free silver," designed to deliver inflation rather than deflation, and as a critic of the railroads and banks. Bryan was seen as a man of integrity, although he also had a second career as a real estate shill for the Florida property developer George Merrick. But if Bryan was principled, there was an unsavory racialist strand in the positions of some of his supporters.[11] Mary Elizabeth Lease, the populist suffragette with whom Bryan campaigned, published a book with the promising title *The Problem of Civilization Solved*, which crudely denounced blacks, Asians, and Jews.[12] In time, what started as a fringe element increasingly dominated the movement. Tom Watson, Bryan's running mate on the 1896 Populist ticket, began his political career as a supporter of black enfranchisement but moved in racialist and nativist directions, attacking blacks and Jews and embracing white supremacism. As the party's presidential nominee in 1904, he appealed to southern white farmers who had not shared in the prosperity of the period by blaming their black neighbors for their plight.[13]

This sense of insecurity and exclusion also manifested itself in anti-immigrant sentiment. If wages stagnated and men of Scots-Irish descent found themselves competing with recent arrivals from Eastern Europe and Asia, then it was tempting to blame immigration for all that was wrong with the world. Already in 1882 President Chester Arthur had signed the Chinese Exclusion Act, barring the immigration of Chinese laborers in response to pressure from native workers. In justifying the measure, he and others invoked racial stereotypes— Senator John F. Miller of California, where much of the population of Chinese extraction resided, disparaged "machine-like" Chinese workers.[14] In that same year Congress passed a general immigration act that clamped down on the entry of other "undesirables." In 1907 the U.S. government succeeded in pressuring Japan to limit the issuance of passports to citizens wishing to work in the United States. The roles of nativism, xenophobia, and economic hardship in the development of these restrictive policies remain hard to disentangle. The safest conclusion is that they were bound up together.

Although Bryan was defeated in 1896, the Populists' complaints did not go unheeded. Mainstream politicians had understood since the 1880s that they had to address the concerns of farmers, miners, and workers or risk losing out to more radical political elements. Their response started with the Interstate Commerce Act of 1887, which required railroad rates to be "reasonable and just." A majority of U.S. states adopted usury laws limiting interest rates or, where those laws already existed, enforced them more vigorously. These laws were passed by state politicians and enforced by local officials directly answerable to the constituents they served.

Beginning in the 1890s, so-called Progressive politicians associated with the two principal parties then pushed through measures designed to restrain the unbridled power of large corporations and address problems of corruption in politics. The Sherman Act and the Clayton Antitrust Act sought to prevent anticompetitive practices. Muckraking journalists popularized the Progressive cause by exposing corporate abuses and focusing attention on political corruption. Reform-minded politicians in both major parties challenged the political status quo.

Teddy Roosevelt campaigned against corruption as New York City police commissioner. Assuming the presidency following the assassination of William McKinley in 1901, he secured additional railway regulation and campaigned against monopolistic practices, earning the sobriquet "trust buster in chief."[15]

President Woodrow Wilson, a political outsider seen as embodying these progressive ideals, then encouraged Congress to address inequality by adopting a graduated income tax, another early demand of the Populists. Wilson's background as an intellectual and president of Princeton University does not single him out as cut from populist cloth. Yet his rhetoric, in the 1912 campaign and then his inauguration speech, in which he warned that "we," meaning the people of the United States, had "reared giant machinery which made it impossible that any but those who stood at the levers of control should have a chance to look out for themselves," echoed classic populist themes.[16]

Financial interests opposed to the free coinage of silver remained an insuperable obstacle to the radical monetary proposals of Bryan and others. But here too the Populist critique registered, convincing even supporters of the gold standard that the monetary system, to survive, had to be reformed. While the Gold Standard Act of 1900 definitively shut the door on free silver, it also halved the amount of capital that banks in smaller towns and cities were required to hold. This encouraged bank entry and competition in rural markets where farmers had long complained about monopoly power and the high cost of credit. Congress next established a National Monetary Commission and passed the Federal Reserve Act of 1913 to provide an "elastic currency" responsive to the needs of the people.[17] This decentralized central bank (notice the juxtaposition of two contradictory adjectives) was an awkward compromise. But the Federal Reserve was tailored this way precisely to address the complaints of Populists and others about the inertness of monetary conditions while at the same time not exciting their suspicion of concentrated financial power.

This may not have been a comprehensive response to the Populists' grievances, but it at least indicated that the politicians were listening. That the United States was one of the few countries with universal (adult, male, and, in practice, mainly white) suffrage meant that the American political system was more responsive than most to popular complaints. There was also the fortuitous fact that the price level stopped falling and that the deflation so harmful to farmers gave way to inflation from the mid-1890s, due to the gold discoveries in the Klondike and Western Australia noted in Chapter 1. Together these factors—policy reform and luck—were enough to contain the third-party threat.

U.S. entry into World War I interrupted politics and economics as usual, but only temporarily. National security concerns were invoked to justify the 1917 immigration act, which imposed a literacy test for immigrants over sixteen years of age and barred "anarchists, or persons who believe in or advocate the overthrow by force or violence of the Government of the United States." The 1917 act excluded Asians outright, with exceptions for the Japanese, immigration of whom was already restrained, and Filipinos, who were U.S. citizens courtesy of the Spanish-American War.

In what sense Asian immigrants threatened U.S. national security during World War I was not exactly clear. More clarity emerged from the debate over the Immigration Act of 1924. A temporary 1921 act had based quotas on the number of foreign-born people in the country in 1910. But much of the "new immigration" of the last decade of the nineteenth century and first decade of the twentieth was from Southern and Eastern Europe. These new immigrants were disproportionately Catholic, Orthodox, and Jewish. In the contemporary stereotype, they were clannish, difficult to assimilate, inclined to radical politics, and prone to syndicalism, anarchism, and terrorism. The arrest and conviction in 1921 of Nicola Sacco and Bartolomeo Vanzetti, alleged followers of the Italian anarchist and advocate of revolutionary violence Luigi Galleani, encouraged this prejudice. Pushing back the date on which quotas were based to 1890, as provided for by the 1924 act, served to better preserve the ethnically and religiously homogeneous United States of the nineteenth century, or an idealized version of it anyway. Barring Asian immigrants worked in the same direction.

Outside New England, Sacco and Vanzetti's home, nativism found reflection in the Ku Klux Klan, membership in which peaked in the 1920s. The Klan attacked immigrants, Catholics, and Jews as much as black Americans. It deplored criminality, immorality, and so-called non-Protestant values. The 1920s Klan was more urban, northern, and western than its nineteenth-century predecessor. Membership responded to the desire of lower- and middle-class white workers to protect their economic status from encroachment by migrants from Eastern Europe and the rural South. Members were drawn from "a backward segment of American society, one trapped by economic insecurity, dying small-town ways, and an inability to adjust psychologically to the 'modern age,'" in the words of the historian Leonard Moore. "The Klan," Moore concludes, "appears to have acted as a kind of interest group for the average white Protestant who believed that his values should remain dominant" in an America increasingly populated by other groups.[18]

Klan members won political office in Indiana, Colorado, and Oregon. They worked through established political parties—both of them.[19] But although membership grew to an estimated 4 million, the Klan never became a dominant force in American politics. Again, economic conditions helped stem the tide. The Roaring Twenties was a time of wage gains for the majority of Americans. Unemployment had fallen to barely 3 percent by the end of the decade. Relative gains still mattered, to be sure: some could complain that they were not doing as well as others, and after 1920 the income share of the top 1 percent took another jump up.[20] But the fact that most people were doing better in absolute terms meant that economic dissatisfaction was limited. Not every household had a radio, a phonograph, or a Model A Ford, but a growing number did.

Support for an open, market-based economy was then undermined by the high unemployment and social distress that developed with the onset of the Great Depression. Foreign trade was an immediate casualty. When Congress had debated the McKinley Tariff in 1890, the United States was an exporter of agricultural commodities and an importer of industrial goods. Tariffs protected American manufacturing while burdening farmers and consumers of imported products. That was one reason the Populists, fundamentally an agrarian movement, broke decisively with McKinley and the Republicans. Over the next quarter century, however, the United States developed into the leading exporter of manufactures by harnessing its natural resources to an industrial complex that depended on fuel- and raw-material-using mass-production methods. By the 1920s, tariff protection was a matter of less urgency to U.S. manufacturers, who were now well positioned to withstand foreign competition, than to the wheat farmers of the Midwest, who found themselves suffering from low prices due to the expansion of production in Canada, Australia, and Argentina.

The movement that culminated in 1930 in the Smoot-Hawley Tariff Act therefore originated as an effort to support the farmer, the expansion of acreage under cultivation in other countries that now depressed world market prices having been stimulated by World War I. But the depression that set in during the second half of 1929 devastated industry as much as agriculture. There was a temptation to point to imports as aggravating or even causing those difficulties and to jump on the protectionist bandwagon. Thus, the tariff bill that emerged from Congress and was signed by President Herbert Hoover in 1930 lacked a clear economic logic: it raised tariffs on agricultural and industrial products alike. Rather than favoring one sector over another, the main thing it did was close off the United States from trade with the rest of the world.[21]

An unemployment rate of nearly 25 percent, like that the United States experienced in the depths of the Great Depression, is fertile ground for anti-immigrant hysteria, isolationist rhetoric, and populist reaction. Other immigrants already having been barred, nativist sentiment now focused on Mexicans working in the United States, who were accused of stealing jobs from native-born workers. Inflated estimates of the number of undocumented immigrants were floated. The Federal

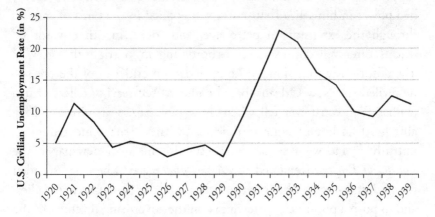

FIGURE 2.1 U.S. Civilian Unemployment Rate, 1920–1939

Source: Susan Carter, "Labor Force, Employment, and Unemployment: 1890–1990." Table Ba470-477 in *Historical Statistics of the United States, Earliest Times to the Present: Millennial Edition*, ed Susan Carter, Scott Gartner, Michael Haines, Alan Olmstead, Richard Sutch, and Gavin Wright (Cambridge University Press, 2006), http://dx.doi. org/10.1017/ISBN-9780511132971.Ba340-651.

Immigration Service was mobilized by Secretary of Labor William N. Doak, a Hoover appointee and former vice president of the Brotherhood of Railroad Trainmen, to make it look as if the administration was doing something about the immigration and unemployment problems. Officers rounded up illegal immigrants using strong-arm tactics designed to impress even legal residents who "looked Mexican" with the idea that they were at risk of being taken into custody, or worse, and consequently to encourage them to leave the country.[22]

A variety of political opportunists sought to capitalize on this hysteria. The most notorious was Huey Long, who served on the Louisiana State Railroad Commission and then as governor before moving to the U.S. Senate in 1933. At each stage Long positioned himself as an opponent of concentrated economic power, be it the railways, the banks, or the oil and utility companies, and as an ally of the common people.[23] He relied on mass rallies and whistle-stop campaign tactics in the manner of William Jennings Bryan, and doled out political and economic favors to attract a loyal clientele. His rhetoric and methods were Trump-like. As Long himself once said, "I used to get things done by saying please. Now I dynamite 'em out of my path."[24] For political advice Long relied on family rather than political professionals. As one supporter put it, "Others had power in their organization, but [Huey] had power in himself." That power was applied in the form of carrots, through the extension of patronage, and sticks, in other words by threats, often veiled but sometimes bordering on "outright thuggery."[25] The notoriously thin-skinned Long traded on criticism of the press— he reviled the New Orleans–based dailies as self-serving tellers of untruths. "You can never tell when those newspapers are sincere. They ain't [got] an honest bone in their body. They don't mind telling an untruth."[26] He went so far as to establish his own newspaper, the *Louisiana Progress* (renamed the *American Progress* when he ascended the national stage), which heaped abuse on the New Orleans dailies, and to push a punitive 15 percent tax on the advertising revenues of the dailies through the state legislature in 1934.[27]

Bankers, as one might expect, were the other prominent targets of Long and 1930s populists generally. Financiers had profited handsomely from the excesses of the 1920s, and they were deeply implicated in the crisis that now followed. That taxpayer funds, disbursed by the

Reconstruction Finance Corporation, were used to prop up the banks hardly seemed fair and right.[28] All this made the banks obvious targets for politicians seeking to whip up populist outrage, an angle on which Long effectively capitalized. He appealed to working-class voters hit by the Depression with a "Share Our Wealth" program focused on taxing the wealthy, starting with wealthy financiers, and redistributing the proceeds to the poor and homeless in the manner of a guaranteed income scheme. Economists pointed out that the sums did not add up, but the details were not of the essence.

In 1933 Long broke with FDR on the grounds that the New Deal was too friendly to finance and business and insufficiently redistributive. The reality was probably that the New Deal was too successful at placating Long's core constituency. Were the New Deal not discredited, it would have been an obstacle to his plan of mounting a primary challenge to FDR in 1936.[29]

Long's leading surrogate was the radio preacher Father Charles Coughlin of Royal Oak, Michigan. Coughlin was early to understand the power of radio in mobilizing a mass movement. He had taken to the medium in 1926 to protest the burning of crosses on the grounds of his church by the Ku Klux Klan but by 1930 was commenting widely on politics. Advocating social and economic justice for the common man, Coughlin, like Long, supported FDR in the 1932 presidential campaign. He supported the New Deal in 1933. But by 1934 he had turned against the program as too accommodating of the "money changers" and against the president as too willing to compromise.[30]

Coughlin's increasingly radical proposals started with direct government control of the Federal Reserve System. (His plan to remove private bankers from the boards of Federal Reserve Banks found an echo in suggestions by Vermont senator Bernie Sanders in the 2016 primary campaign.) They then veered into advocating the free coinage of silver, so as to offset the deflationary effects of the gold standard, and nationalizing the railroads, echoing two long-standing Populist themes, together with guaranteed work and confiscatory wealth taxation. Coughlin praised Hitler and Mussolini for forcefully enlisting industry and finance in advancing their nationalist policy agendas—in contrast, by implication, to FDR. From there it was a short step to anti-Semitic and quasi-fascist rhetoric—the so-called Judeo-Bolshevik threat was one of his favorite tropes—and to advocating a foreign policy of neutrality toward Europe and isolationism for the United States.

By 1934 Coughlin was reaching tens of millions of listeners captivated by his message of hope, change, and elite conspiracy. In 1935, at the height of his popularity, he was receiving more mail than FDR. As in the case of the radio and television hosts Rush Limbaugh and Sean Hannity more recently, it is hard to pinpoint his impact on politics. But by 1936 his statements had grown increasingly extreme and erratic, causing many of his earlier followers to abandon him. That year a Gallup Poll asked respondents whether Coughlin's endorsement would make them more likely to vote for or against a candidate. By this point, Democrats, Republicans, and self-identified Socialists all were more inclined to answer "against."[31]

The other factor undercutting support for Coughlin's brand of populism was evidence that the political establishment was seeking to address the concerns of the insecure and excluded. FDR directly fostered this impression: his "nothing to fear but fear itself" message spoke to Americans' heightened sense of insecurity in terms they could understand.[32] His use of radio to speak directly to the people took a page out of the populist playbook. More generally, his rhetoric was designed to show that he was allied with the common man against business and finance, as in his first inaugural address ("The money changers have fled from their high seats in the temple of our civilization.... The measure of the restoration lies in the extent to which we apply social values more noble than mere monetary profit") and his famous 1936 Madison Square Garden speech ("We had to struggle with the old enemies of peace— business and financial monopoly.... They are unanimous in their hate for me—and I welcome their hatred").

Concretely, the New Deal spoke to the concerns of those who had not shared in the prosperity of the 1920s and were hit hardest by the crisis of the 1930s. The federal government's administrative and organizational capacity, extended during World War I, was now actively put to work. The Agricultural Adjustment Act addressed farmers' concerns with low crop prices. The Rural Electrification Administration and Tennessee Valley Authority brought power to deprived communities, addressing complaints of exclusion. The Federal Emergency Relief Administration provided grants and loans to aid the unemployed.[33]

The Wagner Act obliged firms to bargain with unions selected by a majority of employees. Unemployment insurance and Social Security addressed the insecurity of workers in the transition to the twentieth-century industrial age. Roosevelt's "soak the rich" tax proposal in the summer of 1935 may have been designed to "steal Long's thunder" and was ultimately pared back by Congress, but it was at least a token effort to address long-standing popular concerns over inequality.[34]

FDR's decision to abandon the gold standard in April 1933 responded to a more radical proposal by Senator Elmer Thomas of Oklahoma, advanced on behalf of an inflationist bloc of congressmen representing farmers and small businessmen bearing the brunt of deflation and labor unionists who blamed the monetary regime for unemployment. Thomas's measure would have compelled the Federal Reserve System to issue an additional $2.4 billion of banknotes and the president to devalue the dollar against gold. Roosevelt suggested an amendment limited to permission to devalue the dollar, which he then proceeded to do. The result was sharp upward pressure on prices and production, relieving the plight of the farmers and inaugurating an employment recovery. Adherents to gold standard orthodoxy were horrified, but the policy, or more precisely its effects, helped to solidify popular support for the political mainstream.

Finally, FDR and the New Dealers took visible steps to address problems in the banking and financial system. Banking crises, it will surprise no one, breed resentment of bankers. They foster support for populist politicians who promise to suppress financial excesses and restore the balance between Main Street and Wall Street. The political establishment now visibly sought to address these concerns. The Pecora Investigation of the U.S. Senate Committee on Banking and Currency called the bankers on the carpet. The Glass-Steagall Act forced commercial banks to divest themselves of their risky securities-underwriting activities, while the Securities Exchange Act enhanced the transparency of financial markets. This may not have been the best imaginable regulatory response, but it was enough to bequeath a long period of banking and financial stability, thereby attenuating the link between the banking crisis and populism.

World War II was then followed by further expansion of the welfare state, in the United States as in other countries. The share of the top 1 percent of the income distribution fell, relative to 1920s levels, due to increases in top tax rates, a legacy of the 1930s and especially the war.[35]

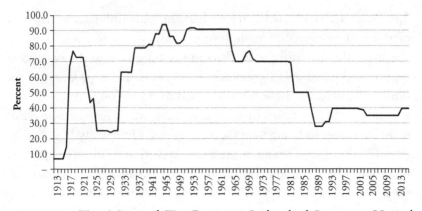

FIGURE 2.2 Top Marginal Tax Rates on Individual Incomes, United States, 1913–2015

Source: Internal Revenue Service, Statistics of Income Division, Historical Table 23.

America's position as an industrial leader, reflecting electrification, the reorganization of factories in the interwar period, and then wartime advances in mass production, generated an abundance of good manufacturing jobs. Economic growth fostered a sense of opportunity, while access to education through the GI Bill enhanced socioeconomic mobility. Against the backdrop of a buoyant world economy, employers saw keeping the assembly line running as even more valuable than before. Manufacturing firms prioritized harmonious labor relations, which they sought to secure by sharing their rents more equitably with their workers. These capsule observations may paint a somewhat one-dimensional picture of the postwar economic and social climate, but they serve to highlight the contrast with both the late nineteenth century and the 1920s, which is what matters here.[36]

This was not a promising economic climate for demagoguery. On the other hand, the international political situation, and specifically the Cold War, remained conducive. In particular they were conducive to the rise of Joseph McCarthy. McCarthy campaigned against the subversive "elites," a term that featured prominently in his 1950 Wheeling, West Virginia, speech warning that there were closet Communists in the State Department. Like Donald Trump, he was not a slave to the facts. And like Trump, he was a skilled practitioner of the politics of fear.[37] A long-standing interpretation of McCarthyism sees the senator from Wisconsin not simply as seeking to situate himself as an opponent of the foreign Communist threat and its domestic fifth column but also as capitalizing on yet another revolt of the masses, this one driven by the status anxiety of white working-class Americans who feared losing their jobs and socioeconomic position to blacks who migrated north and west during the war and to other competing groups. Working-class whites were therefore receptive a kind of distorted midcentury populism championing nationalism and traditional values while ostracizing Jews, intellectuals, and others as Communist sympathizers. They were sympathetic to McCarthyism, in other words.

Subsequent scholarship has qualified this interpretation. Historians Michael Rogin and David Oshinsky established that working-class Wisconsin voters were not, in fact, disproportionately inclined toward McCarthy.[38] Status anxiety there may have been, but it did not dominate American politics in this period, when inequality was falling and growth was lifting all boats. Such status anxiety as existed did not give rise to legions of McCarthys, or prevent Tailgunner Joe himself from crashing and burning. Concern with relative economic status was less when absolute economic status was rising. Resentment against the elites in Washington, D.C., which McCarthy sought to excite, was correspondingly less. Fear of Moscow, of a domestic fifth column, and of the "other" generally there may have been, but that fear was a less potent political force in what was a relatively positive economic environment. To be sure, Barry Goldwater is famous for asserting that "extremism in the defense of freedom is no vice." Richard Nixon never entirely put his association with McCarthy behind him. But the political center held.

Historians disagree about when America's image as the land of opportunity, as inclusive, as a champion of free trade, and as a steward of global peace and security began to fray. On the country's renewed isolationist tendencies, some cite the trauma of the Vietnam War, others America's troubled involvement in Iraq. To explain opposition to immigration, some point to 9/11 and Islamophobia, others to slowing growth, rising inequality, and the stagnation of working-class wages. History suggests a role for all these factors—for failed foreign interventions, for attacks on the homeland, for widening income inequality, and for slower economic growth—but above all for insecurity and the sense of having been left behind.

In hindsight, the only surprise, given this confluence of forces, is that it took so long for a populist reaction to materialize.

3

Luddites and Laborers

ECONOMISTS DISAGREE ABOUT whether technical change or globalization is the main driver of inequality and insecurity. They similarly disagree about the remedies. Some say that society has an obligation to compensate the losers through welfare programs, unemployment insurance, or a basic income, and that politicians would be well advised to do so on both social-stability and self-preservation grounds. Others, seeing globalization as the problem, advocate tariffs, controls on capital flows, and limits on immigration. Still others recommend investing in education and training to ensure that workers can compete in a technologically dynamic, globalized world.

Societies have been grappling with these issues ever since the Industrial Revolution and the first age of globalization in the nineteenth century. Livelihoods and expectations then were already being disrupted by technological change and import competition. Already then, there was a backlash against unfettered markets and free foreign competition, and there were calls for government to restrain these disruptive forces. Recent complaints about the uneven and unfair effects of globalization and technical change, and anger toward government for its failure to do more about them, are far from new.

A classic case in point is the early nineteenth-century English handloom weavers who saw themselves being replaced by less-skilled workers operating stocking frames and power looms, and who mobilized against this mechanization and low-wage competition.[1] Textiles were at the epicenter of the process of technical change that we call the Industrial Revolution. Modern estimates are that cotton textiles accounted for fully a quarter of all productivity growth in Britain between

1780 and 1860.[2] This made for big changes in prices and work organization. It is not surprising that the hand-loom weavers saw their livelihoods as jeopardized by technological forces beyond their control. Nor is it surprising that the first violent acts of the Luddites, as this group came to be known, coincided with the Napoleonic Wars, which depressed economic conditions and dimmed the prospects for alternative employment.[3]

Agriculture also contributed importantly to economic growth in the early nineteenth century, although the point tends to be missed in discussions of the *Industrial* Revolution. The British economy was still heavily agrarian, and technical change in farming was rapid. But, despite this, the real wages of farm laborers rose only slowly from eighteenth-century levels, since many of the gains from increased productivity went to landlords and the owners of farm machinery. Indeed, there is evidence, as in Figure 3.1, that for a time at least their wages in fact declined. Small farmers who relied on the open fields surrounding their villages to gather firewood and pasture their stock were denied access when that acreage was privatized by Parliamentary edict. Under Parliamentary enclosure, the privatization and redistribution of landholdings could be done quickly. Since it could proceed with the approval of the holders of just four-fifths of the land in question, there were complaints that large landlords were expropriating smallholders. The process, the latter complained, had an unseemly political aspect. These complaints may have been exaggerated.[4] But the bottom line is that farm laborers were left wholly dependent on their labor power.

Their reaction was the Swing Riots, an uprising of farm laborers that began in Kent in 1830. "Swing" or "Captain Swing" was the signature on the threatening letters sent to farmers and magistrates, evidently an allusion to the swinging flail used in hand threshing. The protesters focused their destructive energy on labor-displacing threshing machines but also attacked the cattle, haystacks, and barns of landowners using the new equipment.[5]

The reaction of farm labor came later than in textiles, since the Napoleonic Wars, while disruptive to industry, benefited agriculture temporarily. Lack of access to imported foodstuffs pushed up crop prices, bettering the prospects of farmers and farmworkers. But those improved conditions did not last. Admittedly, modern estimates of real wages suggest more than a modicum of exaggeration in contemporary warnings,

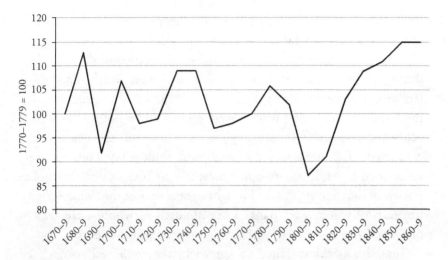

FIGURE 3.1 Farm Laborers' Real Wages, Southeast England, 1670–1870

Source: Gregory Clark, "Farm Wages and Living Standards in the Industrial Revolution: England, 1670–1869," *Economic History Review* 54 (2001): 477–505. doi:10.1111/1468-0289.00200.

like that of Lord Carnarvon, that the English farm laborer had been "reduced to a plight more abject than that of any race in Europe."[6] What had been reduced were the laborer's income security, his employment security, and his future security: income security because households that had once received income from their labor and land now depended entirely on the former; employment security because hiring contracts ran for increasingly short periods with the commercialization of agriculture and the growing social and economic gulf between landowner and farm laborer; and future security because threshing machines augured the development of even more ingenious labor-saving machinery.

To refer to these popular rebellions as populist would be stretching the term. But they had in common with populist movements that they were rebellions against the economic and political establishment. Farm laborers in southern England, like the hand-loom weavers before them, were responding to the same heightened sense of insecurity and perceived lack of alternatives that animate populists in other times and places. These uprisings may have had a different character, lacking the charismatic leader and nativist tendencies of archetypal populist movements. But they are a reminder that violent reactions against the dislocations of economic change and the deteriorating economic status of skilled workers are far from uniquely modern phenomena.

Counterfactually, one can imagine these protests spreading and producing a broad-based uprising like that in France, which toppled the landowner-dominated ancien régime. Like the French revolutionaries, the Luddites and Swing Rioters were motivated by political as well as economic concerns.[7] In the English case, however, the reaction was contained. The army was deployed, and some sixty Luddites were prosecuted for violent crimes in a mass trial in York in 1813. The police powers of the state were again brought to bear against the Swing Rioters, nineteen of whom were hanged, six hundred of whom were imprisoned, and five hundred of whom were transported to Australia.

That this backlash failed to spread further reflected two related facts in addition to this show of force by the state. First, real wages, which had fallen economy-wide between 1780 and 1830, began rising as industrialization spread, increasing the demand for both more- and less-skilled labor. Second, there was serious discussion in establishment circles about how best to address the protestors' concerns. That discussion took place under the heading of the "Machinery Question," most elaborately posed by David Ricardo. Ricardo was a stock-market speculator, a parliamentarian, and probably the most influential political economist (we would say simply economist) of his day. In a chapter entitled "On Machinery" added to the third edition of his *Principles of Political Economy and Taxation*, he addressed the "influence of machinery on the interests of different classes of society" and the "opinion entertained by the laboring class, that the employment of machinery is frequently detrimental to their interests."[8] While continuing to maintain, as before, that the introduction of machinery benefited the capitalists and landlords who used it and the industrialists and skilled mechanics who made it, Ricardo recanted his earlier assertion that mechanization necessarily benefited workers as well, because they would enjoy a lower cost of living——as he put it, they would "command an additional quantity of comforts and enjoyments" out of the same "money income." Instead he now acknowledged that displaced workers might have their skills rendered obsolete and no longer enjoy the same money income and purchasing power as before.

Ricardo did not take this as an argument for resisting mechanization, which promised to raise productivity and national income overall. But his observation that there would be losers as well as winners implied that society might have to compensate the losers in order to avoid a negative reaction.

In terms of action, one concrete step was the Reform Act of 1832, which enhanced the political voice of the middle classes. It consolidated and eliminated so-called pocket boroughs, where a single landlord dominated. It reduced the property requirement for voting, enlarging the electorate by half. Although the property requirement remained non-negligible and the franchise was still far from universal, the 1832 reform at least gave better-off commoners the sense that they could advance their interests through established political channels.

By splitting labor into an aspiring middle class with enough property to vote and a working class that lacked that prerequisite, the 1832 reform also gave rise to the Chartist movement. Chartism was "the first (and arguably still the greatest) mass political movement in industrial Britain."[9] It took its name from the People's Charter, a pamphlet circulated in 1838. The Chartists campaigned for greater political voice for the working class and agitated against wage cuts and insecurity of employment. As one Chartist leader, Joseph Rayner Stephens, a former Methodist minister, put it, the movement focused on "knife and fork... bread and cheese question[s]."

Chartism was a moderate political movement, reflecting the fact that the Chartists' objections to the prevailing political system were themselves moderate. Its members were not populist, as the term is utilized here. They simply sought to enhance the access of working-class people to that political system. They pushed for the vote for every adult male, including urban, industrial workers with little or no property. Indirectly they inspired what became the Second Reform Act, in 1867, which enfranchised all male heads of household and doubled the size of the electorate. Another half century would have to pass before the creation of the Labour Party, but disaffected workers already had grounds for thinking that they could pursue their grievances by normal political means. Support for the country's political institutions was solidified, and Britain, in contrast to other European countries, such as France, was able to head off a more violent reaction.

The most straightforward way of compensating those whose incomes were eroded by technological change was of course through direct income support. Here English society actually did less over time, despite growing need. The rise of commercial agriculture and urban employment eroded traditional social support systems at the parish and village levels, and the working classes suffered the consequences. "In England the Industrial Revolution reversed the trend toward a more extensive and more lenient public protection of those who became victims of economic fortune," as one historian put it. "The liberal elements that came to power in the late eighteenth and early nineteenth centuries championed an industrial society based on individualistic principles."[10]

When a Royal Commission on the Operation of the Poor Laws was appointed in the aftermath of the Swing Riots, its members were concerned less with repairing the fabric of society than with limiting the burden on themselves and their kind.[11] Under the Poor Law in existence since the sixteenth century, the earnings of impoverished farm workers had been topped up by public support administered by local Poor Law guardians.[12] This had the effect of shifting the costs from farmers to others insofar as all property owners were taxed to finance rural relief. With industrialization, those others became more numerous and influential—and increasingly vocal critics of the system. The Poor Law was also perceived as subject to abuse by people from outside the parish, who were an additional burden on local ratepayers and therefore a threat to existing recipients of relief. As early as 1662, this had led Parliament to adopt a Settlement Act allowing parishes to remove within forty days of their arrival any newcomers likely to end up on the relief rolls.[13]

These were the problems on which the Royal Commission on the Operation of the Poor Laws now focused. Under its proposals, public support would be provided exclusively in workhouses under conditions tolerable only to the truly indigent. This punitive restriction was designed to limit abuse of the system and remove the incentive to migrate to receive relief.

Although some of the commission's detailed recommendations were not incorporated into the Act Amending the Laws Relating to the Poor in 1834, they guided the decisions of the independent Poor Law

Commission established by that act. Relief was still administered by local guardians and financed by a tax on local property owners, but it was now subject to uniform rules. The commission instructed small parishes lacking the resources needed to construct a workhouse to confederate with other parishes. It allowed for continued outdoor relief (assistance provided without requiring the recipient to enter an institution) given slow progress in constructing workhouses, but only if the recipients were set to hard work. Subsequent regulations restricted the provision of outdoor relief still further. In many respects the new system was less humane than its pre-1834 predecessor, as depicted by Charles Dickens in *Oliver Twist*.

This system was designed to be stigmatizing, and it was. The share of the population receiving relief declined as people went to greater lengths to avoid it. Relief recipients were now mainly individuals with serious medical conditions, and a growing share of relief expenditure was for health care, leaving the able-bodied to fend for themselves. Workers therefore clubbed together in benevolent societies and trade union associations to insure against sickness and lack of work.[14]

The question is why English society didn't go further to address the concerns of the working class, and why its failure to do so didn't provoke a political backlash in this period of rapid technical change and rising trade. The answer, simply put, is that the period after 1830, and especially after 1850, was marked by improvements in living standards and employment opportunities. There were no disruptions to commerce as severe as those of the Napoleonic Wars. The gap between the wages of skilled and unskilled workers peaked around 1850 and then declined through the end of the century, as ongoing industrialization created employment opportunities for less-skilled workers, many at higher wages.[15] Although Britain now had industrial rivals such as Germany and the United States, it remained the single largest exporter of manufactured goods as late as 1913. Exports were produced by an urban industrial sector that was a reliable source of jobs paying better than those in the countryside. There was continuing concern, to be sure, about the underclass of casual labor, individuals only loosely connected to the labor force, and about the conditions of work. But with a rising tide lifting most boats, the backlash against globalization and technical change was contained.

Foreign competition was of special concern in older industries producing clocks and watches, straw hats and bonnets, boots and shoes, gloves, silks and ribbons, woolens and worsteds, and in shipping and iron, all sectors now facing pressure from German, French, and Belgian producers. The industries in question were conveniently concentrated, from the point of view of organization, in a handful of Midland cities: Macclesfield, Coventry, Spitalfields, Preston, Derby, Nottingham, Bradford, Birmingham, and Manchester. Producers complained that French firms enjoyed unduly favorable access to British markets under the 1860 Cobden-Chevalier Treaty. They complained that foreign firms received export bounties—government subsidies—with no analog in British law. A coalition of aggrieved producers formed the Association of the Revivors of British Industry in 1869 with the goal of negotiating a fairer trade agreement. They mobilized their employees to petition Parliament for a remodeling of the customs tariff. Other associations, like the Reciprocity Free Trade Association and the National Fair Trade League, similarly sought to organize manufacturing interests.

This movement is sometimes seen as a revolt against free trade by workers displaced by import competition and disappointed by government's failure to do much about it. But in fact this protectionist agitation was more an elite project of proprietors in old industries than a mass movement of displaced workers, since many of the latter found new opportunities in expanding sectors. To be sure, foreign competition would continue to intensify. In time, the United States would emerge as an industrial power of the first rank. Trade and transport costs would continue to fall with the advent of steel-hulled ships powered by powerful engines and dual-screw propellers, whose effect was not unlike that of containerization after World War II. But at this point, in the late 1860s and early 1870s, the most intense effects were yet to be felt.

Owners of firms producing woolens, worsteds, and iron products felt more strongly because they had sector-specific investments to protect. But in the absence of a spontaneous mass movement, they had to organize to advance their case. They hired promoters to convene meetings where workers were sold the case for protection. Attendees were urged to participate in the Trades Union Congress of affiliated unions in London in 1881 and support a resolution endorsing the so-called fair trade cause. It soon became known that the promoters had offered to pay the expenses of sympathetic workers. News of their attempts to pack the congress highlighted the divergent interests of the wealthy organizers of the Fair Trade League and the working-class rank and file. In response, the congress adopted a motion that "no one shall be eligible as a delegate...whose expenses are paid by private individuals, or any other institution not a bona-fide trade union or trades council." This more or less put an end to the matter.[16]

Outside the Midlands, the sugar-refining industry was the leading center of anti-trade agitation. Foreign governments provided bounties to producers of refined sugar, which worked to the disadvantage of British refiners, whose number fell from more than thirty in 1864 to a mere handful a decade later.[17] This situation was also unwelcome for that handful of laborers whose livelihood was unloading raw sugar from the West Indies on London's docks. When the promoters of the fair trade movement were ejected from the meeting of the Trades Union Congress in 1881, their next stop was the East End, where they agitated among the dockworkers.[18]

But what was unfavorable for workers tied to the sugar trade was favorable for others required to spend less to sweeten their tea. "Sugar," as Gladstone put it in 1889, "is the article second only to corn among the comforts of the population."[19] As a result, the sugar-coated anti-bounty movement attracted only limited support.

If there was as yet limited popular support for a more restrictive trade policy, there was nonetheless no shortage of opportunistic politicians seeking to nurture it. When Conservative candidates performed poorly in the 1880 general election, party leaders such as Lord Randolph Churchill embraced protection as an issue on which to revive the party's fortunes. They saw trade restrictions that promised to prevent the loss of manufacturing jobs in older industries where wages were high and trade unions were well established as a device for attracting the support of union members. As Churchill put it, "The new unionism which goes for eight hours has almost entirely broken down the old unionism which was in mortal hostility to Toryism. Eight hours will I believe carry with it as a necessary consequence on some increased cost of production a return towards protection."[20] Churchill observed that competition from countries where wages were lower was now greater than in the 1860s and 1870s. To the extent that these trends were a source of anxiety for workers in older industries, they provided an opening for the Conservative Party.

Conservative politicians argued further that protection would strengthen the national security. Preferences for foodstuffs imported from the Commonwealth and Empire would draw the so-called White Dominions together, creating a united front against potentially hostile foreigners. Bismarck's success in creating a powerful German empire on the foundation of the Zollverein, or customs union, was both an example to follow and a challenge to be met.

While this pro-tariff agitation met with some success, Churchill was only temporarily its standard-bearer. With his health in decline, he was succeeded in the 1890s by Joseph Chamberlain.[21] Where Churchill was a patrician, Chamberlain had worked from the age of eighteen in his uncle's business, Nettlefold and Chamberlain, the leading English manufacturer of metal screws. He was the first industrialist to scale the highest reaches of British politics. His political start was as mayor of Birmingham, a center of the steel industry. His reputation for employing the blunt tactics of the hardscrabble businessman and successful local politician stayed with him throughout his career.

Chamberlain started political life as a free trader but changed his tune in response to the complaints about German competition of his fellow Birmingham businessmen. By the 1890s he had come to see tariff protection as a way of reviving British industry while not incidentally advancing his own political prospects. Like Churchill, he saw protection as useful for attracting the support of workers fearful of being displaced by import competition, adopting "tariff reform means work for all" as the straightforward slogan of his movement.[22] Aware that other politicians were similarly courting working-class voters, Chamberlain supported the Workman's Compensation Act of 1897, which partly indemnified people injured on the job. Tariff revenues, he observed, could be used to fund social reforms, not just workman's compensation but also old-age pensions, that appealed to working-class political constituencies, not unlike Bismarck's strategy in Germany.[23] The Tariff Reform League, the pressure group of Chamberlain's followers, is said to have been less opposed to large-scale government expenditure "than any other political group in Edwardian Britain."[24] Indeed, it may have favored lavish government expenditure precisely because doing so strengthened the revenue-raising rationale for protection. Where others regarded any discussion of taxes on imported foodstuffs as politically toxic, Chamberlain, when asked in 1894 by a fellow member of the Royal Commission on the Aged Poor how he would fund a pension scheme, replied, "By an import duty on wheat…Nothing that I have ever said or written would prevent me from advocating a tax on corn for a specific purpose."[25]

Chamberlain was "the most dynamic politician of late Victorian and early Edwardian Britain," a forceful platform speaker and a political loose cannon in the populist mold.[26] He was more comfortable tilting at windmills than with the confines of office, however—not unlike Donald Trump, it is tempting to add. Nonetheless, when the Conservative leader Lord Salisbury offered him the post of secretary of state for the colonies in 1895 on the grounds that he posed less danger to the government inside than out, Chamberlain accepted. He used the post as a bully pulpit to advocate tariffs with preferences for the empire, with the goal of creating an imperial federation, complete with imperial parliament, to counter the rise of Germany and the United States.[27]

Chamberlain's invocation of an imperial customs union also had a racialist strand, reflecting the "Anglo-Saxon imperialism" of his friend and political consort, the Liberal member of Parliament and author Sir Charles Dilke. A Radical, or English progressive, on domestic matters, Dilke also believed in manifest "Saxon" destiny and the innate superiority of the "Anglo Saxon race."[28] In 1897, on his installation as lord rector of Glasgow University, Chamberlain echoed his friend's language, portraying empire as "fulfilling the manifest duty of our race."[29]

Effectively, tariff reform divided Britain along the same lines as Brexit in 2016. It pitted industry against finance, the merchant banks that exported financial services understandably opposing Chamberlain's plan. It set cosmopolitan London against the regions. It spoke to Britons yearning, in an increasingly diverse economic and political world, for the unity of an imagined English race encompassing not just the British Isles but also the so-called settler colonies. It was regarded skeptically by the educated elite.

Given the ranks from which his political colleagues were drawn, Chamberlain's campaign met with less than enthusiastic cabinet support. He therefore adopted the populist tactic of speaking directly to the people. Using tariffs to bring the Empire together, he declaimed at Birmingham Town Hall, the scene of his early political triumphs, was the only way for Britons to "recover our freedom, resume the power of negotiation and retaliation whenever our own interests or our relations between our Colonies and ourselves are threatened by other people."[30] It was a way of regaining control of the nation's fate. It was a way of countering predatory foreign competition. And it was an expression of the will of the people.

In the event, this vaulting political rhetoric convinced true believers but few others. It didn't help that Chamberlain was unschooled in economics. He preferred his own statistics to those of the Board of Trade and his own advisors. His protectionist apostasy horrified his Liberal colleagues, free traders all, who dismissed his arguments as "reckless" and "criminal."[31]

Chamberlain's was still not a winning coalition, in other words, given Britain's free trade tradition and the working-class belief that tariffs meant higher food prices. But if his campaign was less than fully successful, it nevertheless demanded a political response. If protectionism was to be rejected, it would be necessary to demonstrate that the social reforms to which Chamberlain linked it could be funded by other means. In this way Chamberlain's proposals empowered the left-leaning, social-reform-oriented wing of the Liberal Party.

In particular, they empowered David Lloyd George when he was appointed Chancellor of the Exchequer in the government of H. H. Asquith in 1908. From a rural background, Lloyd George may not have been intimately familiar with the condition of the urban working class, but he was an astute politician.[32] Among his first acts, tailored to appeal to working-class constituencies, was to push through a second reading of the Old Age Pensions Bill, now to be funded, given Liberal opposition to import duties, by a tax on land payable on sale or death of the owner. Other Liberal reforms completed during his chancellorship included state stipends for the sick and infirm and the National Insurance Act of 1911, which laid the basis for state-supported health and unemployment insurance.

This was less an attempt to preempt labor-led opposition to economic openness, opposition that remained largely latent in the event, than to prevent the opponents of free trade, principally businessmen in import-competing sectors, from engaging their workers in the campaign against foreign competition. The poor physical condition of many of the recruits enlisted to fight in the Boer War in 1899, in addition, was an eye-opener for the political class. It created genuine concern over working-class living standards and heightened fears of a political reaction.[33] There was also support for the view that strategic intervention to reorganize the labor market would enhance the efficiency of British industry, thereby beating back competition from Germany and America and, not incidentally, obviating the need for tariff protection.

A leading center of these arguments was the Fabian Society, founded in 1884 with the goal of improving the condition of all Englishmen, including the least advantaged. The Fabians exposed poverty among the working class in a series of publications, many authored by the economic sociologists Sidney and Beatrice Webb. They made the case for a minimum wage and universal health care not just on equity grounds but also to enhance the efficiency of the labor force. They advocated labor exchanges to better match workers with jobs. They established the London School of Economics in 1895 and were centrally involved in the creation of the Labour Party. They counted among their early members such prominent figures as George Bernard Shaw and H. G. Wells. This is not to claim them as populists; the Fabians were nothing if not members of the elite. But it is to observe that this elite was conscious of working-class concerns, and that those concerns received a hearing, which helps to explain the limited traction of more radical movements.

That hearing took the form, perhaps predictably, of yet another investigation, this one a Royal Commission on the Poor Laws and Relief of Distress. Formed in 1905, the commission spent four years laboring over a pair of reports. Beatrice Webb, together with her husband, Sidney, coauthored a minority report advocating child support, universal free education, a living wage, guaranteed health care, and pensions for the retired and disabled. This was not yet a cradle-to-grave welfare state in which young people received the education and training needed to compete in a globalized world and older workers received state-supplied insurance against insecurity and misfortune. Nor were the proposals of the Webbs enthusiastically embraced by Asquith's Liberal government when the commission reported in 1909.

But there was a straight line from the work of the Webbs to the Beveridge Plan, the seminal 1942 document laying the groundwork for the post–World War II British welfare state. Indeed, William Beveridge himself, while still in his twenties, worked at this time as a researcher on the Webbs' project.

The immediate response, in the form of publicly administered social benefits, was limited because the threat to the political establishment was limited.[34] The British parliamentary system was firmly established. There was no equivalent of the 1871 Paris Commune, and no need, unlike in Bismarck's Germany, to bind the working class to a newly established state. Modest social protections sufficed to address the insecurity of workers confronted by technical change and foreign competition.

Limited health benefits were already provided, as we have seen, by friendly societies, voluntary associations of workers organized along industrial, regional, and religious lines. Commercial insurance companies meanwhile developed a market in funeral benefits. The 1911 Insurance Act built upon these foundations while modifying their administration and funding. Manual workers in key industries were now required to sign up for insurance in which the worker's contribution was matched by his employer. The resulting funds were administered by a recognized friendly society or by a commercial insurance company once the latter created a health insurance subsidiary.[35]

Unemployment insurance was extended, in the first instance, only to shipbuilding, engineering, iron-founding, and the building and related construction trades, sectors where seasonal or cyclical unemployment was chronic and where workers had a reputation for militancy. Applicants for benefits had to demonstrate that they had been employed for at least twenty-six weeks in each of five previous years. Moreover, those benefits could be drawn for no more than fifteen weeks in any twelve-month period. Thus, the resulting system excluded the floating underclass of casual laborers, dockworkers, and others only loosely tied to a particular job, as well as regular workers permanently displaced by changes to the economy.

Pensions were more difficult to organize on a contributory basis. The aged were in no position to contribute, while requiring contributions only from the young would create problems of intergenerational equity. Absent steps to regularize irregular employment, it was impossible to organize contributions from the floating underclass of laborers moving from one casual position to another.[36] The government therefore opted for a noncontributory scheme funded out of general revenues. But since there were other pressing demands on the government's income, payments averaged just five shillings a week, less than a fifth the average wage and below the level of subsistence. Only men over seventy qualified, and even these payments were eliminated on evidence of other income.

Although the programs created in this period were modest, they still helped to insulate workers from the elevated sense of insecurity created by industrial change, buttressing support for openness and the market system. They indicated that the political class was listening. None of this prevented the rise of the Labour Party nor, after World War I, the formation of a Labour government, as conservative supporters of these programs, perhaps naively, had hoped. They did not preempt the turn to a more restrictive, empire-oriented trade policy when conditions deteriorated in the 1930s. But the response of the establishment at least delayed these developments by several decades. And they pointed a way forward for those who understood that the British system rested on a measure of social cohesion, something that could not be taken for granted.

4

Voyage of the Bismarck

THE GERMAN EMPIRE plays an iconic role in the literature on the social insurance state. Imperial Germany pioneered health insurance, accident insurance, and old-age insurance in the 1880s, earlier than Britain, which adopted its own limited form of social insurance at the turn of the twentieth century, and earlier than the United States, which took similar steps only in the 1930s. For those concerned with how states respond to economic insecurity and why some respond faster than others, it helps to understand what informed this precocious state-sponsored action. It helps, specifically, to understand what motivated the Reichstag, the German parliament established in 1871, and Otto von Bismarck, the towering figure who served as chancellor for two decades.

In answering these questions, some invoke the traditional obligations of Prussian landowners to their agricultural tenants, Prussia being the largest member of the German Confederation. Others point to time-honored associations of artisans that had long provided disability insurance to their members. Still others emphasize the rapidity of German industrialization, which outstripped the capacity of these traditional arrangements to provide protections against insecurity, and to the uncertainties of a rapidly changing work environment. They point to the active role of the state in German economic growth—to the role of the Reich in mobilizing resources for the expanding industrial sector, for example.[1] That the state should similarly play a role in providing protections that markets left to their own devices were unable to supply was part and parcel of this experience.

The alternative is to emphasize personalities, much as historians of the British welfare state emphasize David Lloyd George and American historians emphasize Franklin Roosevelt. The role of the state as problem solver was exalted by no less than Georg Wilhelm Friedrich Hegel, who by the 1820s had relocated to Berlin, the seat of Prussian government, and become something of an academic celebrity. Hegel's pupil Lorenz Stein, longtime professor at the University of Vienna, elaborated his mentor's vision of Prussia as a social kingdom whose benign monarch was responsible for the welfare of his subjects.[2] Stein's arguments were then taken on board by economists of the German historical school, starting with Gustav von Schmoller, who coined the term "social policy" and made it the focus of his research.[3]

Bismarck himself was no radical seeking to overturn the prevailing order. He was, to the contrary, a conservative seeking to strengthen the state precisely in order to secure the established state of affairs. Shepherding health, accident, and old-age insurance through a Reichstag dominated by conservative politicians was his strategy for convincing the working class that there were alternatives to the Socialist Party for advancing their interests, something that was imperative once imperial Germany adopted universal male suffrage in 1871.[4] It was a way of heading off more-radical political movements. It gave workers an interest in the stability of the state insofar as their pensions now depended on it. All this was important for a German Empire whose unity was still to be forged.

To be sure, Germany was not the only place where workers complained of insecure factory employment, farmers protested capricious market forces, and industrialists clamored against unfair foreign competition. It was not the only country with political, regional and religious divisions. The United Kingdom had its Welsh, its Scots, and, most nettlesome, its Irish. America's Populist Revolt set the agricultural South and West against the industrial East. But Germany was the one place where the response took the form of tariffs for agriculture and manufacturing together with state-mandated social insurance to protect workers against the insecurities of industrial life.[5]

Before the 1870s, German states relied on tradition and custom to aid their destitute and disabled subjects. Catholic and Protestant churches supported indigent believers. Craft guilds pooled the resources of their members and supported invalids and other unfortunates. Lords acknowledged their obligations to their serfs as well as the other way around until Prussia abolished serfdom in 1807, and even then many *Junkers*, the landowning nobles who dominated East Prussia, retained a sense of obligation to their tenants. Bismarck himself, not incidentally, was a sixth-generation *Junker*.

In addition, Prussia, whose policies set the pattern for other German states, had a poor law not unlike England's, under which the state delegated the administration of poor relief to localities. The Prussian poor law reform acts of 1842 gave those local measures a modicum of uniformity, similar to what happened in England with its 1834 reforms. As in England, the generosity of relief was limited by fears that excessive support would "impair the energy of self-help."[6] And as in England, there were worries that overly generous support would attract opportunistic migrants and heighten the burden on local ratepayers. Prussia's 1842 legislation therefore allowed towns to deny residence to destitute newcomers.[7] As a further brake on migration, a three-year waiting period was established, only after which was an individual entitled to relief.[8]

Compared to England, the Prussian system focused more on industrial workers.[9] Attention to their condition was heightened by riots by weavers in Silesia in 1844. Like the Luddites before them, the weavers of southeastern Prussia suffered wage cuts due to the substitution of machinery and less-skilled workers. The difference was that this substitution now occurred as much abroad—in Lancashire—as at home, and the vehicle was cheap imports, inciting unhappiness about foreign competition along with mechanization.

The weavers responded by destroying machinery, burning warehouses, and attacking the homes of local merchants, which were rather more accessible than the textile mills of Lancashire. Having adopted the same tactics as the Luddites, they met the same fate. The army was deployed. Eleven protesters were killed, and the leaders were arrested, flogged, and imprisoned. The weavers' tragic end was memorialized by the German poet Heinrich Heine in his "Song of the Silesian Weavers," published in Karl Marx's newspaper *Forward!*[10] Friedrich Engels may have succumbed to wishful thinking when he wrote how "the working classes...have been aroused from their lethargy by misery, oppression, and want of employment, as well as by the manufacturing riots in

Silesia and Bohemia" and claimed that one could not "go on board a steamer, or into a railway-carriage, or mail-coach, without meeting somebody...who agrees with you, that something must be done to reorganize society."[11] But there is no question that something was in the air.

That something unsettled the conservative aristocracy. Baden, the Palatinate, the Rhineland, Bavaria, Saxony, and Prussia all saw political uprisings, inspired by protesting French workers, in 1848. The workers demanded better wages and working conditions. Middle-class elements inveighed against the clannish, poorly run autocratic governments of Germany's fragmented states and called for modernization of their archaic civil and criminal codes. The two groups met at the barricades.

Accommodating middle-class demands was straightforward. Baden broadened the franchise. Prussia's King Frederick William IV agreed to popular election of a national assembly to draft a constitution together with the Crown.[12] Calls to replace the many anachronistic principalities with a Greater Germany were met by expanding and deepening the customs union, setting the stage for eventual creation of the German Empire.

It was less clear how to placate the workers. Bismarck, having been elected to the first Prussian diet (the Landtag) in 1849, initially favored a reactionary response, namely restoring the guild system of mandatory membership and self-insurance.[13] But this conservative approach, in which artisans banded together on the basis of craft to support one another and limit unwelcome competition, was not well suited to an economy on the cusp of industrialization. Workers were moving into industrial employment, where there was less stability. Factory labor associated with an industry rather than a specific set of skills was not easily organized into guilds. Workers might have been encouraged to form industrial unions capable of providing health, disability, and old-age insurance to their members, but employers realized that members might also make other demands, including higher wages and shorter hours. If encouraged to organize, they might form a political movement that diverted popular support from established parties.

In 1849 the Prussian diet, still seeking to build on the traditional approach, authorized municipal authorities to order factory workers to join mutual welfare funds without at the same time recognizing their right to bargain. The result was some two hundred such funds. But membership was spotty, benefits were limited, and funds to which employers as well as workers contributed were the exception.[14] The weakness of these schemes was their local nature. Employers could object that mandating substantial contributions might render them unable to compete with firms in neighboring jurisdictions.

Discussion of these problems acquired urgency in the 1860s with more ferment in the ranks of industrial workers. The weavers were battered again, this time by cotton shortages caused by the American Civil War. The German labor movement created new associations, the most important of which, the German Workingmen's Union, sought to advance the interests of its working-class members in the electoral arena. It quickly acquired 125,000 members—an ominous number from the conservative standpoint—mainly urban and factory based. The Workingmen's Union then merged with a competitor, the Social Democratic Workers' Party, to create the Socialist Workers' Party, renamed the Social Democratic Party in 1890.[15]

Above all, there was the industrialization of Germany itself, powered by unification of its formerly independent polities into a federal state with an imperial chancellor in 1871. Employment in industry, unlike that in agriculture, did not follow predictable seasons. Protections from poverty and insecurity afforded rural workers by a local poor law authority and charitable bodies were not available to their urban counterparts, or at best were available only after an extended waiting period.

Bismarck, previously preoccupied by the territorial consolidation of Germany and war with France, now turned his attention to the internal unity of the empire. Unity required the allegiance of the working class, and social insurance was a means to this end. The chancellor, one author writes, "wanted the worker as a loyal and obedient ally, and to accomplish this the worker's interest had to be closely tied to the state. The state, therefore, had to become the protector of the workingman."[16] This was strategic statecraft, not altruism. It was a policy "born in fact not of love, but of fear" of a populist or revolutionary working-class reaction.[17]

The initial result was the Employer Liability Act of 1871, which anticipated similar British legislation by several decades.[18] It made the employer liable for a worker's injury even when fault lay not with the employer directly but with other workers.

Although this was a significant step, there was as yet no equivalent of the modern Federal Ministry of Labor and Social Affairs to enforce standards and establish procedures for adjudicating claims. To obtain a judgment, a worker had to sue his employer, a challenging task for someone with limited financial resources. To collect, he had to convince the court that the fault lay with others and not himself. Thus, the 1871 act was important more for the precedent than for actual compensation.

But, having started down this road, German legislators were in a position to go further. When a financial crisis erupted in 1873, it strengthened the hand of those favoring a more interventionist state. The crash inaugurated a period of slow growth and falling prices referred to by contemporaries as the Great Depression (or Long Depression), not to be confused with the Great Depression of the 1930s. Workers experiencing wage cuts and unemployment rallied around the Social Democratic Party, which, alarming establishment politicians, polled 9 percent in Germany's 1877 election—almost the exact same share polled by the People's Party in the U.S. presidential election fifteen years later.

The insecurity associated with industrial change, slower growth, and heightened foreign competition also manifested itself in nationalist and nativist sentiment. It found expression as the convenient belief that someone other than hardworking Germans themselves was responsible for these unpredictable and not uniformly desirable changes in economic life. In the United States, it was expedient to blame immigrants and to pass the Chinese Exclusion Act. In Germany, a country of emigration, it was easier to target the Jewish minority. Jews were blamed for the 1873 stock market crash by the magazine publisher Otto Glagau, who took heavy financial losses and channeled his frustration in anti-Semitic directions, and whose inflammatory publications attracted a considerable audience.

Bismarck, meanwhile, had just launched the *Kulturkampf*, his culture war against the Roman Catholic Church, with the goal of weakening religious control of education and thereby strengthening the role of the federal state. By highlighting religious differences, the *Kulturkampf* cleared the field for anti-Semitism. Not least, it encouraged anti-Semitism among Catholics who sought to deflect blame for the perceived sufferings of the German people onto others.

More generally, the newly created empire was fertile ground for anti-Semitism because Bismarck and others, in an effort to further strengthen support for the state, also sought to foster the notion of a German *Volk*. Jews were impugned as not fully German, making it possible to single out what was now characterized as not just a religious minority but also a racial group.[19] Thus, the same resentments, fed by economic insecurity and nationalism, that would give rise to anti-immigrant sentiment in the twenty-first century fostered ant-Semitism in the nineteenth. And then as now, there was an effort by politicians and others to use that nationalistic, anti-other sentiment to advance their policy agendas and political careers.

Fortifying the imperial state required securing the allegiance of not just workers, of course, but also industrialists and landholders. In the United States, where the depression triggered by the Panic of 1873 led similarly to falling crop prices and to difficulties for capital-heavy industrial firms that made profits only when plants ran at capacity, the response took the form of the McKinley Tariff, which protected manufacturing from cheap foreign imports. In Britain too, tariff reform was fiercely debated, although in the end allegiance to free trade proved too strong. In Germany, building a winning coalition required forging an alliance between heavy industry, whose political influence, while growing, remained limited, and the country's still powerful Prussian agriculturalists. This was the so-called marriage of iron and rye. Agriculture and industry were both suffering from the post-panic slowdown in growth. Large landowners felt competition from foreign cereals as railways and steamships lowered the cost of importing grain from Russia, the Danube Basin, and the United States. These transport improvements similarly made it less costly to import iron and steel products from Belgium and France, where producers received government-financed export bounties.[20] And even where Germany remained the low-cost producer, tariffs were needed in order for firms to limit output and raise prices, cartel behavior being German industry's preferred way of limiting price cuts when demand weakened.[21]

Industrial interests therefore formed the League for the Protection of the Economic Interests of the Rhineland and Westphalia, also known, for self-evident reasons, as the "Long Name Society." They emphasized not just foreign bounties but also domestic security as justifying import duties.[22] Large landowners, for their part, established the more parsimoniously named League for Tax and Economic Reform to lobby against the grain invasion.

Bismarck's own conversion to protectionism occurred in the 1870s. He was responding to the complaints of industrialists and agriculturalists—four hundred Rhenish-Westphalian producers who met in 1877 to petition against unfair foreign competition, for example—and seeking their political support. He was searching for a source of federal revenue, since the Reich still depended on transfers from its constituent states. That this was a period of mounting tensions in the Balkans and between Germany and Russia made obtaining this dedicated fiscal and military capacity seem all the more urgent.

Bismarck was also maneuvering politically, having broken with the Liberal Party and its left wing. He saw the tariff as a way of attracting industrialists and agrarians affiliated with the *Junker*-dominated Conservative Party and the Catholic-based Center Party.[23] On July 12, 1879, his tariff bill was approved by a coalition of Center and Conservative Reichstag members together with fifteen rebellious members of the right-wing National Liberal Party. The chancellor thus achieved much of what he wanted, though not the full increase in federal revenues, being forced by the Center Party to cede a significant fraction of the increase in import duties to the states.

Although industrialists and landowners had now received the olive branch of protection, something still had to be done to pacify labor, more so insofar as taxes on imported grain made for higher bread prices. Expert opinion acknowledged the linkage. Adolph Wagner, the Berlin-based professor of economics and fiscal policy expert who helped to found the Social Policy Association (Verein für Sozialpolitik), a group of academics and parliamentarians seeking state-sponsored solutions to social problems, advanced import tariffs as a way of raising revenues to fund social programs, thereby strengthening the state. Von Schmoller, the preeminent economist of the time and leader of the German historical school, similarly supported tariffs on the grounds that these could be used to raise revenues for social programs.[24]

Bismarck's preferred design for health, accident, and old-age support was compulsory insurance for industrial workers, with contributions from employers and workers together with state subsidies, all administered by an imperial insurance office. He described these as ideas for heading off international socialism in an audience with King Ludwig II of Bavaria in 1880 and again in an interview with sympathetic journalists in 1881. Creating an imperial insurance administration could highlight the social role of government and foster worker allegiance. Public subsidies would give workers a financial stake in the stability of the state.[25]

This was a bitter pill for conservative social groups to swallow. Right-wing Liberals criticized Bismarck's administrative centralization for undermining self-reliance and private charity. Members of the Conservative Party opposed it for intruding on the organic relations between workers and employers. The Center Party, dominated by Catholics from Bavaria jealous of their regional autonomy, opposed anything that smacked of a strengthened role for the federal government and, by implication, the Protestant north.

Progress required compromise, even by an iron chancellor now firmly ensconced in office. The eventual compromise delegated the administration of health insurance to associations of workers and employers, dominated in practice by the latter, which reported to regional insurance offices.[26] One is reminded how regional opposition to New Deal programs in the United States was similarly overcome by delegating their administration to the states.

The way was thus paved for health insurance in 1883, the further extension of accident insurance in 1884, and old-age and disability insurance in 1889. While this was an impressive array of initiatives, in each case benefits were far from generous. Health-related payments, for example, were targeted at those with temporary ailments. Benefits, including sick pay and access to specialized medical attention, were provided for no more than thirteen weeks and capped at half the average wages of the insured.[27] With its limit of thirteen weeks, the program promised to create only temporary ties between the worker and the state, which rendered it one of Bismarck's lower priorities. The chancellor therefore acquiesced to suggestions that health legislation should build on the foundation of existing guild, factory, and union sickness funds. New funds were created for trades that lacked them, and local funds were established for workers who did not fit into existing categories. Regional offices administered these new insurance funds for workers not served by factory, industry, or union insurance. The federal role was limited to mandating the creation of additional funds and standardizing contributions, which averaged about 1.5 percent of the wage and came two-thirds from workers and one-third from their employers. All this represented a considerable scaling down of Bismarck's ambitions, but it was at least something.

In contrast to health benefits, payments to permanently disabled workers were provided for an extended period, promising to more firmly attach the individual to the state. Bismarck therefore pushed harder for subsidies to top up the contributions of workers and firms. The new accident insurance law covered all industrial accidents. It was administered by associations of employers. But there remained opposition to federal subsidies from Liberals who saw the idea as creeping socialism, and from Center Party members jealous of states' rights. In the final compromise, the financial role of the state was limited to providing a backstop in the event that private contributions proved inadequate.

Old-age insurance was administered by local pension boards controlled by civil servants and overseen by a state government ministry, giving government (albeit state rather than federal government) a more prominent role. In this case, moreover, Bismarck's proposal for state subsidies was retained. Subsidy supporters in the Reichstag heralded the role of pensions in "support[ing] ... the total economic and social order."[28]

The insurance laws of the 1880s focused on industrial workers, who felt economic insecurity most strongly and were especially prone, in the prevailing view, to radical socialism. Insurance was finally extended to white-collar workers earning less than 2,000 marks a year in 1900 in the case of pensions, and in 1903 in the case of health insurance. The same year, 1911, in which Great Britain put in place its own social policy legislation then saw passage of the Reich Insurance Law, which provided health insurance to all employees, including agricultural workers, and benefits for dependents of the elderly and disabled.[29]

Germany's early start in adopting social insurance thus reflected long-standing awareness of the role of the state in governing the economy and of the need for public intervention as the country industrialized. Urbanization and the shift from agriculture to industry occurred even faster than the comparable transitions in Britain and the United

States, heightening insecurity and limiting the effectiveness of traditional institutions for addressing it. Worries that those industrial workers might unite in an anti-market, anti-establishment movement were thus more immediate than in other countries.

These concerns fused with Bismarck's desire to tie the working class to the new federal state. They combined with the reaction against globalization by still-influential German agriculturalists and with the complaints of powerful industrialists about lack of market access and unfair foreign competition. These dissatisfactions too, like those of the workers, had to be harnessed. It was necessary to tie these additional interest groups to the state and to Bismarck's base in the Conservative and Center Parties.

This confluence was what made possible Germany's distinctive response to the pressures of globalization and industrial change, which included precocious development of the social insurance state combined with tariff protection for both agriculture and industry, a response that effectively suppressed anxiety about economic change on both the Left and the Right. It was not a confluence that was equally evident in America, where both revolutionary ferment and confidence in the administrative capacity of government were less. It was not as evident in Britain, where parliamentary institutions were well established, calming fears of revolution, and where agriculture had declined to the point where it no longer figured importantly in political calculus.

Politicians in other countries observed the German recipe of tariff protection for agriculture and industry together with health, accident, and old-age insurance for workers facing the uncertainties of industrial life. The German precedent influenced design of the McKinley Tariff and the health and pension benefits provided to Union Army veterans and their spouses in the United States. It informed the views of Beatrice and Sidney Webb and Britain's National Insurance Act. It led Denmark, Sweden, Norway, and other countries to create commissions to investigate the social question. In all these instances, legislators made reference to Germany's earlier measures and drew on them for inspiration and support.

But agreement on those German measures required compromise. As a result, the import duties agreed to in 1879 limited international trade only to a degree. Tariff rates fell from the mid-1890s, as industrialists

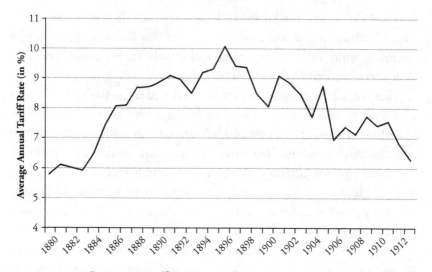

FIGURE 4.1   German Tariff Rates, 1870–1913

Source: B.R. Mitchell, ed. *European Historical Statistics, 1750–1970* (Springer, 1975).

gained political leverage relative to landowners and post-Bismarck governments lowered duties on imported agricultural commodities.[30] Health, accident, and old-age benefits were funded mainly by the workers themselves. Administration was delegated to employers, to corporative associations of firms and workers, and to local and regional agencies. The federal government's role in subsidizing the system was circumscribed. The precocious measures taken by the German Empire in response to globalization and the dislocations of rapid industrial change were real, but they are also prone to exaggeration.

Above all, those measures were important as a model. They were a model that some countries but not others, in their wisdom, ultimately chose to follow.

5

The Associationalist Way

THE GREAT DEPRESSION was the gravest economic and social crisis of the twentieth century. The United States was plunged into the deepest recession in its history as recorded rates of unemployment soared to 25 percent. Much of the rest of the world quickly followed.

A crisis of this magnitude deeply damaged support for free and open trade and for the market system generally. Communist Party activists in the United States formed Unemployed Councils, distributing leaflets at breadlines, flophouses, and employment offices in an effort to organize the out-of-work. The party declared March 6, 1930, "International Unemployment Day," organizing marches and rallies demanding action to support the unemployed. Demonstrations in San Francisco were peaceful, but in Washington, D.C., tear gas was used to disperse the protesters. In New York City, responding to exhortations by protest leaders to march on city hall, the police waded into the crowd. As the *New York Times* described the scene: "Hundreds of policemen and detectives, swinging night sticks, blackjacks and bare fists, rushed into the crowd, hitting out at all with whom they came into contact, chasing many across the street and into adjacent thoroughfares and rushing hundreds off their feet." Subsequent rallies and marches inveighed against not just unemployment but also police brutality, as Black Lives Matter would many years later.

In 1932, impoverished World War I veterans marched on Washington, demanding that the government pay out the bonuses servicemen were promised.[1] The Bonus Army set up camp in Anacostia Flats, across from the Capitol. But President Hoover and the Republican-controlled Senate were less concerned with indigent veterans than with maintaining a balanced budget, which the politicians saw as critical for restoring investor confidence. On June 17 the Senate voted down a bill to disburse the bonus money. With the Bonus Army showing no sign of dispersing, Attorney General William D. Mitchell then ordered the removal of protesting veterans, instructions with which the Washington, D.C., police were tasked. The protesters resisted. Shots were fired, and two demonstrators were killed. With the situation spiraling out of control, Hoover instructed the army, under the command of General Douglas MacArthur, to clear the Capitol grounds. Exceeding his orders (not for the last time), MacArthur instructed his troops, with bayonets fixed, to dismantle the Anacostia camp. In the subsequent battle, 50 veterans were wounded and 135 arrested.

These events, played out against the backdrop of a collapsing economy, did not go unnoticed by the voting public. They resulted in the landslide victory of Franklin Delano Roosevelt in November 1932 and in the Democrats capturing both houses of Congress. This realignment set the stage for the New Deal, through which the government provided relief work for thousands of idled people, and for the Social Security Act of 1935, under which it provided old-age pensions, disability insurance, unemployment insurance, and public assistance for the elderly and dependent children. In the symbolic capstone, the veterans finally got their bonus in 1936.

Together these measures were enough to ward off existential threats to the market system. That said, the response was limited by the standards of other advanced countries. And it had some peculiar features, such as the omission of anything resembling national health insurance.

Understanding why requires looking back at the history of social provision in the United States. America was late to develop the kind of government-mandated protections pioneered by Bismarck's Germany and elaborated by Britain and other European countries. At first glance this seems peculiar. U.S. manufacturing expanded rapidly in the final quarter of the nineteenth century, following the discovery of high-quality iron ores in the Mesabi Range in Minnesota and the exploitation of petroleum in Pennsylvania. But that expansion was far from smooth. It was punctuated by downturns, often accompanied by financial crises. Dislocation and insecurity accompanied these movements. Factory workers typically did not have a farm or an extended family on which to fall back. Joblessness was chronic among the floating class of un-skilled workers loosely attached to a particular occupation or firm.[2]

All this suggests that there should have been a demand for state-sponsored unemployment, health, old-age, and disability insurance. Yet, prior to World War I, the only significant such measures were old-age, disability, and widows' benefits for former members of the Union Army. Benefits were paid only to disabled veterans and war widows initially, but the criteria for qualifying, including self-reported injury or disability, were progressively relaxed. By the turn of the century, fully half of all elderly native-born men in the North were receiving veterans' benefits, averaging 30 percent of typical earnings.[3]

These pensions were funded out of revenues from tariffs, following the German model.[4] As in Germany, the connection served to create a coalition of manufacturers and workers with a stake in the economic status quo. Workers appreciated disability and widows' payments, while manufacturers were sheltered from import competition. Republican Party leaders, for whom import duties were standard economic fare, supported veterans' pensions precisely because funding them required higher tariffs, the latter being the government's principal source of rev-enue. This provided a link between the McKinley Tariff and the Disability Pensions Act of 1890, which allowed faster qualification by veterans and the extension of benefits to more widows.

But these arrangements left little in the way of an enduring legacy. As Union Army veterans died off, so did their pension system. By World War I, Civil War pensions had come to symbolize everything to be avoided. Democrats and Progressives portrayed them as riddled by false and equivocal claims. Their true rationale was less justice and generos-ity, these critics argued, than "a desire to cultivate the 'soldier vote' for [Republican] party purposes."[5] The image they painted of inefficiency and favoritism clashed with Progressive efforts to counter corruption in government.

Patronage, not unrelatedly, was the other principal source of public social support.[6] At the end of the nineteenth century, the federal gov-ernment employed some 150,000 civilians. Just 20 percent were hired competitively through a process resembling the modern-day civil service. The rest were mostly employees of the post office, mail delivery being one of the core functions of America's still-limited government.

Many of these civilian employees obtained their positions through demonstrations of political fealty to their congressman or local officials.

In the years bracketing World War I, a number of states then passed legislation extending aid to widowed mothers, presaging the advent of the Aid to Families with Dependent Children (AFDC) program in 1935.[7] Permitting children to remain in parental care resonated with Progressive emphasis on family and motherhood. "Home life is the highest and finest product of civilization," as the point was put by the 1909 White House Conference on the Care of Dependent Children. "Children should not be deprived of it except for urgent and compelling reasons."[8] Women, still denied the vote, organized the National Congress of Mothers and the General Federation of Women's Clubs to advance this argument. The enactment of measures providing aid to widowed mothers and dependent children was closely tied to the lobbying efforts of these groups.[9]

Even where such measures were adopted, however, eligibility was limited to "deserving widows," not also impoverished parents with children, as under AFDC.[10] Administration was assigned to juvenile courts and social workers, themselves by-products of the Progressive movement, thereby eliminating the tinge of favoritism and corruption associated with patronage and Civil War pensions.

Around the same time, a growing number of states adopted workers' compensation laws to help workers deal with the consequences of workplace injury, anticipating the Social Security Disability Insurance program finally adopted in 1956. These laws were similarly a product of the Progressive movement. The positive case was made by the American Association for Labor Legislation, a group of progressive academicians. The association drafted model bills. It pointed to government-mandated disability insurance in Germany as an example to follow. Employers were not strongly opposed, since they could already be taken to court for compensation by injured workers.[11] Neither were legislators, since compensation could be funded directly by the employer, avoiding a burden on the taxpayer. But compensation covered workers in industry only.[12] And accident-prone industries were able to limit the payments for which they were liable, citing the danger, real or imagined, that accident insurance would encourage recklessness on the part of their employees. Still, passage of these laws constituted a recognition that industrial change, and specifically continued mechanization of the workplace, created new risks with which neither workers and employers nor even the courts were fully prepared to cope.

The question is why there wasn't more extensive social insurance for disability, joblessness, poverty, and old age at the federal level, as in Germany. The answer starts with the absence of a strong state. Two oceans gave America natural protection from enemies, making central power less imperative. Internal divisions there might be, like those between North and South, but these too worked to limit federal powers. The last thing southern employers with a captive black labor force wanted was a northern-dominated federal government making social policy for the region. This concern continued to shape the design of such policies through the 1930s and beyond.

Relatedly, there were doubts about the competence of a government riddled by waste, fraud, capture, and sheer ineptness. As Theda Skocpol, the authority on such matters, more clinically puts it, "Only around 1900 did U.S. governments at local, state and federal levels begin to develop significant bureaucratic capabilities."[13] Even organized labor shared these concerns, union leaders worrying that business would capture the federal bureaucracy and turn it to its advantage. Thus, Samuel Gompers and the American Federation of Labor lobbied for strict liability laws and judicial recourse rather than government-sponsored workmen's compensation.

The federal landscape was altered in 1912 by the election of Woodrow Wilson, who "ushered into full bloom the progressivism [William Jennings] Bryan had demanded since 1890" (and who not incidentally appointed Bryan, the icon of Populism, as his secretary of state).[14] As Progressive governor of New Jersey, Wilson had pushed workmen's compensation legislation through the state legislature. Following his lead, Congress now passed the Kern-McGillicuddy Act, providing workmen's compensation for federal employees. Wilson supported a graduated income tax (as noted in Chapter 2), which was adopted once the states ratified the Sixteenth Amendment to the Constitution, providing revenue for new federal programs. While tax rates started out low, they jumped once the United States entered World War I, to 67 percent in 1917 and then to 77 percent in 1918 on incomes above $1 million.

Wartime also saw considerable expansion of the federal government's administrative powers. Not only did military recruitment and production increase, but new agencies such as the War Industries Board, which oversaw production of essential inputs, and the War Trade Board, which granted import and export licenses, demonstrated the capacity of federal agencies to carry out additional tasks. Prominent among these agencies was the U.S. Food Administration, directed by an ambitious administrator with an engineering background by the name of Herbert Hoover. Hoover created the U.S. Grain Corporation to purchase foodstuffs, and the Sugar Equalization Board to purchase and allocate Cuba's sugar crop, developments that went at least some way toward demonstrating that the federal government was competent to assume additional tasks.

The 1920s, as a decade of peace and prosperity, did not provide many new demands for government action. Although farmers complained again about low crop prices, the prosperity of the period did not create particularly fertile ground for populist agitation. The Republican Party, traditionally opposed to the income tax, regained control of the Congress and White House and rolled back top tax rates to 25 percent. Wartime boards and agencies were abolished, reducing government's reach and dimming the prospects for a Bismarckian insurance state. Europe, now engulfed in economic and social chaos, no longer was seen as a shining city on a hill but rather was considered an example to be avoided.

The United States turned instead to welfare capitalism, that is, to welfare provision by enlightened employers. Enlightened employers, the argument ran, understood that old-age pensions and disability insurance promised a more stable labor force. Pensions and insurance went hand in hand with scientific management and with the personnel departments now created to more efficiently recruit and retain productive workers.[15] Voluntary provision promised to limit inroads by organized labor, which had unionized additional workers during World War I.[16] Seeing the lay of the land, Congress amended the Internal Revenue Code in 1926 to provide tax exemptions for employer pension contributions.[17]

Welfare capitalism thus promised an alternative to federal government administration, about whose efficiency Americans harbored doubts. In his stint as head of the wartime Food Administration, Hoover had championed corporatist initiatives like Price Interpreting Boards, which brought together wholesalers, retailers, and consumer representatives to negotiate an acceptable balance between prices and profits. As secretary of commerce under Presidents Harding and Coolidge, the Great Engineer, as he was known, applied this vision of an associative state more broadly.[18] He organized a 1921 President's Conference on Unemployment to mount voluntary, cooperative responses to the postwar recession. He established a Bureau of Unemployment in the Commerce Department to provide information about local conditions to charitable organizations. He encouraged employers to coordinate the provision of pensions and voluntary assistance.

These visible initiatives paved the way for Hoover's presidential run in 1928. But the reality did not match the vision: in 1930, at the outset of the Great Depression, the United States still had just 420 industrial pension plans covering a mere 100,000 retirees.[19] Other workers who had paid into these systems for a limited period lost their jobs in the downturn, consequently failing to satisfy the qualification period and never becoming eligible for pension payments.

This was an unpromising setting for a constructive response to a populist backlash, which was what the Great Depression now threatened to unleash. Along with rallies by the urban unemployed and marches by veterans, there was mounting anger and protest in the Farm Belt. Members of the Farm Holiday movement, protesting low prices, blocked highways to disrupt the crop markets of Omaha and Des Moines until police dismantled the roadblocks. They demonstrated against foreclosure auctions, threatening sheriffs and justices that they would be ridden out of town on a rail. Farmers allied with the Ku Klux Klan and the Communist Party—sometimes both at the same time.[20] They marched on state capitols, forcing legislatures in twenty-five states to declare foreclosure moratoria. By dramatizing the farmers' plight, these protests set the stage for the Agricultural Adjustment Administration, which was a key building block of the New Deal.

A second, more unconventional response was the Townsend movement. This push for universal old-age pensions was the spontaneous reaction to a letter by an unsuccessful California physician, Francis E. Townsend, published in September 1933 in the author's hometown paper, the Long Beach *Press-Telegram*. The letter went viral, and within months petitions endorsing the Townsend Plan had gathered thousands of signatures, leading to the formation of hundreds of Townsend Clubs. People unaffiliated with the two mainstream political parties, including the unemployed, were disproportionately represented. By 1936 there were as many as 2 million active club members, nearly one in five of all Americans over the age of 60. In all, the movement claimed 30 million supporters.[21]

Townsend's letter proposed that the federal government should pay a basic income of $150 a month, $2,700 in today's dollars, to every person sixty years or older, conditional on his quitting work and immediately spending the money.[22] Thus the plan claimed not only to address the needs of the indigent elderly but also to solve problems of unemployment and depression by removing older workers from the competition for jobs and providing a proto-Keynesian stimulus.

Townsend himself was self-promoting and naive and drew an excessive salary from what became the Townsend Plan Corporation. He had the poor judgment to ally with the Reverend Gerald L. K. Smith, an anti-Semitic proto-fascist former aide to Louisiana politician Huey Long who was seeking a new political movement to latch on to following Long's assassination.[23] Be that as it may, the Townsend movement was the first true mass movement of the elderly in any country. It was the first significant precursor to the American Association of Retired Persons (AARP), the mid-twentieth-century American lobby.[24] It was logical that this movement gained traction in the 1930s, when assembly-line methods displaced experienced labor in manufacturing and Depression-era unemployment disproportionately impacted older workers.[25] Furthermore, it was logical that it originated in the United States, where there had been little progress in the public provision of pensions and there was no Labor Party to advocate on behalf of older workers. The Townsend movement thus confronted the established political parties with a new interest group strongly invested in including old-age protection in what ultimately became the Social Security Act.[26]

There were thus a variety of pressures for government action. Yet the Hoover administration's response to them, and to the Depression generally, was almost comical for its impotence. The president himself continued to call for an associationalist approach. In November 1929, with the economy clearly turning down, he invited business and labor leaders to the White House and urged them to maintain wages and employment. By working together, Hoover argued, leaders could successfully address problems whose solution would otherwise elude them. While it might not be feasible for any one firm or industry acting alone to maintain the prevailing level of wages, if all firms and industries did likewise then the additional spending of workers in some sectors would help absorb the output and defray the costs of firms in others. The press release following Hoover's November 1929 White House meeting referred, additionally, to "human considerations" militating against wage reductions. It spoke optimistically of "the development of cooperative spirit and responsibility in the American business world."[27]

If this was the ultimate test of welfare capitalism, then it was a test that was failed unequivocally. High wages for some did not guarantee employment for others given heightened uncertainty, which rendered workers receiving additional income reluctant to spend it.[28] Firms playing the associationalist game saw their profits squeezed, forcing them to curtail production.

In a limp effort to address calls for public employment and relief, Hoover supported the creation of the Emergency Relief Administration to loan funds to the states. Other than this, however, his administration took few meaningful steps. The 1932 election therefore became a referendum on the competence of economic management and the need for government action.

But if voters resoundingly rejected Hoover's associationalist way, they did not vote for progressives or socialists in any number. Norman Thomas's Socialist Party campaign drew almost no attention. Voters simply switched their allegiance from one mainstream party to the other. But now it was imperative for this other mainstream party to mount a concerted response to the crisis if it was to head off a more radical political reaction and keep power out of the hands of the likes of Huey Long.

The New Deal and the Social Security Act of 1935 are often seen as that concerted response. They are portrayed as a break with the country's small-government past and a decisive step toward the modern welfare state. In fact, they were something less. FDR did not champion large-scale public employment or ambitious public works. Rather than advocating sharply higher public spending to replace the private spending that had evaporated, he moved in 1934 to balance the budget. He did not push for comprehensive social insurance at the federal level, instead delegating administrative functions to the states.

This, in turn, raises two questions. Why did the president, with his own party firmly in control of both houses of Congress, fail to do more? And why did these measures, despite their limitations, succeed in repelling the populist challenge to the status quo?

The answer to the first question is political constraints. As noted, FDR had to contend with Southern Democrats opposed to any expansion of federal powers that threatened to weaken the control of southern businessmen and farmers over their black labor force. He was not making policy in a parliamentary system: Democrats in Congress could challenge his leadership and reject his program without bringing down the government and exposing themselves to loss of office in an immediate election. Those Southern Democrats insisted on the decentralization of New Deal programs and delegation of their administration to the states. They may have been happy to see a federal government committed to promoting the economic development of the rural South, but only on their terms. People sometimes ask why the American welfare state is less extensive than its European counterparts. There can be no more basic explanation than this historic divide between North and South and between black and white.[29]

Relatedly, Roosevelt inherited a Supreme Court with four conservative justices, the so-called Four Horsemen, and a fifth unpredictable swing voter, the Hoover appointee Owen Roberts. Ambitious initiatives, especially when they were seen as infringing on states' rights, could be invalidated by the Court, as happened in 1935 when the justices struck down key provisions of the New Deal on the grounds that they usurped prerogatives reserved for the states. This separation of powers was an established part of the American political landscape, as FDR learned in 1937, at considerable cost to himself, when he attempted to expand the Supreme Court in order to add justices sympathetic to the New Deal but saw his bill go down in flames in the Senate.

A final countervailing force, along with Congress and the courts, was business, which mobilized against policies that threatened to interfere with labor relations and against taxes that would increase costs. The nominally bipartisan American Liberty League, founded in 1934, was in fact dominated by businessmen affiliated with the Democratic Party, who opposed their own president's interventions on precisely these grounds.

FDR might have sought to advance a more ambitious agenda and over-ridden these sectional, judicial, and business constraints by building a co-alition of urban liberals, progressive Republicans, and southern blacks. But the obstacles were formidable. Acknowledging this reality, he instead sought to forge a centrist coalition that addressed poverty, inequality, and insecurity while at the same time respecting the priorities of business and the states and maintaining the economic and political status quo.

The result was less a rejection of Hoover's quasi-corporatist approach than a balancing act. It involved balancing the views of conservatives such as budget director Lewis Douglas against those of liberal activists including Rexford Tugwell, Harry Hopkins, and, not least, the First Lady, Eleanor Roosevelt. It included legislation mandating a minimum wage but also measures to compensate business through, inter alia, the suspension of anti-trust laws. It relied on investment for reviving the economy, which implied avoiding measures that antagonized investors.

This moderate approach to social reform also suited Roosevelt tem-peramentally. The president was committed to reform but in the con-text of the prevailing system. His goal was not to overturn the market economy but to repair it. The purpose of reform, in his own words, was "to save our system, the capitalistic system."[30] FDR was a card-carrying member of the economic and political establishment—in other words, not a populist firebrand.

FDR also sought to decouple immediate steps to address the eco-nomic emergency from social reforms designed to solidify support for the market system. His emergency measures included the bank holiday, taking the country off the gold standard, and asking Congress to estab-lish the Federal Emergency Relief Administration, or FERA. These ini-tiatives succeeded in meeting the immediate emergency without funda-mentally altering the market system. By declaring the bank holiday, for example, FDR avoided having to nationalize the banks, a more radical step. Most banks were able to reopen after two weeks, confidence having returned as a result of the cooling-off period, inspection of their balance sheets by the regulators, and new powers for the Federal Reserve System to provide liquidity under the Emergency Banking Act of 1933.

Taking the country off the gold standard in April was a shock to the status quo and a focal point for those accusing FDR of despotic and Communistic tendencies.[31] But taking control of monetary policy through the powers of the Reconstruction Finance Corporation and buying gold at progressively higher dollar prices enabled the president and his advisors to bring deflation to an end. This allowed FDR to re-peg the dollar to gold in January 1934 at a price of $35 an ounce, up from $20.66, changing the structure of U.S. monetary policy rather less than feared by his more alarmist critics.

Finally, FERA, though providing work for some four and a half million Americans at its peak, was only temporary. Once it was replaced in 1935 by the Works Progress Administration, the commitment to public employment waned.[32] Southern, business, and farm interests all opposed the extension of federal employment programs. There was nothing like the increase in public employment in some European countries in the 1930s and then after World War II.[33]

These initiatives were visible. They responded to the immediate crisis. But they worked in the context of the prevailing system and bought time to contemplate more far-reaching measures.

The emergency having been addressed, Roosevelt appointed a Committee on Economic Security chaired by labor secretary Frances Perkins to consider those more far-reaching changes. The name of the committee is indicative of the president's awareness of the pervasive sense of insecurity created by the Depression. But even this committee reflected FDR's commitment to a middle way. Both radical reformers and reactionary business representatives were excluded from the deliberations of the committee and its advisory council. The committee was insulated from extremists on the Left and the Right, allowing its proposals to be situated firmly in the middle. Social insurance was framed as a technical problem to be solved by experts like Edwin Witte, the committee's staff director, professor of economics at the University of Wisconsin, and onetime executive secretary of the U.S. Commission on Industrial Relations. The administration's continued reliance on technocrats is a reminder that this was not populism in action; to the contrary, the goal was to head off a populist reaction.

FDR and his committee still had to contend with pressure from the Townsendites for a noncontributory retirement scheme financed out of general revenues. But the president and his advisors worried that direct government grants to citizens were subject to abuse. This preoccupation, a legacy of the Civil War pension system, lived on even if not everyone understood its historical origins. Hence the old-age security program that the administration offered Congress involved no federal subsidy; it was designed to be funded by matching employer and employee contributions. Given this limit to funding, benefits for the aged were necessarily modest.[34]

In terms of administration, this was the one time Roosevelt and his advisors went to the mat, insisting on a federally administered program on the grounds that the tendency for people to move between states in the course of their working lives made a patchwork of state systems infeasible.

But when it came to unemployment insurance, arguments for states' rights and local provision carried the day. The Social Security Act of 1935 therefore appropriated funds for grants to the states for administering unemployment compensation, old-age assistance, and aid to dependent children rather than creating federal agencies to provide these services. Disbursal of funds was conditioned only on a state passing an acceptable law and submitting a conforming plan to the Social Security Board.[35] These conditions regarding laws, plans, and administration were again designed to address concerns about corruption and patronage and tensions between North and South.

Coverage of these social insurance programs was uneven, reflecting differences in state resources and the limited ability of the Social Security Board to enforce uniform standards. Benefits were further limited by the contributory nature of the scheme and the requirement for matching state funds. Ultimately, regular monthly Social Security benefits started only in 1940 due to the need to first build up a reserve.

Moreover, some risks, including exceptional health care costs and disability, were not covered at all.[36] FDR had initially supported including health care in the Social Security Act. But compulsory government-run health insurance was opposed by the American Medical Association (AMA), which feared government intruding in ways that undermined the autonomy, not to mention the compensation, of medical professionals. The AMA was an encompassing organization, since membership in the local medical society, which conferred hospital privileges, patient referrals, and malpractice liability protection, required joining the national association.[37] Public support for government-run health care was hard to mobilize, medical care being complicated and the American public being instinctually averse to government bureaucrats in the exam room. Forced to pick his battles, Roosevelt concluded that unemployment insurance, lent prominence by the Depression, and old-age insurance, having been highlighted by Townsend and his clubs, were the priorities, and so he agreed to removing the health care provisions of the Social Security bill.[38]

Later, in response to World War II wage and price controls, employers offered health insurance to their workers in lieu of additional pay.[39] After the war, tax breaks and the continued opposition of the AMA to socialized medicine allowed the arrangement to persist.[40] And so was born the peculiar U.S. system where workers obtained health coverage from their employers, and where the AMA allied with the critics of big government in opposition to mandatory health insurance and a role for the public sector in providing it. The absence of national health insurance in the United States was a prominent exception to the growth of social welfare spending across the advanced economies in the postwar years. This exception and the distinctive approach to the provision of health insurance in the United States are clear examples of history's long shadow.

This brings us finally to the question of why these limited measures were enough to repel populist challenges to the status quo. The answer lies partly in the success of FDR's emergency measures. Relief work helped millions of Americans hardest hit by the slump, if only for a time. Economic recovery, supported by repair of the banking system and monetary policies that removed the specter of deflation, helped millions more. Putting aside the double-dip recession of 1937–1938, the U.S. economy expanded between 1933 and 1941 at an annual rate of nearly 10 percent. The 1940 unemployment rate, at 14 percent, though still elevated, was barely half the disastrous levels of 1933.

And then there was World War II, which made for the quick restoration of full employment, if nothing else could.

6

Unemployment and Reaction

THE 1920S AND 1930S were years of crisis not just in the United States but globally. High unemployment, collapsing incomes, and all the associated socioeconomic ills—rising poverty, declining family formation, and deteriorating health status—were widespread, especially in the 1930s, when economic turbulence was greatest. In some places the political reaction developed even earlier, in Italy, for example, in response to the postwar recession and banking crisis, and in Germany in the chaos of post–World War I demobilization and then hyperinflation in 1923. Inflation in the 1920s and unemployment in the 1930s undermined confidence in the ability of mainstream politicians and governments to manage the economy. The failure of the political establishment to do more to help those feeling the most damaging effects and instead curtailing even those limited programs of social support of greatest value to the masses—the decision to opt for what today we would call austerity at the cost of the working class—bred support for political extremists on the Left and Right.

In the worst cases, such as Hitler's Germany, the demagogues assuming power targeted religious and ethnic minorities as responsible for society's ills. They repudiated free trade and prohibited a broad swath of cross-border financial transactions. They renounced the market and brought large segments of the economy under government control. They undermined checks and balances and more generally the institutional foundations of the political system. They showed scant respect for individual rights.

Benito Mussolini's assumption of power in Italy similarly owed much to the chaos that engulfed the country after World War I. Like

Hitler, Mussolini used an aggressive nationalism to cultivate support in a turbulent economic environment, when many Italians already had doubts about their government's competence in light of its pathetic performance in the war. He cultivated the image of a strongman to appeal to those who believed that only an authoritative, even authoritarian leader could restore order. He organized visible demonstrations of his economic prowess, commissioning roads, bridges, and most famously the Monumento Nazionale a Vittorio Emanuele II, crowned by two bronze statues of Winged Glory, in 1925. He undermined political and economic institutions, substituted personal decision-making for judicial and constitutional rule, and superseded the market system, all with the goal of limiting individual liberty and strengthening the state. "The Fascist conception accepts the individual," as he explained in a 1932 article for the *Enciclopedia Italiana*, "only in so far as his interests coincide with those of the State."[1] Mussolini maintained his power base by showering favors on cronies, attacking the hostile media, and cultivating sympathetic journalists. If his impact was ultimately less catastrophic than Hitler's, this only reflected his more limited competence.

In other cases, like that of Britain, the fascist reaction failed to command widespread support. Influenced in part by Mussolini's example, the aristocratic and temperamentally impatient Oswald Mosley formed the New Party in 1931 and then the British Union of Fascists in 1932.[2] As a member of the Labour Party, Mosley had been charged with developing policies toward unemployment for the MacDonald government, formed in 1929. His proposals, which included tariffs, nationalization of major industries, and an ambitious program of public works—all characteristic populist initiatives—were spurned by a cautious prime minister and a cabinet anxious to establish Labour's financial bona fides. Rejection of his populist agenda precipitated Mosley's resignation, his political turn to the Right, and his conversion into an antisystem politician.

It was not immediately clear, however, that Mosley's was a losing bet. Labour's failure to contain the spreading economic crisis created political disarray. It led to the collapse of the MacDonald government in August 1931 and then to popular repudiation of the party and its program in the subsequent general election. These conditions were just the type on which an authoritarian, quasi-fascist leader could conceivably capitalize.

But though Mosley shared Mussolini's military bearing, his image as a strongman, and his oratorical skills, his movement never caught fire. Mosley's rallies and marches remained small. All but two of twenty-four candidates fielded by his New Party for the October 1931 general election failed to win the 5 percent vote share needed to obtain a refund of the deposit tendered to stand. (Mosley himself was one of the two.) The Mosleyites were then unable even to contest seats in the next general election, in 1935. At its height, the British Union of Fascists numbered no more than twenty thousand members.[3] At the other end of the political spectrum, twenty-six Communist candidates stood for election in 1931, but none was victorious, and only two received more than ten thousand votes. Instead, the National government, made up of a coalition of mainstream politicians with various party affiliations, but in practice dominated by the Conservatives, won a landslide victory and controlled British politics for the balance of the decade.

There is no single explanation for these contrasting outcomes. Still, there are some general lessons for those seeking to understand the roots of anti-system reactions and how they are successfully contained.

First, the economic legacies of World War I were fundamentally less amenable to conventional policy solutions in some countries than in others. Germany experienced high unemployment not just in the Great Depression but earlier, in the wake of World War I. Already in the early 1920s, inflation, by expropriating the middle class, undermined the legitimacy of the mainstream politicians who presided over it and weakened faith in the country's political institutions. Nor were these challenges that even a competent German government could meet. The country's economic and financial problems, and its internal struggle over distribution and inequality, were linked to the reparations burden imposed by France and the other victorious Allies, which raised the intractable question of who, within Germany, would pay.[4] There was no way for a reasonable government to extricate Germany from the reparations tangle and transcend its domestic political consequences. A solution would be found, ultimately, only by that least reasonable of governments.

Britain, in contrast, while not without economic problems, was not burdened by reparations.[5] And unlike in other countries, there was no banking crisis to radicalize public opinion. While there was much debate about the causes and consequences of the economic downturn, the fact is that the depth of the Great Depression, as measured by the fall in real GDP, was less than in virtually any other country, and that decline in GDP was successfully arrested by 1932.[6] The authorities took a number of visible steps to jump-start growth: abandoning the gold standard, allowing sterling to depreciate, and cutting interest rates to historically low levels. There was also the imposition of a tariff, more on which below. This proactive response solidified support for the political status quo.[7]

In Germany, in contrast, there was no resumption of growth at the end of 1931, nor even the distant prospect of such under the Grand Coalition of mainstream parties led by Hermann Müller from 1928 or the Center Party–led government of Chancellor Heinrich Brüning, in power from 1930 to 1932.

This leads to the second point, that different governments went to different lengths to address economic insecurity. The signal economic problem of the interwar period was unemployment. There was more consciousness of unemployment as an aggregate phenomenon now that

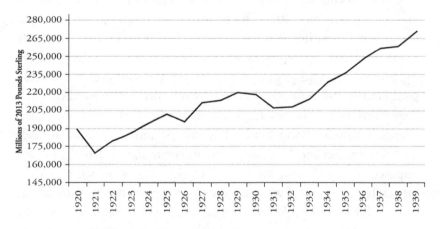

FIGURE 6.1 GDP in the United Kingdom, 1920–1939

Source: Sally Hills, Ryland Thomas and Nicholas Dimsdale, "The UK Recession in Context – What Do Three Centuries of Data Tell Us?" *Bank of England Quarterly Bulletin* (2010), Data Annex – Version 2.1.

academicians had given it a clear definition and governments gathered statistics on it. There was more awareness of unemployment as an economic and political problem to be solved, or else, now that the franchise had been broadened, unions had acquired additional strength, and labor and socialist parties had come on the scene.

In Britain, many of these changes were already under way before World War I, resulting in adoption of that country's pioneering unemployment insurance system in 1911.[8] That system now provided a basis for the further development of public policy. As a result of the precedent and of a consensus for building on that foundation, Britain elaborated one of the most comprehensive unemployment insurance schemes of any country, with near-universal adult male coverage. The British system was not without its critics, but it succeeded in providing assistance to many of those most directly affected by unemployment, defusing more radical political reactions.[9]

In Germany, in contrast, state-organized insurance had never covered joblessness. A limited unemployment insurance scheme was finally agreed in 1927, but benefits quickly came under the gun with deepening financial difficulties in 1929.

The French and Italian economies, by comparison, were more heavily agrarian. In 1921, 59 percent of employment in Italy was in agriculture; fifteen years later, the figure was 52 percent. Italy and France had little need for extensive unemployment insurance programs, either before or after World War I, because urban industrial workers had the option of returning to family village and farm.[10] In France, unemployment insurance organized by trade unions on behalf of their members and by municipalities on behalf of their residents covered just 171,000 people as late as 1931.[11] Small landowners and shopkeepers saw no need for unemployment insurance. A compulsory system of contributory insurance was considered by legislators in 1928 but rejected as unnecessary.[12]

Yet despite mounting only a limp institutional response, France did not experience a German-style political reaction. In 1936 the French electorate threw out the latest in a series of conservative governments for a short-lived socialist administration under Léon Blum, but that reaction was mild compared to what took place east of the Rhine. The structure of the French economy, still heavily village and household based, helps to explain this response.

Finally, the weakness of political institutions empowered political extremists hostile to the system to a greater extent in some places than others.[13] The British parliamentary system was well established, and successive reform acts tinkered with it only at the margins. There might be important changes in the political landscape, such as the rise of the Labour Party and the decline of the Liberals, but these could be accommodated by the country's well-established parliamentary institutions. In turn, this capacity to accommodate new parties and movements gave those dissatisfied with the political status quo reason to work within the system rather than seeking to overturn it.[14]

German institutions, by comparison, were weak. The Weimar Republic had been born of weakness; it was declared in Weimar, in the state of Thüringia, in February 1919 because Berlin was still occupied by the Communist-inspired Spartacists and other dissident groups.[15] That the new German constitution bore little resemblance to earlier political arrangements did not inspire confidence or promote allegiance. Pure proportional representation opened the door to representation in the Reichstag of scores of small political parties whose members had little incentive to move to the political middle, unlike the United Kingdom's first-past-the-post electoral system. Political fragmentation made for a succession of unstable, ineffective coalition governments, weakening support for the constitution. Key groups that might have been expected to defend it instead displayed their apathy, starting with the army's failure to intervene on behalf of the government during the Kapp Putsch, the unsuccessful coup attempt organized by the right-wing autocrat Wolfgang Kapp in 1920.[16] Article 48 of the constitution, which gave the president decree powers, including the power to suspend civil liberties, acknowledged these weaknesses but was readily exploited by political opportunists like Hitler, who invoked it, using the Reichstag fire as a pretext, less than a month after taking office. Poor design thus contributed to the vulnerability of Weimar's institutions, although so too did lack of familiarity with and fidelity to the new arrangements.

In Italy, Mussolini gained office by conventional means, being asked by the king to form a government, but the weakness of the political system allowed him to entrench and extend his power. These problems of institutional weakness had a long history. With only slight exaggeration it can be said that the unification of Italy had essentially been based on the transplantation of Piedmontese institutions to the rest of the country, where they failed to firmly take root. Political unrest centering on strikes by peasant farmers and workers in Sicily had led Prime Minister Francesco Crispi to declare a state of emergency, suspend civil liberties, and place the island under military law in 1894. In 1898 Crispi's successor Antonio di Rudini had called in the military to break up strikes and food riots in Milan. These events in Sicily and Milan were both indications of the sense, on the part of working-class Italians, that the political system was inadequately responsive to their needs. Then in 1900 King Humbert I was assassinated by the anarchist Gaetano Bresci. The 1907 financial crisis and Italy's disastrous foray into World War I, highlighted by the catastrophic Battle of Caporetto, fanned dissatisfaction with the political mainstream and fed support for the Socialists, who made significant gains in the 1919 general election.

Next there was a slow-motion banking crisis starting in the summer of 1920 involving Ansaldo, an engineering conglomerate that both was the principal shareholder in the troubled Banca Italiana di Sconto and had borrowed extensively from it. This was conflict of interest at its most blatant. In the straitened circumstances following the war, Ansaldo predictably found it difficult to repay its loans. A central-bank-organized rescue put off the day of reckoning, but with the troubled bank continuing to take losses on its loans, it was forced to declare bankruptcy in November 1921. The episode provoked not unjustified complaints of cronyism, and popular anger at all involved.[17]

Meanwhile, successive left-liberal coalitions under Francesco Nitti and Giovanni Giolitti, seeking to stem inflation and balance the budget, proposed a capital levy on wealth-holders, which incited the Right, along with cuts in bread subsidies and welfare-related government spending, angering Catholics and the reformist Left, and leaving everyone unhappy with the prevailing state of affairs. The status quo, it seemed, was fractious coalitions, governmental instability, and economic and financial chaos all around.

This political vacuum created the desire for a strong leader. It enabled Mussolini to secure the king's instructions to form a government despite his party having won only 19 percent of the vote in the 1921 election. It allowed him to argue that only a strong, Fascist-led government was capable of balancing the budget, ending inflation, and restoring stability.[18] It gave him cover to close opposition newspapers, ban public protests, and outlaw labor unions, strikes, and competing political parties. It allowed him to embark on a series of quasi-authoritarian initiatives despite Italy's constitutional monarchy.

Seen from this perspective, Britain's success in developing a mechanism for addressing unemployment and beating back radical political elements was exceptional. In fact, the two achievements went hand in hand. Unemployment insurance, put in place for a limited set of relatively volatile sectors, was extended in wartime to cover workers in munitions-producing industries. The precedent having been set, coverage was extended further in 1920. The authorities' motives were clear: there was fear of unrest like that in Germany and Italy if poverty and lack of work accompanied demobilization. As one historian has put it, "The government genuinely feared civil disorder 'if something were not done to provide economic security for the British working man.'"[19]

By 1920 the insurance system covered more than 11 million workers, up from 2 million before the war. This was virtually the entire civilian labor force.[20] The Fabian Socialists had evidently made a compelling intellectual and political case for unemployment insurance. And confidence in Britain's political institutions fostered the belief that government could be entrusted to administer a centralized scheme without capture by special interests.

The British system was supposed to be self-financing on the basis of matching contributions from the worker and his employer. But its expansion in 1920 coincided with a sharp postwar recession, creating an immediate deficit in the insurance fund, which the Treasury was forced to fill using general revenues. This was an unhappy situation, to say the least, for a government committed to running a balanced budget in order to return to the gold standard and then to stay there.

The problem returned, with a vengeance, with the onset of the Depression. Unemployment soared to still higher levels, increasing benefit payments and reducing contributions at the same time. The Labour government that assumed power in 1929 appointed a Royal Commission on Unemployment Insurance to assess the situation and, it was hoped, provide some reassuring words. In the event, its words were anything but reassuring. Sir Richard Hopkins, a high Treasury official, in his evidence to the commission put it in apocalyptic terms.

Unfunded unemployment insurance liabilities, he ominously warned, were "bringing the country to the brink of a chasm in which her credit might be lost."

In February 1931 the government therefore assembled a committee of conservative financial experts to recommend corrective action. The committee was chaired by Sir George May, recently retired secretary of the Prudential Assurance Company—an odd choice, perhaps, for a Labour government, but who better than an insurance company executive to recommend measures to restore the financial viability of an insurance scheme? Predictably, given its composition, the committee in its July 1931 report proposed swingeing economies, headlined by a 20 percent cut in benefits. This was not something the left-leaning members of MacDonald's cabinet were prepared to accept, however. Its inability to agree was the precipitating event that led to the collapse of the Labour government in August.[21]

The National government, the Conservative Party–dominated coalition formed following the Labour government's fall, went ahead with cuts in benefits of 10 rather than 20 percent. While those cuts were not popular, they were accepted as legitimate because the government adopting them received a popular mandate, 67 percent of the vote, in the general election that followed the next month. Keynesian hindsight suggests that these perversely pro-cyclical policies were the height of folly in the midst of an unprecedented slump. That said, the fact that cuts were imposed against a baseline where the unemployed received relatively generous support and coverage was widespread meant that the destabilizing consequences, both economic and political, were less than they might have been otherwise.

It helped, as noted above, that the government took other steps to stabilize the economy. Cutting interest rates to 2 percent and allowing sterling to depreciate on the foreign exchange market halted deflation, removing one immediate obstacle to the resumption of growth. Abandoning the gold standard made the maintenance of strict budget balance less imperative and helped to stimulate recovery, which allowed the 10 percent cut in benefits to be reversed in 1934. Parliament created the Unemployment Assistance Board to run training schemes and provide assistance for workers seeking to move to regions where employment prospects were better.

The most controversial aspect of the response, given the role of free trade in British history, was a temporary across-the-board tariff in November 1931 and then a permanent 10 percent tariff with preferential rates for the Commonwealth and Empire in 1932.[22] As tends to be the case whenever unemployment rises, critics of various stripes pointed to unfair foreign practices as the source of the country's ills. The argument for shutting out imports to provide jobs was compelling so long as the gold standard prevented the government from adopting other fiscal and monetary measures to stimulate employment—so long as there was a fixed lump of spending to be distributed between imports and domestic production. Even sophisticated observers such as John Maynard Keynes supported the adoption of trade restrictions on these grounds, despite awareness of the risk of foreign retaliation.[23]

There remained a reluctance to move in this direction, however, given Britain's history and ideology of free trade and Labour's opposition to import taxation on "dear bread" (cost-of-living) grounds. In the end, Parliament went ahead only after the Conservative-dominated National government succeeded Labour, a shift in political power that should, if anything, have reduced the pressure to address the unemployment problem (unemployed workers not exactly being the Conservatives' core constituency). Even more curiously, it went ahead only after the gold standard was abandoned. Keynes had argued that a tariff was needed to boost the demand for British goods because the constraint of the gold standard ruled out other employment-friendly measures. But now this constraint had been lifted, allowing the Bank of England to cut interest rates and give the British economy the boost it needed.[24] The Bank, for its part, was quick to move in that direction, but no matter. The Conservatives were committed to delivering something to their long-suffering industrial constituency. And the new Chancellor of the Exchequer, Neville Chamberlain, younger son of Joseph, wished to secure his father's protectionist legacy.[25]

But by limiting imports, the tariff insulated British industry from the chill winds of foreign competition, reducing the incentive to innovate. It slowed productivity growth, most visibly in the sectors that were most generously protected.[26] If in the short run the tariff was redundant, in the long run it was counterproductive. And those counterproductive effects—lack of competition, high markups, failure to innovate—persisted not just through the end of the 1930s but even after World War II. This is a reminder that quasi-populist arguments, even when advanced by mainstream politicians, can have unintended, and enduring, consequences. If you are reminded of the Brexit vote in 2016, another proto-populist rejection of economic integration with far-reaching and potentially damaging implications, then you're not alone.

On balance, then, the British policy response in the 1930s had costs as well as benefits and in this sense was far from ideal. Unemployment, in particular, remained a chronic problem—how could it not given the severity of the Great Depression? The October 1936 march from the Tyneside town of Jarrow to London's Hyde Park, organized in protest against chronic unemployment and poverty, symbolized how even after several more years the battle was still far from won. But the fact that Britain developed an encompassing unemployment insurance scheme administered by institutions in which there was a relatively high level of confidence, together with the fact that other measures were taken to stabilize the economy, meant that populist forces gained only limited traction.

Why, then, was unemployment more conducive to political disaffection and extremism in Germany? Insurance against unemployment there was still a recent innovation when the Depression struck, as noted above. There was strong resistance to supporting the jobless on moralistic grounds and for fear that doing so would encourage indolence. Bismarckian social insurance had focused, therefore, on helping the elderly, the ill, and the destitute, who, it could be argued, had little scope for gaming the system. Before World War I, employment in agriculture had actually not been that much less important in Germany than in Italy and France, given the tariff protection enjoyed by growers of rye and other farm products, and the same argument that self-sufficient farmers, and even farm labor, didn't need unemployment insurance also had currency there. Large landowners prominent in the Conservative Party worried, moreover, that unemployment insurance would prevent idle industrial workers from returning to agriculture. Employers generally warned that income support for the unemployed would drive up wages. They resisted national unemployment insurance, arguing that the costs of already existing social insurance programs were straining their resources.[27]

While some trade unions operated unemployment funds for their members, these were self-financed, not unduly burdening employers or taxpayers.[28] But the beneficiaries of union unemployment benefits were few, since only some 5 percent of employees were unionized prior to World War I.

The exigencies of war modified this situation. The German government introduced a temporary program of unemployment assistance in 1914 to pacify the labor force, since disruptions on the home front could now threaten national security. This program was extended in November 1918, just weeks after the Sailors' Revolt in Wilhelmshaven, when enlistees in the German High Seas Fleet refused an order from the Admiralty to put out to sea, mere days after the outbreak of the November Revolution against the Empire. The need to placate the unemployed understandably came to be seen as pressing. Then the volatility of the economy following demobilization made eliminating this program, as originally envisaged, inconceivable.[29]

Formally this was still only temporary assistance for the unemployed, not a permanent insurance system. Benefits were not linked to prior work or to contributions to a fund. They were not related to an individual's earlier wages. The requirement that recipients genuinely seek work and related qualification provisions were not imposed.

But temporary assistance changed the terms of the debate. It challenged the presumption that government should not aid the unemployed, as distinct from the elderly, infirm, and destitute. If the choice now was between ad hoc assistance and a properly organized unemployment insurance system, and no longer between unemployment insurance and nothing at all, then employers had good reason to change their tune.[30] By replacing ad hoc assistance with a proper insurance scheme, qualification could be linked to prior employment, eliminating help for those with no record or intention of working. Replacing the earlier flat rate with a payment linked to wages and contributions would avoid subsidizing low-wage workers so much that they had no incentive to work. Employers, as participants in the debate over program design, would be better positioned to limit abuse of the system.

This shift in thinking took time, as shifts in thinking generally do. A majority of employers came around to supporting unemployment insurance only in 1926, and the law on unemployment insurance and employment services was finally passed only in July 1927, scarcely a year before Germany began its descent into the Great Depression. The country succumbed to the Depression even earlier than Britain and the United States because Germany, burdened by reparations and other debts, depended so heavily on foreign finance. That foreign finance dried up abruptly in the summer of 1928, as Wall Street, in the throes of its boom, sucked up capital previously directed elsewhere, including to Germany. With this, spending in Germany began to fall. There was then the further blow of an unusually cold winter in 1928–1929 and slowing growth abroad.

Consequently there was little time to get the German unemployment insurance system fully up and running before it was clobbered by recession and the financial difficulties that followed in its train. Although the insurance fund was permitted to borrow from the Treasury, it could do so only temporarily and in limited amounts. And what Hopkins had said about the cost of unemployment benefits in Britain, that it threatened to bring the country to the brink of a chasm in which her credit was lost, applied to Germany in spades. The German economy depended on foreign credit. Its ability to attract it was tenuous, given uncertainty over reparations.[31] With memories of hyperinflation still fresh, maintaining the mark's peg to gold was paramount. And budget balance was critical to the maintenance of gold convertibility, as politicians like Chancellor Brüning asserted with almost religious fervor.

As a result, the German government was quick to cut benefits when a deficit developed in the insurance fund and, more generally, whenever fiscal problems deepened. It did so even though the unemployment rate, as measured by the number of people registered as unemployed as a share of the workforce, peaked at even higher levels than in Britain and came down more slowly. Coverage was restricted in November 1929. The earnings limit was raised, and benefits for seasonal workers were cut. In June 1930, the Reichstag adopted a bill cutting benefits yet again. This bill allowed the Treasury to lend the insurance fund no more than half of any projected operating deficit, requiring the balance to be eliminated through benefit cuts and increased contributions. Another expert commission was appointed in January 1931 to examine the scheme's finances, and in June the government, adopting its recommendations, cut benefits once more.

As the crisis deepened, so did the cuts. It didn't help that Germany suffered one of the worst depressions of any country, as measured by the peak-to-trough fall in real GDP.[32] In response, the hyperconservative Franz von Papen, who succeeded Brüning in June 1932, issued an emergency decree under powers granted the chancellor by the Weimar constitution, reorganizing the insurance scheme and reducing benefits by an additional 23 percent. As this and related responses were described by a group of American academics: "Most of the changes [imposed by Brüning and von Papen were] . . . designed to maintain solvency rather than to overcome defects or improve procedure."[33] Even less were they intended to help the unemployed. That the most dramatic cuts were imposed by decree, circumventing normal legislative deliberation, did not foster popular admiration of the politicians then in office or enhance the legitimacy of the constitutional system. Contrast the British situation, where cuts were applied by a National government with an overwhelming electoral mandate.

A standard measure of these policies is the "replacement rate," the share of average after-tax wages replaced by unemployment benefits for

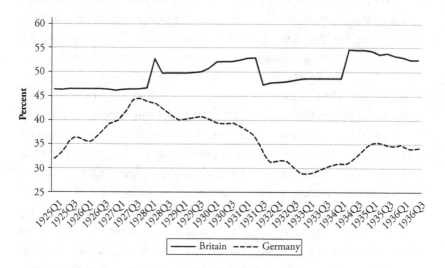

FIGURE 6.2 Unemployment Benefit Replacement Rates for Britain and Germany, 1927–1936

Source: Nicholas Dimsdale, Nicholas Horsewood, and Arthur van Riel, "Unemployment and Real Wages in Weimar Germany," Discussion Papers in Economic and Social History no.56, University of Oxford (October 2004), and author's calculations.

the typical newly unemployed worker. In Germany the replacement rate declined from 38 percent in 1928 to less than 34 percent at the beginning of 1933, when Hitler took power—that is to say, by more than a tenth. Although wages were also falling in this period of deflation and depression, benefits were falling even faster.[34] Again, the contrast with the United Kingdom is revealing. Although benefits there were cut as well, the replacement rate rose rather than falling, from less than 50 percent in 1929 to rather more in 1933.[35] In Britain, benefit cuts lagged behind wage declines instead of leading them, as in Germany.

A single statistic is not an adequate explanation for why political extremists assumed power in one country but not the other. Unemployment was not the only form of personal and economic insecurity about which people cared, and income replacement by the state was not the only plaster applied to the sore. That said, it is hard to reject the view that the failure of German society and government to do more for the unemployed was consequential in the worst possible way.

7

The Age of Moderation

SEEN IN THE rearview mirror, the third quarter of the twentieth century looks like a golden age of political moderation. The period was not without its populist firebrands, from Pierre-Marie Poujade in France to Enoch Powell in Britain and George Wallace in the United States.[1] No doubt it felt less moderate to those who lived through it. The perception of an earlier era as a utopia of economic stability and political equanimity is something to be guarded against, especially by those whose untroubled childhoods coincide with the period.

Still, figures don't lie. The vote shares of extreme left-wing and, especially, right-wing parties across twenty advanced economies (the United States, Canada, Australia, Japan, and sixteen European nations) were lower in the third quarter of the twentieth century than before 1939 and after 1975.[2] No anti-system party, defined as one actively seeking to subvert the established political system, formed a government. No charismatic leader flaunting the three key populist traits—anti-establishmentarianism, authoritarianism, and nativism—actually took office.

This is not to deny that governments sometimes lost votes of confidence. Parliaments could be fragmented into many party groupings, complicating efforts to form stable coalitions. Street protests indicated the frustration of those unable to make their voices heard through conventional channels. Recall the events of May 1968 in France and the demonstrations at the 1968 Democratic National Convention against the Vietnam War. Not everyone was satisfied by the political status quo or prepared to work for change by conventional means. That said, the traction of anti-system parties and politicians, as judged by votes garnered and offices held, was unusually low.

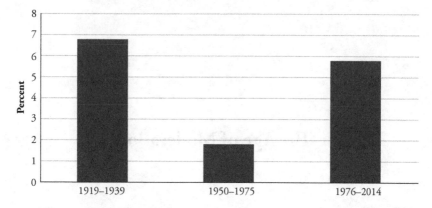

FIGURE 7.1 Average Vote Share for Far Right Parties in Twenty Democracies, Three Periods

Source: Author's calculations, based on Manuel Funke, Moritz Schularick, and Christoph Trebesch, "Going to Extremes: Politics After Financial Crises 1870–2014," *European Economic Review* 88 (2016): 227–260.

A combination of factors accounts for this peculiar state of affairs. Most obviously there were memories of extremism gone wrong. In countries like Germany and Austria, those memories now delimited the politically acceptable. Nativism that spilled over into hate speech was unacceptable. Nationalism encouraging militarism was unacceptable. Government would be by a rules-based system that constrained elected and appointed officials. In Germany, these ideas coalesced into the doctrine of "ordoliberalism," a body of economic and social thought emphasizing rules as the basis for an orderly society, as barriers to intervention in the economy by grasping government, and as obstacles to arbitrary action by a charismatic leader. This is a doctrine that continues to shape German thought and policy down to the present day, as noted by critics of the country's cautious approach to the euro crisis.[3]

This postwar consensus on the limits of acceptable political thought and action was embedded in the constitution of the German Federal Republic (the Basic Law) and its Civil and Criminal Codes. Hate speech (*Volksverhetzung*, literally "instigation of the people") was punishable by imprisonment under Section 1 of the Criminal Code. Although Germany was no longer prevented after 1955 from raising an army, and restrictions on its military vanished with German reunification in 1990, self-imposed restraints on the foreign deployment of German forces remained in place, something that is still the case today.⁴ These can be changed only by a two-thirds vote in the Bundestag (the legislative lower house) and a majority vote in the Bundesrat (the upper house). These self-imposed restraints merely formalize what was already understood about the limits of the permissible.

To be sure, even West Germany had its extremists. Reactionary nationalists began forming political groups in the American and British zones of occupation almost immediately following the cessation of hostilities.⁵ By 1949 the Socialist Reich Party, or SRP, a radical nationalist splinter group with fascist tendencies, was prominent in northwest Germany. But the party's high-water mark came in 1951, when it polled 11 percent of the vote in Lower Saxony's state elections. Its vote share was highest where unemployment was worst. Ultimately, however, the SRP was unable to broaden its appeal, in part because the German economy was doing better. In 1952 the government then invoked Article 21 of the Basic Law, which banned political parties seeking to undermine the democratic order, dissolving the party and seizing its assets. The SRP had few hard-right successors of consequence.

At the other end of the spectrum, the German Communist Party never developed into a mass political movement because of its rigid allegiance to Marxism-Leninism and its association with Soviet authoritarianism. It was banned by the Constitutional Court in 1956. Its successor, the ideologically less hard-line League of Germans (BdD), fared little better. The German Peace Union (DFU), founded in 1960, attracted Communist front members but few others and rarely polled more than 2 percent of the vote.

With time, memories faded and the Third Reich's atrocities no longer discouraged support to the same extent for political parties and movements espousing nativist and nationalist sentiments. Memories of the brutality of the Soviet army no longer deterred militant far-left groups such as the Baader-Meinhof Group (subsequently the Red Army Faction) from bombings, kidnappings, and assassinations.⁶ But so long as those wartime memories were still fresh, as they were in the 1950s and even the 1960s, they worked to suppress radical tendencies.

Political reform further limited the operating space of anti-system figures and parties. Countries with electoral systems of pure proportional representation that had previously experienced high levels of parliamentary fragmentation now imposed thresholds, typically 5 percent of the vote, to be exceeded before a party gained parliamentary representation. In Germany a party had to attract a minimum of 5 percent of the vote nationwide or else had to win at least three directly elected provincial seats. New parties with a significant following could still gain representation, but small splinter parties were excluded, making it easier to form a coalition.

Under the new German federal constitution, moreover, the chancellor could no longer be dismissed by a simple vote of no confidence, only by a "constructive vote" that included majority support for another candidate. This provision was designed to avoid the kind of revolving-door leadership that had bedeviled Weimar. So it did: there were no constructive no-confidence votes between the adoption of the new constitution in 1949 and when Helmut Schmidt was voted out in favor of Helmut Kohl in 1982. The same change was adopted by other countries that drew the same conclusion, for example Belgium.

At the time, these changes did not entirely preclude the formation of parties and movements with views far out of the mainstream. Nor have they prevented the rise of new extremist parties in recent decades. But the practical appeal of such parties was less, insofar as supporting them was tantamount to throwing away one's vote unless one was convinced that others would vote likewise. The ability of their representatives, even when elected, to disrupt the government by supporting a no-confidence vote was less, insofar as they were unlikely to agree on a constructive alternative.

The Cold War further suppressed support for radical anti-system parties. The Soviet threat raised the value of national solidarity and undercut support for hard-left Communist parties taking instructions from Moscow. The United States had troops stationed in Germany, and its financial support was needed for postwar reconstruction. The United States conditioned its assistance to France and Italy on the expulsion of Communist parties from their governments. Voters in these and other countries drew the obvious conclusion: U.S. aid was predicated on their own electoral support for centrist politics.

Then there was the favorable economic performance of the advanced economies after World War II. Not for nothing was the 1950–1973 period known as a golden age of economic growth.[7] In Western Europe, real GDP per capita rose by 3.8 percent per annum, nearly four times as fast as in 1913–1950 and at more than twice the rate of 1973–1993. Living standards in the United States grew more slowly, by 2.5 percent a year, but even this was a significant acceleration.[8] Japanese growth, approaching double digits, was the most miraculous of all. In all these places, there was less reason to attack the economic status quo when that status quo was delivering the goods.

In a sense, the postwar growth miracle was not all that miraculous; it was just a matter of making up lost time. Investment had been depressed in the 1920s and 1930s. War did not favor the consumer goods industries that were the drivers of demand in the second half of the twentieth century. Avoiding a repetition of earlier disasters allowed countries to exploit the resulting backlog of investment opportunities. Investment rates after World War II were half again as high as they had been between 1913 and 1950.[9] The United States had leapt ahead in developing mass production methods, with Henry Ford's moving assembly line, the reorganization of production to take advantage of electric power, and wartime mobilization of industry. By investing in these same technologies and methods, Europe and Japan could now follow its lead.

The roots of modern mass production in the United States stretch back further to the country's pioneering development of the large corporation in the second half of the nineteenth century.[10] As a result, by the end of World War II a very considerable gap had opened up between Europe and America that could now be closed by straightforward investment in technology and organization.[11] Europe had a literate and numerate labor force. It had apprenticeship and vocational training to equip workers with the skills needed to implement American technologies. It had labor to draw out of underemployment in agriculture and be put to work in manufacturing, the movement of smallholders from southern Italy to the Fiat factories of Turin being a classic case in point.[12] Germany had refugees from the East to work in its expanding industrial sector. Between 1947 and 1950, nearly a million people of German and Polish descent, many with prior industrial experience and in their prime working years, moved from Eastern to Western Europe.[13] And the countries of the Continent now had stable political institutions to reassure investors.

Producers, for their part, had access to American know-how, from the multidivisional corporate form to modern personnel management practices and numerical inventory control, all aspects of the scientific management revolution associated with the efficiency expert Frederick Winslow Taylor. Multinationals like the Ford Motor Company, which invested heavily in Europe, provided a vehicle, as it were, for transferring this knowledge. European labor and management gained exposure to American techniques on productivity missions sponsored by the Marshall Plan. What they encountered in the United States they brought back and adapted to local conditions.[14] American business and trade union representatives traveled to Europe to spread their "gospel of productivity."[15] Under other circumstances the Americans might have attempted to husband their technical and organizational secrets. But they understood that extraordinary steps to boost European productivity and security were warranted by the circumstances of the Cold War.

Though the technological and organizational backlog was least in the United States, American economic growth accelerated as well, as we have seen. The 1940s were the decade with the most rapid increase in four-year college graduation rates, courtesy of a GI Bill enabling veterans to attend college at federal expense.[16] More education meant more literacy and numeracy, enhanced analytical skills, and greater facility in operating complex machinery in factory and office.[17]

On the capital side, there was continuing investment in electricity and the assembly line. Electrically generated horsepower in American factories rose by 70 percent between 1940 and 1950. These investments constituted a significant increase in the quality of the capital stock, commensurate with the increased quality of labor. And not only was there higher-quality investment, there was more investment, not just in general but in industry in particular. Investment in producers' durable equipment as a share of GDP was half again as high in 1948–1957 as in the 1930s (6.2 percent of GDP as opposed to the earlier 4.1 percent).

Finally there was government, which had invested in machine tools and other equipment used by American industry as part of the war production push. Now it invested in the Interstate Highway System, allowing manufacturing to cluster in advantageous locations and its output to be distributed nationwide. This allowed full realization of the efficiency advantages of mass production, the internal combustion engine, and trucking.

Growth, besides being faster, was also more stable. The European economy expanded steadily in the 1950s and the first half of the 1960s, the only interruptions of note being mild recessions in France in 1957–1958 and Italy in 1964–1965.[18] GDP growth was only half as variable as it would become in the 1970s and 1980s.[19] Although the United States experienced mild recessions in 1954 and 1958, U.S. growth was steady as well.[20] Together, stability and growth meant that only a small fraction of the workforce was exposed to extended spells of unemployment, attenuating the insecurity associated with economic change.

An obvious contributor to this stability was better policy: it wasn't hard, after all, to improve on the policy disasters of the 1920s and 1930s. While active countercyclical monetary and fiscal policy was still more in the realm of theory than action, the spread of Keynesian ideas at least prevented governments and central banks from repeating their worst mistakes. On top of that, there was the simple fact that public spending was more stable than private spending. When the economy slowed, the growth of tax receipts slowed with it, and budgets moved into deficit. Because these mechanisms worked automatically, they were known as automatic stabilizers. And because the public sector had grown, the induced change in tax receipts was now larger as a share of GDP. Automatic stabilizers thus worked even more powerfully than before to dampen the business cycle.

Moreover, there was no high inflation like that of the 1920s, aside from a brief period immediately following World War II. There was no reparations tangle to blow a hole in government budgets. To the contrary, U.S. insistence that demands for German reparations be subordinated to other goals, namely, social stability and the resumption of growth, was what led to the final break with the Soviet Union, the one power committed to extracting reparations by force.

A further stabilizing factor was the Bretton Woods international monetary agreement. Under the Bretton Woods System agreed to in 1944, other countries committed to keeping their currencies stable against the dollar. So long as the United States kept inflation low, as it did successfully in the 1950s and much of the 1960s, it conferred comparable stability on other countries.[21]

The stability of the Bretton Woods System was reinforced by the stability of the international economic environment generally. The latter was partly a matter of good luck: there was no serious interruption to Middle East oil supplies when the Six-Day War between Israel and the Arabs erupted in 1967, and there was no OPEC oil shock before 1973.[22] But there was also good judgment. International trade was liberalized cautiously. Tariff barriers were lowered gradually through not one but a succession of periodic GATT negotiating rounds.[23] Domestic markets were not thrown open to foreign competition before they were ready. There was no shock to the global trading system as large as China's accession to the World Trade Organization in 2001.[24]

Controls on international financial flows were relaxed even more cautiously, governments having learned from the 1930s that unrestrained capital movements could be destabilizing. Removing capital controls was not an obligation of signatories of the Bretton Woods Agreement. Even as they dismantled barriers to merchandise trade, Japan and Europe retained their restrictions on capital movements, in some cases only finally removing them in the 1980s as part of the broader push for financial liberalization and deregulation. Memories of the destabilizing effects of capital flows, much like memories of political excesses, faded with time, and eventually did less to shape decision-making. For the moment, however, the lessons of the 1930s ruled.

Prudent management of globalization thus accentuated its positive impact. Countries were allowed to specialize along lines of comparative advantage and do more of what they did best while avoiding trade and financial shocks.

Another dimension was banking and financial stability. There were no systemic banking and financial crises in the advanced countries in the period through 1973. Banks still failed, but in no case did their failure imperil the banking and financial system.[25] More countries adopted deposit insurance, in the manner of the United States, limiting the danger of depositor panic. They more tightly regulated their financial institutions, discouraging risk taking so as to avoid banking crises like those that riddled the 1930s. Banking crises regularly breed populist reactions against the financiers and plutocrats who are seen as profiting at taxpayer expense, as noted in Chapter 1, and induce political swings to the extreme left and right.[26] Between 1945 and 1973, quite remarkably, there were no banking crises of consequence in the advanced countries to provoke this reaction.

Besides being rapid and stable, growth was widely shared. Real wages rose strongly in the third quarter of the twentieth century, in contrast to their subsequent stagnation. Low unemployment meant that the gains were distributed widely. Labor's share of national income was stable or rising. The share of national income accruing to the top 1 percent of high earners fell in continental Europe, Japan, the United Kingdom, and even the United States.[27] High growth and low inequality went hand in hand: as Robert Gordon writes of the United States, the remarkable fact "is not just that incomes grew at roughly the same rate for the bottom 90 percent, the top 10 percent, and the average, but that the real incomes for each group grew so rapidly."[28]

Wartime had seen higher taxes on the rich, both more progressive individual rates that hit those with high incomes, and higher corporate profit taxes. During the war, top marginal individual income tax rates peaked at 95 percent in the United Kingdom, 92 percent in the United States, and 90 percent in Germany. The political scientists Kenneth Scheve and David Stasavage argue that mass warfare is a key catalyst for taxes on the rich.[29] Taxes on high incomes are ratcheted up because mobilization makes extraordinary demands on the working class and thus creates an argument for taxing the rich on grounds of equal sacrifice. The argument is general, but World War II is a case in point.

Those high top tax rates persisted. In Britain, the top tax rate in the 1960s was still 83 percent, and the wealthiest few paid an additional 15 percent on investment income. In the United States, the highest marginal tax rate was still 91 percent in the early 1960s. Deductions and loopholes there were, but these high top tax rates reduced the income share of the top 0.1 percent of the distribution by as much as half.[30]

Higher tax rates persisted because the hardships of mass mobilization didn't vanish with the end of the war. Higher taxes on the wealthy can thus be seen as part of the same social bargain prompting adoption of the GI Bill's education and home-loan provisions in the United States and analogous measures in other countries.[31] Taxing high incomes more heavily, moreover, changed norms about acceptable rates of taxation. It created a new status quo. The fact that higher rates on top incomes didn't destroy economic growth, as their critics had warned, changed assessments of the equity/efficiency trade-off.[32]

Technological progress also leveled incomes. The diffusion of machine tools and the spread of assembly-line methods to additional sectors stimulated the demand for semi-skilled workers. It created employment opportunities for people who lacked technical training but who could solder and weld. Workers learned these skills at Henry Kaiser's shipyards in Richmond, California, where the Pacific Fleet was built, and then applied them in enterprises supplying consumer durables, such as one in San Francisco that made fireplace screens and tool sets for sale by catalog retailers including Sears and Montgomery Ward.[33]

Eventually, programmable machine tools, computers, and robots allowed capital equipment to be substituted for semi-skilled labor, reducing the number of workers needed to run a forge or man an assembly line. Automatic teller machines (ATMs) were substituted for bank tellers, and barcode scanners were substituted for supermarket clerks. But this came later. The first ATM debuted in North London only in 1967, its first U.S. equivalent in Rockville Centre, New York, in 1969. The first supermarket scanner entered service in Troy, Ohio, only in 1974.[34] The development of numerically controlled, programmable machine tools had started during World War II, when the U.S. Air Force and Sikorsky Aircraft experimented with their use in the production of helicopters, but their practical application was limited until the advent of minicomputers in the late 1960s. Numerical control was so slow to catch on that the U.S. Army, to popularize its use, built 120 numerical control machines and leased them to manufacturers.[35]

And if technology favored the employment of semi-skilled labor, the international environment was especially conducive to its employment in the advanced economies. Tariffs, though falling, were not yet insubstantial. Transport costs were still to be reckoned with, especially before the logistics and containerization revolution reduced them significantly in the fourth quarter of the twentieth century.[36] Until then, however, it still made sense to produce close to final demand, which meant in the advanced countries, and first and foremost the United States.

And even where low labor costs were a decisive advantage, as in textiles, apparel, and footwear, the advanced economies could still compete. South Korea, Hong Kong, Taiwan, and Singapore, the first wave of "newly industrializing economies," only began industrializing in the 1960s. Not until the 1970s did they start moving up the technology ladder from textiles, apparel, and footwear into shipbuilding and machinery. China, at this point, was not even a blip on the radar screen of the most acutely sighted observer. Competition from developing countries in manufactured goods may have begun to materialize, but it remained significantly less intense than it would be subsequently.

A growing demand for blue-collar workers makes for rising blue-collar wages, the textbooks tell us. But, in addition, when firms have market power, they enjoy above-market returns that they can share with, or withhold from, their workers.[37] Those workers, if well organized, can secure a portion of those above-market returns, or rents, by threatening to disrupt production. Such disruptions were frequent in the 1920s and 1930s, leading U.S. manufacturers to now worry that the same could happen again. During World War II, government-designated business and labor leaders had cooperated in setting wage standards and maintaining industrial peace. Unions then emerged from the war with newfound respect.[38] Walter Reuther's United Auto Workers, for example, famously supported the war effort with a no-strike pledge. In return, an appreciative President Harry Truman convened a presidential summit in Detroit in 1945 bringing together representatives of management and labor. The president campaigned, albeit unsuccessfully, against the Taft-Hartley Act, which prohibited shops where only union members could work and limited certain kinds of strikes. He made a point of delivering a strongly pro-union Labor Day speech in Detroit's Cadillac Square in 1948.

This political support from a sitting president was not without effect. There was also the fact that automakers had invested heavily in new capacity, so they stood to lose financially if production was idled by lockouts and strikes, whereas pent-up demand left over from wartime rationing promised strong sales if labor disputes were avoided.

The result was a series of long-term contracts with the Big Three automakers. The template was the contract signed by the United Auto Workers and General Motors in 1950. In return for five years of labor peace, GM offered a $125 monthly pension, medical coverage, a schedule of annual wage increases, and a cost-of-living escalator. This, then, was finally the welfare capitalism envisaged by Herbert Hoover in 1929.

Ford and Chrysler quickly emulated the "Treaty of Detroit," as this agreement came to be known. Their contracts set the tone for labor-management relations in the 1950s and 1960s in Big Steel and other manufacturing sectors.[39]

In Europe, resistance members who had led the fight against the Nazis were now prominent in labor organizations, which acquired new legitimacy and respect as a result of their leaders' wartime actions. Labor was in a stronger position in European countries, where it did not have to contend with anything resembling Taft-Hartley. The share of the workforce that was unionized was also higher in Europe, reflecting the earlier development of union movements there. An example of the consequences was the German Coal and Steel Codetermination Act of 1951, which gave workers representation on the supervisory boards of directors of companies in those sectors.[40] Board approval was required for all major business decisions, not excluding wage settlements. There had been experiments along these lines under the Allied occupation and even earlier, during Weimar.[41] Bismarck himself had advocated the creation of a *Wirtschaftrat* (economic council) to bring together representatives of capital and labor.[42] But where these precursors had met with mixed success, they were now durably codified into law.

Over time, codetermination was extended to the public sector and then to all companies with at least two thousand employees. Similar laws were adopted in Austria, the Netherlands, Sweden, and elsewhere. It is hard to think of a more direct mechanism for ensuring a fair division of rents between capital and labor. This is a reminder that more than rapid productivity growth contributed to rising working-class living standards. In addition, a supportive institutional framework on the shop floor, in the courtroom, and in parliament enabled labor to secure its share of the spoils.

Other countries developed their own variants of these arrangements, reflecting their distinctive national circumstances and histories. Europe's small countries, which were most directly exposed to external shocks, had previously reached framework agreements—the Basic Agreement in Norway in 1935, the Peace Agreement in Switzerland in 1937, the Main Agreement in Sweden in 1938—designed to enhance domestic stability. In each case the participants sought to identify wage and employment levels consistent with economic and social peace. Labor was recognized as a social partner, providing a basis for industry- and economy-wide negotiations in which the parties sought to agree on the division of profits and rents. In the Netherlands these arrangements grew into product and company boards (*publiekrechtelijke bedrijfsorganisatie*, or PBOs) made up of employers' representatives and union leaders, who jointly negotiated employment and investment decisions. In Sweden they developed into the Cooperative Body for Increasing Exports and Production, under whose auspices industry, labor, and government officials met to set wages at levels consistent with both rising living standards and continued export competitiveness. Under the so-called Scandinavian model, large engineering companies, including Volvo, ASEA, Alfa-Laval, and SKF, first reached rent-sharing agreements with their workers, after which similar agreements were extended by firms in other sectors.[43]

These arrangements were easiest to reach in small countries, open economies, and ethnically homogeneous societies.[44] They were most durable in West Germany, where they were buttressed by a historical legacy that discouraged labor strife. They worked least well in the United Kingdom, which inherited a fragmented craft-based union movement from its early industrialization. Labor-management relations there were contentious, creating disputes over staffing levels, discouraging investment, and causing productivity growth and incomes to lag. It is not a coincidence that a politician like Enoch Powell, who gained notoriety in 1968 with an explosive speech blaming immigrants for the nation's economic woes, found support among disaffected working-class voters facing chronic unemployment, stagnant living standards, and deteriorating neighborhoods.[45]

Finally, a more expansive welfare state provided insurance against economic displacement. Scholars dispute how best to measure the extent of the welfare state, but there is no question that it expanded considerably in this period.[46] By the 1970s, more than 90 percent of the Western European labor force was covered by state-sponsored insurance against income loss in old age and due to disability and sickness. More than 80 percent possessed accident insurance; 60 percent had coverage against unemployment. Whereas some 10 to 20 percent of GDP had been devoted to social expenditure in the 1960s, this share rose to between a quarter and a third of national income, depending on country, in the mid-1970s. Economic growth helped to fuel this expansion of state social expenditures, but the expansion of social expenditures also laid the basis for economic growth.[47]

By the end of the period, the contradictions of the welfare state were becoming apparent. Overly generous unemployment and disability insurance was discouraging recipients from actively seeking work and encouraging some to drop out of the labor force. Poorly designed old-age and health insurance was promoting early retirement and inflating health care costs. There was much to criticize about these government programs, as there is about all government programs. But without them it is hard to imagine that there would have been a durable consensus for policies that delivered rapid economic growth and tolerance of structural change.

Altogether, then, the third quarter of the twentieth century was exceptional for a constellation of forces that strengthened the political mainstream and limited support for populist leaders and anti-system parties. Fascism and the Cold War discredited extremism. Stronger political institutions improved governance and stability. Catch-up growth after three decades of depression and war promised to raise all boats.

Moreover, this growth was shared. The technical change associated with the adoption of mass production methods generated good blue-collar jobs. Globalization had not yet eroded the demand for semi-skilled workers. Labor's sacrifices during World War II legitimized its demand for a fair share of the pie, which was met through trade union recognition and institutions such as industrial codetermination. The welfare state helped those who couldn't help themselves. Strikes and street demonstrations did occur throughout the period, but the dominant impression was that social and political institutions were responding adequately to the needs of the majority.

But if special circumstances contributed heavily to this happy outcome, there was already reason to think that those special circumstances wouldn't last.

8

Things Come Apart

AFTER 1973, EVERYTHING ran in reverse. The growth of GDP per head in the United States slowed to 1.2 percent between 1973 and 1992, down from 2.4 percent in the period 1950–1973.[1] Growth similarly fell by half in Western Europe, from 3.8 to 1.8 percent. In Japan, where growth in the golden age had run fastest, the deceleration from 8.0 to 3.0 percent was even more dramatic.

Slow growth made everything harder. It was harder for governments to find the resources to help displaced workers. It was harder to credibly maintain that the benefits trickled down. Governments deriving support from their success in delivering growth saw their popularity wane. Jimmy Carter may have lost the 1980 presidential election because of Iran's failure to release the fifty-two American hostages it was holding (a release that happened shortly after Ronald Reagan finished giving his inaugural address), but he also lost because of his less than stellar management of the economy. An econometric model by the Yale economist Ray Fair pinned Carter's loss on a handful of economic indicators, notably inflation and unemployment.[2] As the economist Sidney Weintraub put it, Carter succeeded "where all Democrats—and Republicans—have failed—namely, in making his own name a synonym for economic mismanagement and expunging memories of Herbert Hoover dawdling at the onset of the Great Depression."[3]

Disaffected voters in the United States and elsewhere turned initially to other mainstream parties and leaders. But the grasp on power of those leaders hinged on their ability to deliver the economic goods. In some cases, such as those of Reagan and Margaret Thatcher, they could claim some success. But Reagan's policies pushed up the dollar, which accelerated the deindustrialization of the heartland. Thatcher's policies of disinflation were accompanied by a sharp rise in unemployment. In no case were governments able to restore growth to the heights of *les trente glorieuses*, the thirty glorious years after World War II.

Blaming political incompetence was tempting insofar as there was no other convincing explanation for the slowdown. The slump in the advanced economies was necessarily a slump in productivity, since productivity accounts for the majority of GDP growth. Popular accounts emphasize the OPEC oil shocks of 1973 and 1979, queues at the pump being visible signs of economic distress. But energy is too small a part of GDP to explain more than a fraction of what happened to the economy as a whole. If higher energy prices depressed productivity by causing the obsolescence of energy-using capital equipment, moreover, then we would expect to see a sharp fall in the secondary-market price of such equipment, where no such fall in fact occurred.[4]

Some analysts blamed business-cycle volatility for discouraging investment and innovation.[5] This argument had appeal insofar as not just energy-price shocks but also other factors, from the resignation of Richard Nixon to rising inflation, could have contributed to that volatility. But there was no agreement on the sources of business-cycle fluctuations and, in particular, on whether one such source was the inept and destabilizing policy response of central banks and governments (the Jimmy Carter effect)—something that again pointed the finger of blame at establishment politicians.

Maybe the post-1973 slowdown was just the inevitable by-product of success. In the 1950s and 1960s growth had flowed from improvements in the quality of labor. With higher incomes it then became possible to invest still more in education. The 1940s had seen the fastest increase in U.S. high school and college graduation rates of any decade, as noted in Chapter 7, an upward trend that continued for an additional twenty years. But now high school graduation rates plateaued at 75 percent. It was hard to boost graduation rates still further with such a large share of capable students already completing school. The share of American men with university degrees plateaued at about the same time, at roughly 25 percent.

But the same was not true outside the United States. The high school movement of the 1910–1940 period was a distinctively American phenomenon.[6] The rise and broadening of educational attainment began later and proceeded more gradually in other countries. Average years of education of people between ages fifteen and sixty-four therefore continued to rise in Europe and Japan in the 1980s and after, continuing well after the growth of productivity slowed.[7]

Or maybe the growth slowdown just reflected the end of catch-up. Europe and Japan could grow rapidly so long as there existed a backlog of technology to be acquired from the United States, and so long as there was still underemployed agricultural labor to be shifted to more productive uses in manufacturing. By the 1970s, however, the technology gap vis-à-vis the United States had been closed, and the pool of underemployed agricultural labor was drained.

But this perspective suggests a gradual deceleration, when in fact productivity fell off a cliff. The pool of underemployed rural labor did not evaporate on a single day. The United States offered a range of technologies, some more advanced than others. European producers could start with the most attractive, but there was no reason to stop there, on a single day or in a single year like 1973. Similarly, the fact that the United States, which had no one to catch up to, suffered an equally pronounced slowdown underscores the limits of this interpretation.

By process of elimination, we are left with the possibility that the scope for productivity-enhancing technological progress had diminished. Robert Gordon has famously argued that productivity growth in the United States and more widely was supported by one great wave of innovation—the railway, the internal combustion engine, synthetic chemicals, electricity, radio, jet propulsion, and antibiotics. But after 1970 boosting output through the application of these products of nineteenth- and early twentieth-century science became harder. Nothing since has had comparable productivity-enhancing potential.[8]

This begs the question of why there was only one great wave of scientific advance. Maybe post-1970s governments invested too little in basic research to maintain the momentum. Maybe they provided inadequate incentives for private-sector R&D.[9] Maybe by raising hiring and firing costs as a low-cost response to labor market insecurity they discouraged start-ups and entrepreneurship. This was the view of critics of European policy who, from the early 1980s, spoke of "Eurosclerosis."

But to the extent that all this was true, the finger of blame pointed, once again, at inept governments.

Working-class living standards stagnated not just because income growth slowed but also because the income growth that did occur accrued disproportionately to the wealthy. While the growing gap between the incomes of more and less skilled workers was widely noted in the wake of the 2008–2009 financial crisis, the increase in inequality in the United States in fact dates back to the 1970s.[10] This is how the median earnings of prime-age working men, adjusted for inflation, could fall by 4 percent between 1970 and 2010, despite the fact that the economy as a whole was continuing to expand.[11] While this trend toward greater inequality was most prominent in the United States and United Kingdom, it was similarly evident in a range of other advanced economies in the 1980s and 1990s, especially when one focuses on full-time male wage earners.[12]

If there is a shortage of convincing explanations for the productivity slowdown, then the problem for inequality is the opposite, namely, an embarrassment of riches. These start with changes in technology, which for decades, if not centuries, had favored unskilled workers but now favored the skilled. The mechanization of weaving in nineteenth-

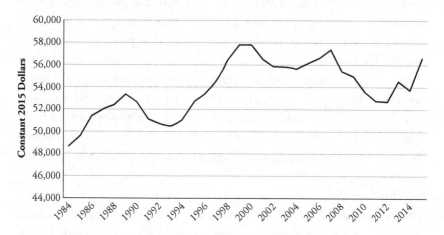

FIGURE 8.1 Real Median Household Income in the United States, 1984–2015

Source: U.S. Bureau of the Census, [MEHOINUSA672N], retrieved from FRED, Federal Reserve Bank of St. Louis; https://fred.stlouisfed.org/series/MEHOINUSA672N, February 23, 2017.

century Britain had undermined the demand for skilled handloom weavers, allowing them to be replaced by women and children tending automatic looms.[13] The Luddites were skilled workers who lost out to technical change, in other words. More generally, the transition from the workshop to the factory and assembly line allowed artisans, who spent years in apprenticeship, to be replaced by workers responsible for only a narrow set of tasks who could be trained up in a short period of time. Henry Ford famously observed that assembly line workers could be trained up to their peak productivity in a matter of days.[14]

In the language of production theory, new technology and unskilled labor now complemented one another. In other words, the introduction of assembly-line technology and the creation of additional good jobs for unskilled and semi-skilled workers went hand in hand. Because this situation persisted through the third quarter of the twentieth century, American, European, and Japanese factories, fitted out now with machinery and assembly lines, offered an abundance of good manufacturing jobs.

But then the direction of technical progress shifted. New kinds of machinery replaced assembly-line workers undertaking routine tasks. General Motors installed the first industrial robot, UNIMATE, in its New Jersey assembly plant in 1962. Robots were first used in significant numbers on assembly lines in the 1970s and 1980s, when they replaced less skilled workers engaged in routine tasks. Maintaining this machinery required relatively high levels of literacy and numeracy; it required education and skill. Capital and unskilled labor were now substitutes (the more machines, the fewer jobs for unskilled and semi-skilled workers), while capital and skilled labor were complements (the more machines, the more need for skilled operatives to maintain them).

This change visibly affected the demand for more- and less-skilled workers and therefore their compensation. Whereas in 1965 American workers with college degrees earned just 24 percent more than high-school graduates, that gap widened to 47 percent in the mid-1980s and 57 percent in the mid-1990s.[15] The situation in Europe and Japan differed in extent but not in kind.[16]

This change in technological trajectory is best understood as a response by employers to rising educational attainment. So long as skilled workers were few, it didn't pay to design jobs for them, or to install machines that required tending by skilled operatives. Instead firms hired less-skilled workers, trained them on the job, and gave them positions where they worked with limited amounts of complex machinery. But as the supply of high school and college graduates rose, it paid to design jobs expressly for them and to invest in advanced machinery for them to oversee. The result was higher productivity for skilled workers and fewer well-paying jobs for the less skilled.[17]

But this was not just a matter of machinery; it was also a matter of organization. Firms with ample supplies of skilled labor had an incentive to group workers into teams whose members were responsible for solving problems and developing ideas about how to better organize production. This was the essence of the Toyota Production System, pioneered by that company in the 1950s but adopted more widely in the 1970s and 1980s as workers with the requisite skills became more widely available.

This is an appealing story because it explains not just why technical change took the form it did—it was a response to increased educational attainment after World War II—but also how it was that the earnings premium for college graduates rose despite the fact that the supply of graduates was rising as well.[18] And there is evidence of its operation in a wide range of countries.[19]

The unskilled-labor-saving bias of technical change is not the entire explanation for the post-1970 increase in inequality, to be sure.[20] In a 2003 study, the economists David Autor, Frank Levy, and Richard Murnane concluded that computer-enabled technology, of which industrial robots are perhaps the most visible manifestation, accounted for no more than 30 to 40 percent of the shift in earnings toward college graduates in the preceding three decades.[21] Subsequent studies put the share attributable to technology a bit higher, perhaps because the full impact of computers and robotics was not yet evident at the turn of the century. But those subsequent analyses don't change the basic conclusion that more than robots matters.

Import competition and immigration are the other usual suspects for the shift in income toward skilled labor. One of the most robust propositions in international economics is that foreign trade doesn't raise all boats. Some groups benefit disproportionately, while others lose in relative and absolute terms.[22] In the case of the advanced countries, skilled labor benefits, since it is the abundant factor used in the production of exports, while unskilled labor is left worse off. Because skilled workers already have high incomes, the result in this case is additional inequality.

This is not a controversial proposition, although there is less than full agreement on the magnitude of the effects. Most investigators agree, however, that those effects were "appreciable," in the judiciously chosen terminology of one recent study.[23] Their impact on the skilled-unskilled wage differential was roughly equivalent to that of technology.

Moreover, the negative effect on some workers and communities is strikingly persistent. Studying the impact of import competition from China on the United States, David Autor, David Dorn, and Gordon Hanson found substantial and persistent distributional consequences and adjustment costs. Wages and employment in local markets that were home to industries suddenly exposed to Chinese competition remained depressed for more than a decade. Workers formerly employed in the affected industries found it hard to secure stable employment in other sectors. They experienced income losses not just in the short run but over the balance of their working lifetimes.[24]

The mystery is why these impacts were neglected by economists and downplayed by politicians—and, equivalently, why globalization was embraced so wholeheartedly by the intellectual and political elites. The populist answer is that the elites knew on which side their bread was buttered. As skilled workers themselves and as investors in high-tech companies and multinationals, they were self-interested promoters of globalization. A less cynical response is that it took time for the full negative effects to materialize. Prior to the 1970s, when growth was rapid, it was still possible to argue that foreign trade raised all boats. As late as 1990, most trade flows were among advanced countries with similar factor endowments and average incomes, limiting the distributional consequences.[25] The trade-to-GDP ratio worldwide remained more or less flat through the 1980s; there was no massive globalization shock. All this changed with the rapid growth of exports from emerging markets in the 1990s and China's accession to the World Trade Organization. The decline in U.S. manufacturing employment accelerated, and the inequality trend grew more pronounced.[26]

None of this challenges the presumption that trade can be beneficial for advanced countries as well as emerging markets. But if trade has

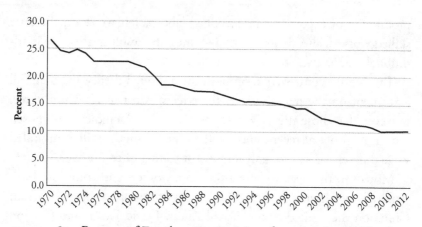

FIGURE 8.2 Percent of Employment in Manufacturing in All Nonfarm Employment in the United States Since 1970

Source: Retrieved from FRED, Federal Reserve Bank of St. Louis; https://fred.stlouisfed.org/series/USAPEFANA.

distributional consequences and adjustment costs, then these must be addressed by income transfers, training schemes, and regional policies if there is to be a political consensus in its favor. These observations are straightforward, but they run headlong into free market ideology, skepticism about the problem-solving capacity of government, and budgetary constraints. They were paid lip service but little more in the countries now experiencing an anti-trade backlash.

The impact of immigration is even more contentious, given that there is no agreement on its overall effects. Its impact on native-born workers depends, moreover, on whether immigrants are skilled or unskilled. It depends on how directly immigrants compete with natives—whether their skills and experience are different, and whether they choose similar occupations. It depends on the size and suddenness of the immigrant inflow, since larger flows mean higher adjustment costs.

In the United States, the immigration issue is fraught because the distributional impact is the same as that of trade. Most immigrants are less-skilled workers.[27] Their impact has thus been to depress the living standards of natives who are not high school graduates while raising those of U.S.-born workers with at least a high school diploma. Workers in fast food outlets and poultry processing plants earn less, but skilled workers consuming McChicken sandwiches see their earnings go further. Most studies conclude that the positive effects on the wages of native-born workers dominate on balance.[28] But the fact that the losers from immigration are the same folks who have lost from trade makes the issue socially and politically problematic.

Studies of other advanced economies reach similar conclusions. Research on the United Kingdom suggests that "immigration has a small impact on average wages of existing workers but more significant effects along the wage distribution: low-wage workers lose while medium- and high-paid workers gain."[29] But if the direction of the effect is the same as in the United States, the operative word here is "small." Half of all immigrants in the United Kingdom are from other EU countries.[30] They are more likely than natives to have some post-high-school education. Hence they do not have a pronounced effect on the wage distribution or disproportionately impact workers at its lower end. Even U.K. regions with a large influx of immigrants from Eastern Europe after 2004 did not see larger-than-average falls in the wages of native-born workers or a larger rise in inequality.[31] More generally, most immigrants to European countries possess at least some post-secondary education, the opposite of what is the case in the United States. It follows that those immigrants have done little to raise inequality in the recipient countries and may have even reduced it. Recent inflows of undocumented immigrants and refugees from Africa and elsewhere, many of whom lack the same education and skills, are a different matter—which is one reason why their presence and the inability of governments to control the influx are so contentious.

Even after taking all these factors into account, recent changes in income distribution vary across countries. It's not all about technology, trade, and immigration, in other words—it's also about institutions. We saw in Chapter 7 how the increased strength and legitimacy of unions after World War II enabled their members to share in the rents accruing to employers.[32] This was true of not just union members but also nonunion workers, whose pay was similarly influenced by union wage norms. It was true even in the United States, never a hotbed of unionism, following the Treaty of Detroit in 1950. We also saw how the existence in Germany of strong trade unions with a seat in the boardroom helps to explain why that country didn't share in the more general decline in full-time male real wages experienced in other countries in the final decades of the twentieth century.

It follows that declining unionization has been a factor in rising inequality. The share of American workers covered by unions fell from

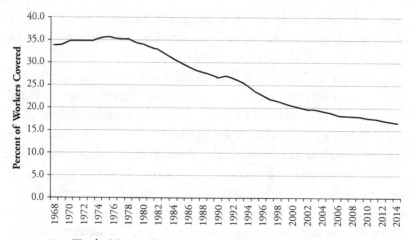

FIGURE 8.3 Trade Union Density in OECD Countries, 1968–2014
Source: OECD.Stat, https://stats.oecd.org/Index.aspx?DataSetCode=UN_DEN#.

27 percent in 1973 to barely 17 percent in 1993 and 11 percent in 2016. Some authors ascribe as much as a third of rising inequality over the period to this decline in union coverage.[33] Since unions also help to restrain CEO pay, their decline may have also facilitated the explosion of compensation at the top. It is revealing that the rise in inequality was greatest in the United States and United Kingdom, where the fall in union coverage was most pronounced.

An extended analysis of why unionization declined would take us far afield. One factor was the falling share of the workforce in manufacturing, where unions traditionally organize. That fall resulted from automation, globalization, and simple economic maturation, as we have seen. But it had negative implications for the union movement, given the greater difficulty of organizing workers in the service sector.[34] Another factor was the same skill-biased technical change described above. Changes in technology and organization favoring skilled workers, by creating new high-paying opportunities, weakened their support for union policies of wage compression, from which those skilled workers stood to lose. Those changes thereby undermined the coalition of skilled and unskilled workers traditionally supporting unions.[35]

The result was a vicious spiral of deunionization and inequality. As jobs were reorganized, improving opportunities and pay for skilled workers, those same skilled workers withdrew their support for union organizing efforts. Weaker unions were less able to enforce norms of wage compression—they were less able to raise wages for less-skilled workers. Inequality rose further, advantaging skilled workers more. This in turn undermined the skilled-unskilled worker coalition still further, weakening the union movement even more and reinforcing the wage-inequality trend.

In addition, there was the changed political climate. By the 1980s, the role of union members in having helped win the war was a distant memory. A postwar settlement that spoke of social partners and shared wage norms was valued only so long as it successfully delivered fast growth. Hence as growth slowed, those norms were increasingly questioned by skilled workers who now saw themselves as sacrificial lambs. They voted in growing numbers for Reagan and Thatcher, who defined their political reputations in opposition to the air controllers and coal miners unions. In this changed political climate, employers were empowered to intensify their opposition to unionization efforts and free to relocate to regions like the U.S. South, where union tradition was weak.

Elected officials were also less inclined to embrace labor's legislative agenda. Organized labor was less effective in countering those who argued for lower top tax rates. Minimum wages were allowed to lag inflation where unions were in decline. A substantial body of evidence suggests that that increases in the minimum wage reduce inequality, and that reductions in the real value of the minimum wage have the opposite effect.[36] Modest increases in the minimum wage push up the earnings of those at the bottom of the income ladder at the cost of few if any jobs. They reduce turnover in firms employing low-wage workers, enhancing efficiency and encouraging hiring. The debate about the minimum wage may be ideologically charged, but the facts are reasonably clear. Similarly, that a more progressive tax system reduces inequality is self-evident.[37] But these inequality-reducing policy interventions became harder when organized labor was in decline.

Finally there was welfare state retrenchment. Slower growth meant tighter budgets, making some welfare state cuts unavoidable. This was especially true in Scandinavia and the Netherlands, where the provision of social benefits overshot sustainable levels.[38] Unemployment benefits, pension payments, public employment, the public share of health care spending, and sick pay were all ratcheted up in response to the economic volatility of the 1970s.[39] Norms adapted to enable workers to exploit permissive aspects of the social-welfare system. By 1980, for example, fully 10 percent of Dutch workers were claiming sickness and disability benefits.[40] This situation, clearly, was unsustainable, a realization that led the Dutch to overhaul their system in 1987.

Welfare state retrenchment was as much political as economic, of course. Inequality meant greater social distance between more and less skilled workers and less inclination to contribute to collective goods.[41] Where unions were in decline, they were less able to support political candidates favoring an extensive welfare state.[42] Pension payments were cut back in the 1980s as aging populations put pressure on pay-as-you-go systems.[43] Unemployment replacement rates were cut in six OECD countries, with the largest cuts in the United Kingdom.[44] Sick pay was cut in another half dozen OECD countries besides the Netherlands. And even where welfare programs were not cut, their growth slowed or stopped. Replacement rates were lower in absolute terms at the turn of the century than they had been in 1975 in eight of seventeen countries in the case of sick pay, and in ten of eighteen in the case of unemployment insurance.[45]

Popular support for welfare-state institutions meant that these changes were incremental, not radical.[46] Pay-as-you-go pension systems, for example, were formidably difficult to reform. But the era when the welfare state grew faster than the economy was now over, and significant cuts were no longer the exception.

Indeed, the same pattern of cuts occurred both where the welfare state was most extensive, in Northern Europe, and where it was least, in the United States. It was evident in countries with left-of-center and right-of-center governments. Retrenchment was undertaken in response to slower growth, aging populations, and fiscal strains. It reflected changes in technology and workplace organization that made for greater inequality and social distance between those up and down the economic ladder. It was influenced by ideology and by changed perceptions of the welfare state, ideology and perceptions that themselves flowed from underlying economic conditions. And the same factors operated, with broadly similar effects, across the advanced economies.

The bottom line is that there was now a more limited safety net protecting unfortunates who fell from the economic trapeze. The hopeful response to this was that the economy was now more stable, so fewer participants were at risk of losing their grip. This, recall, was the era of the "Great Moderation," from the second half of the 1980s through the first half of the 2000s.[47] Business cycle volatility declined not just in the United States but across the advanced countries. Economists credited a combination of improved policy (the stable monetary policies of inflation-targeting central banks) and good luck (the absence of commodity-price shocks and then improved productivity performance, especially in 1995–2005, when the boost from new information and communications technologies was greatest). Some observers credited financial deregulation and innovation for making it easier for households to borrow and smooth their spending over the cycle.[48]

Subsequent events, in the form of the global financial crisis, showed the Great Moderation to have been an illusion. The same factors credited with having reduced business cycle volatility—low and stable inflation, financial deregulation, and the absence of shocks as an inducement to risk taking—set the stage for an exceptional episode of volatility and economic loss. And that episode, it turned out, was one with which Western societies were singularly ill prepared to cope.

9

Trumped Up

AMERICA WAS THUS ripe for a populist insurrection. Growth had slowed. Inequality had risen. Globalization and automation heightened insecurity for workers lacking vocational training, trade union funds, or an extensive insurance state on which to fall back. A financial crisis undermined faith in the competence and integrity of decision makers. These are the classic preconditions for a populist reaction. Or so 20/20 hindsight suggests.

The obvious objection to this readout of the 2016 election is that the results were driven by more than just economic insecurity. They reflected fears about national security, more specifically security from terrorism. They reflected insecurity around national identity, the feeling that the identity of the United States as a country of Judeo-Christian values, in which Anglo-Saxon males held the power, was under threat from ethnic and racial minorities, from women's rights advocates and LGBT activists, and from acceptance at the elite level of the very concept of diversity.

The best response to this objection, as in Chapter 1, is that these national, social, and personal security concerns are most compelling against a backdrop of economic insecurity. In the United States, worries about national security fused with economic insecurity to feed opposition to immigration. Donald Trump's signature speech on immigration, in Phoenix, Arizona, in August 2016, referred to the concerns of "working people" that immigrants were negatively affecting "their jobs, wages, housing, schools, tax bills, and general living conditions," while also highlighting "the issue of security," asserting that "countless innocent American lives have been stolen because our politicians have failed in their duty to secure our borders and enforce our laws." The threat to economic security and threat to national security were thus ascribed to a common source, illegal immigration. If mass shootings in San Bernardino and Orlando were not the work of illegal immigrants, or if Mexican immigrants took jobs that natives were unwilling to accept, then these facts could be conveniently ignored. This immigrant-centered diagnosis of mutually reinforcing economic security and national security concerns was simply too compelling as a way of mobilizing "the [working] people" against the other. Moving on, Trump spoke to the identity concerns of the once-dominant white working class in passages warning that "not everyone who seeks to join our country will be able to successfully assimilate" and asserting the right of America as a sovereign nation "to choose immigrants that we think are the likeliest to thrive and flourish here."[1]

This narrative makes Trump's electoral victory look preordained, which of course it wasn't. The outcome might have been different without FBI director James Comey's decision to discuss the issue of Hillary Clinton's use of a private email server in a July 2016 press briefing and then his announcement, just eleven days before the election, that he might reopen the case. It might have been different in the absence of Vladimir Putin and Russian hacking into Democratic National Committee servers. It could have been different had the opposition fielded a candidate who spoke more effectively to working-class concerns and hadn't given $250,000 speeches to Goldman Sachs.

But if populism is a theory of society, a political style, and an economic approach that rejects convention and constraints, then Trump effectively embodied each of these populist traits. He embraced the theory that divides society into the virtuous people and the corrupt elite. His campaign was first and foremost anti-establishment. "The establishment," he argued in a final television ad a few days before the election, "has trillions of dollars at stake.... For those who control the levers of power in Washington and for the global special interests, they partner with these people that don't have your good in mind.... The only people brave enough to vote out this corrupt establishment," he concluded, "is you, the American people."[2]

Reinforcing this message, Trump positioned himself as an enemy of Republican Party orthodoxy. He showed scant regard for the party's stands on social policy, foreign policy, and trade policy and even less for its other candidates. He refused to make common cause with his rivals for the nomination. He had little use for the Republican National Committee and shunned its operatives in the general election campaign.

Instead, Trump spoke directly to voters in rallies at which he flamboyantly arrived via personal jet, echoing William Jennings Bryan's dramatic arrival by railway. He appealed to the people and their common sense in classic populist fashion. As CNN wrote in its election postmortem, "Donald Trump and his political advisers decided early on that two words would drive the billionaire's campaign for president: Common sense."[3] The people, Trump asserted, understood what ailed the country. If the problem was simple, say a decline in manufacturing jobs, then so was the solution: common sense suggested using threats and inducements to prevent companies from building factories abroad. If the problem was illegal immigration, which the people understood was occurring in larger numbers than the official statistics allowed, then common sense dictated building a wall. The wall became a symbol of U.S. national security and a commitment by the candidate to secure the nation's borders. Conceived in opposition to Hispanic immigration, it symbolized the Anglo-Saxon desire to regain control of the country's cultural boundaries. The wall also symbolized the divide between the people and the elites on which Trump sought to capitalize. So too did the idea of a 35 percent tariff on imports, which promised to do for trade what the wall would do for immigration and set Trump apart from expert opinion in his own party. And no sooner did Hillary Clinton denounce Trump's supporters as "deplorables" than they and the candidate embraced the label precisely to distance themselves from the elite and so-called respectable opinion.

Trump's political style was fundamentally populist in its use of colorful and off-color language. It was populist in its disregard of political and personal niceties and its reliance on blunt talk to communicate strength of personality. It was populist in its undercurrent of violence against opponents. It was populist in its denigration of the establishment press and use of alternative media like Twitter to speak directly to the people.

Trump's campaign was also populist in its approach to economics, which emphasized growth and distribution while denying constraints.

A Trump administration would double the rate of economic growth, the candidate asserted, without specifying how. Trump's emphasis on infrastructure spending echoed earlier populists who commissioned monumental projects in which the public could take pride and with which the leader would be forever identified, from Mussolini's Monumento Nazionale to Gamal Abdel Nasser's Aswan Dam. Here Trump's background as a builder stood him in good stead. The wall along the Mexican border was only the most symbol-laden such project.

Trump's resort to tariffs was another characteristic populist move. Populist leaders can deny the existence of constraints on their ability to cut taxes and raise growth, but it is beyond even their power to abolish the balance-of-payments constraint. The additional spending stimulated by their policies will include additional spending on imports, like it or not. Populist politicians generally don't like it and therefore impose trade restrictions to limit imports and protect industry from foreign competition. One thinks of the import-substitution policies of Latin American populists such as Juan Perón and Getúlio Vargas or, perhaps stretching the point, the even more draconian trade restrictions of Mussolini and Hitler.

Tariffs appeal to the populist temperament as an assertion of national autonomy. For Bismarck they were a way of uniting industry and agriculture against economic competition from abroad. For Joseph Chamberlain they were a way of uniting the British Isles and White Dominions against foreign nationalities and races. Tariffs are especially appealing when they are used to protect industry, which is associated with economic self-sufficiency and military might. They protect the good manufacturing jobs promised by the leader. Whether these policies in fact create jobs and stimulate growth is another matter. But that other matter is beside the point for a charismatic leader for whom taxing foreign goods is a visible assertion of national authority.

For Trump, running as a Republican, tariffs were also a way of breaking with party establishment. The Republican Party had not always been the party of free trade, it is worth recalling. Nineteenth-century Republican presidents from Abraham Lincoln to William McKinley had supported tariffs to protect industry from foreign competition. The Fordney-McCumber Tariff was adopted in 1922 during the Republican presidency of Warren Harding, the Smoot-Hawley Tariff during the

Republican administration of Herbert Hoover. Before World War II, tariffs were thus very much in the party mainstream. This changed with the Cold War, when congressional Republicans reluctantly embraced foreign trade and aid to support the Western alliance. Comforted by the unassailable position of American manufacturing, Republican members of Congress agreed to grant foreign producers unfettered access to U.S. markets while allowing Japan to pursue restrictive industrial policies and European countries to create a preferential trade area.[4] Exposing a robust manufacturing sector to limp foreign competition was a small price to pay for cementing Western unity, getting the Allies back on their feet, and repelling the Soviet threat. There was still the possibility that the Republicans would revert to their traditional protectionist stance when they regained the White House in 1952. But Dwight D. Eisenhower, a general first and a student of economics second, was swayed by the geopolitical argument.

While this rationale for an open U.S. economy dissolved with the collapse of the Soviet Union, Republican support for free trade did not dissolve with it. Opposition to protection became part and parcel of the post-Reagan Republican Party's ideological objection to government intervention in the economy. It was hard to argue for deregulation in other spheres but stricter regulation of trade. By the 1990s, in addition, a large number of Fortune 500 companies had factories overseas and sourced inputs abroad. In return for supporting other elements of the Republican agenda, they expected fidelity to free and open trade. Moreover, there was growing recognition by corporate strategists and politicians alike that America benefited from the existence of a rules-based multilateral trading system that obliged other countries to open their markets to U.S. exports.

None of these rationales was particularly compelling to Trump, an interventionist by temperament who was less beholden to free-market ideology than a run-of-the-mill Republican. Alliances with other countries were not his priority. Using commerce to cultivate harmonious security relations was not high on his list. Nor did Trump obviously appreciate the importance of multinational production and global supply chains for U.S. manufacturers. He was more inclined to deploy threats and sanctions in bilateral negotiations than to put his faith in international organizations. He regarded the reciprocity rules of the

World Trade Organization (WTO) as undesirable restraints on unilateral decision-making and infringements on U.S. autonomy. If some of his more extreme proposals threatened to violate WTO rules, then this was a feature, not a bug. And if the party elite was antagonized by this stance, all the better, given the candidate's position as an outsider.

Trump's criticism of the Federal Reserve was also straight from the populist playbook. Inveighing against concentrated financial power had been a constant of American politics ever since Andrew Jackson went to war with the Bank of the United States and vetoed the congressional bill renewing its charter in 1832. Jackson's background was not unlike Trump's in that he had engaged in property speculation and suffered a series of financial setbacks, notably in the Panic of 1819. Where a less headstrong individual might have ascribed those reversals to his own flawed judgment, Jackson blamed them on the Bank of the United States. The bank had manipulated monetary conditions, Jackson complained, inflating and then depressing land prices, and in so doing had bankrupted Jackson's counterparties in a series of land deals.[5] For his part, Trump in his first week chose a portrait of Jackson to adorn the Oval Office.

Damage to the people from concentrated financial power is, of course, a constant of American history. It was a central complaint of the Farmers' Alliance and the People's Party in the final decades of the nineteenth century. Those complaints resulted in the creation of a peculiarly atomized central bank, structured to avoid the centralization of financial power. Similar objections cropped up whenever times were tough and politicians sought to appeal to working-class voters. Huey Long attacked financial interests when gathering himself to run for the presidency in 1934–1935, tarring both the Fed and banks controlled by the Morgans and Rockefellers. FDR, hardly a political outsider, sought to position himself as a critic of the banks when seeking reelection in 1936 in the face of a 17 percent unemployment rate.[6]

One suspects that Trump, like FDR before him, was mainly seeking to portray himself as a friend of the people rather than really preparing to break up the banks. In the run-up to the election, he took the position, unusual for a populist and a property developer both, of criticizing the Fed for keeping interest rates low. He argued that Fed policies were supporting a "very false economy," artificially inflating asset prices and favoring his Democratic opponent. But on other occasions he described himself as a "low-interest-rate person."[7] Be that as it may, the Fed typified the kind of elite institution that always has and continues today to be a target of populist ire. Trump showed no compunction during the campaign about weighing in on Federal Reserve policy, something mainstream politicians including his opponent Hillary Clinton warned was irresponsible. Not that he was deterred. That final campaign ad where Trump inveighed against "those who control the levers of power" and "don't have your good in mind" left no doubt about whom he had in mind, overlaying the candidate's voice on an image of Fed chair Janet Yellen.[8]

Other elements of Trump's policy agenda are more difficult to cast in populist terms. Nineteenth-century American populists were uncompromising critics of monopoly power. Huey Long campaigned against Standard Oil, denounced FDR as too cozy with big business, and condemned the New Deal as regulated monopoly. This anti-big-business, anti-monopoly stance is also typical of Latin American populism: in the 1970s, in Salvador Allende's Chile, large domestic business firms with international ties were tarred as "the monopolies."[9] Trump, with a background in business, appeared to want it both ways: to use business as a whipping boy when companies moved facilities abroad, but to enlist it in bringing manufacturing jobs back home. This personal background plausibly explains why Trump turned to businessmen such as Wilber Ross to fill cabinet posts and advisory positions. It explains why the anti-monopoly stance typical of populist movements did not feature prominently in his campaign, aside from some critical remarks about the pharmaceutical industry, and why Trump ceded the issue of market power to Elizabeth Warren, Bernie Sanders, and populists of the Left.

The same tension with standard populist positions also characterized Trump's fiscal plans. The more typical populist stance, typified by Long's "Share Our Wealth" campaign, is to raise taxes on the wealthy and large corporations to finance increases in social spending and guaranteed incomes. In 1934 Long would have assessed a graduated capital levy on all individuals with a net worth of more than $1 million. He would have used taxation to cap annual incomes at $1 million and inheritances at $5.1 million. He would have used the revenues to finance a basic income of $2,500 (roughly one-third of average annual family income), provide pensions for people over sixty years of age, extend universal health care to veterans, and guarantee free education and training to college and vocational-school students.

Trump's fiscal plans cut in the opposite direction. They envisaged lowering marginal tax rates for high earners and abolishing the inheritance tax. They proposed cutting corporate tax rates, where corporate profits that translate into dividends and capital gains accrue disproportionately to the wealthy. Trump proposed a 10 percent reduction in government spending while ramping up outlays on defense and security, thereby putting social programs squarely in the crosshairs. The new president's pledge to abolish the Affordable Care Act (Obamacare) with its subsidies for low-income households was a move away from universal social insurance. Applying the federal hiring freeze ordered in his first week in office to the Veterans Administration and its hospitals was the opposite of the posture adopted by Huey Long. Proposing to give the states fixed blocks of federal funds for Medicare, Medicaid, and food stamps, rather than increasing federal funding as use of these programs increased, similarly augured less, not more, support for low-income households.

This approach to fiscal issues may have reflected the fact that Trump was, in reality, more pro-business than pro–working people. It may have been an attempt to appeal to mainstream Republican skepticism about government intervention in the economy and to the party's opposition to legislatively mandated redistribution. If so, it indicated that Trump understood the need to broaden his appeal from disaffected voters to the Republican mainstream.

An alternative in a more traditional populist vein is that Trump was attempting to ground his opposition to social spending in identity politics. Welfare benefits, he explained to his supporters, were exploited by illegal immigrants and minorities. "The Center for Immigration Studies," he noted in his Phoenix immigration speech, "estimates that 62 percent of households headed by illegal immigrants used some form of cash or non-cash welfare programs, like food stamps or housing assistance. Tremendous costs, by the way, to our country. Tremendous costs."[10] We saw above that the more heterogeneous a society and the greater the distance between social groups, the more reluctant are its members to fund public programs that benefit not just themselves but also others. In advocating reductions in social spending, Trump was tapping into the belief of his white, working-class, small-town supporters that these programs were being exploited by racial minorities, immigrants, and aliens.

Other aspects of the Trump phenomenon fit the Populist mold more closely. There was an almost perfect inverse relationship between the size of a metropolitan area and voters' proximity to it, on one hand, and the share of the vote going to Trump, on the other.[11] Andrew Jackson's bank war, the Farmers' Alliance, and the People's Party were all rural revolts by individuals sensing that they were no longer in control of their economic destinies as a result of urbanization, commercialization, and other changes to the economy. The swing in the Republican share of the vote between 2012 and 2016, between Romney and Trump, was largest in small cities and towns, especially those geographically remote from major metropolitan centers. These smaller towns and rural areas were disproportionately white. Their residents were older and less mobile geographically and socioeconomically. While they were not disproportionately poor, they had a disproportionate fear of poverty, reflecting the lack of alternatives that comes with remoteness. They were less likely to have college degrees, where college education enhances mobility.[12] Their homes and families were physically removed from the global cities where new employment opportunities in high tech and finance were concentrated. They were therefore likely to regard elites in Washington, New York, and Silicon Valley as out of touch with their reality.[13]

Metropolitan areas predictably swung in the other direction. The election of 2016 was the first time Orange County, California, went for a Democratic presidential candidate since FDR in 1936. Among metropolitan districts and counties, those with the largest increase in import competition from China in the decade prior to the election had the greatest likelihood of opting for Trump. More generally, such districts had a greater tendency to vote for candidates at one or the other end of the political spectrum.[14]

Moreover, counties where the swing from Romney to Trump was 15 percentage points or more were virtually all in the Midwest. The Midwest is a diverse and complicated place, but scholars of the region

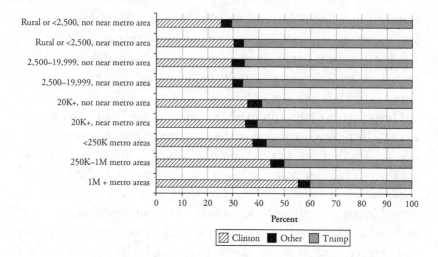

FIGURE 9.1 U.S. Presidential Votes, Urban Versus Rural Areas, 2016

Source: Danielle Kurzleben, "Rural Voters Played a Big Part in Helping Trump Defeat Clinton," *NPR* (14 November 2016), http://www.npr.org/2016/11/14/501737150/rural-voters-played-a-big-part-in-helping-trump-defeat-clinton.

generally characterize it as more traditional than the country as a whole when it comes to issues such as women's and LGBT rights.[15] Midwesterners were less likely to feel that they were benefiting from economic growth. The region had a lower concentration of immigrants and therefore a greater fear of the unknown than the West Coast, the Southwest, the Northeast, and Florida. It may be coincidental that the People's Party held its 1892 convention in Omaha and that its 1892 presidential candidate, James Weaver, was from Iowa. It may be coincidental that William Jennings Bryan was from Nebraska. Or it may be that midwesterners are, subconsciously at least, aware of their populist tradition.

Finally, Trump did especially well in states that enjoyed a temporary fracking boom but suffered subsequently from depressed energy prices. There is an obvious analogy with crop prices in the 1870s and 1920s: a temporary boom that created expectations of good times, followed by a slump.

What, in terms of economic policy, could mainstream politicians have done to head off this populist reaction? Answering this question requires one to take a stance on whether the decline in manufacturing employment in the United States was due mainly to trade or to technology. The argument that it was due mainly to automation and the declining labor intensity of industrial production starts with the observation that the fall in the manufacturing employment share predates the rise of competition from low-wage countries, and from China specifically. It goes back half a century, to when manufacturing firms learned to do more with less and employment shifted toward the service sector. Consider the coal industry, which, though the subject of much impassioned rhetoric in the 2016 campaign, was not directly exposed to Chinese competition. The amount of coal mined in the United States rose by more than 150 percent in the half century ending in 2011, but employee hours fell by more than 20 percent as the industry adopted open-pit mining, self-advancing longwall mining machines, and other mechanized processes.[16]

This diagnosis suggests that a more restrictive trade regime won't be good for American workers. It will be good mainly for American robots insofar as it shifts spending back toward the products of domestic manufacturing firms. Eliminating regulatory restrictions on coal will benefit mainly the skilled-labor- and capital-using producers of longwall mining machines, not the long-suffering residents of Appalachia. Similarly, this diagnosis suggests that had Presidents Bill Clinton and George W. Bush been slower to embrace NAFTA or to agree to Chinese membership in the WTO, this would have done little to arrest the decline in manufacturing employment.

To be sure, import competition negatively affected specific local markets that were home to labor-intensive industries facing Chinese competition. If you had the bad luck to live in a county that was home to firms producing luggage, furniture, textiles, apparel, or electrical appliances, the impact could be devastating, just as in the English Midlands towns producing boots, shoes, gloves, and silks and facing foreign competition in the 1870s.[17]

Because displaced workers lack the resources to move, there is an argument for attempting to bring jobs to them. The Tennessee Valley Authority, begun in 1933 in an effort to bring manufacturing to the region by investing in hydroelectric power, is a case in point. But evidence on the effectiveness of the TVA and its modern equivalent, Empowerment Zones that subsidize the provision of infrastructure, training, and other forms of business assistance in depressed regions, is mixed at best. Moreover, studies suggest that to the extent that the TVA succeeded in attracting new industries, it did so mainly at the expense of other regions.[18]

This is not an argument against trying if the goal is to aid regions and workers displaced by imports. Moreover, the experience of countries like Germany, where manufacturing employment remains more important than in the United States, points to still other measures politicians might try: investing in apprenticeship and vocational training and keeping the national currency at competitive levels, for example. These are not new observations. President Obama proposed a $2 billion apprenticeship training fund in his fiscal year 2016 budget, and economists who believe that manufacturing matters have long criticized the country's strong dollar policy.[19]

These changes are more easily imagined than implemented, however. Germany's apprenticeship system is historically rooted. It is the product of a culture that values what Germans proudly call "blue-collar work." It requires patient employers prepared to invest in their workers, and strong trade unions to help coordinate the operation of the system.[20] Most un-American of all, it requires government, working with employers and unions, to establish standardized occupational profiles, define training curricula, and help pay the bills.

On the competitive-currency side, it's hard to imagine other countries welcoming U.S. efforts to push down the dollar. When smaller countries engage in this behavior, they can be safely ignored. But since the United States is a global heavyweight, other countries would almost certainly respond by pushing down their own currencies along with the greenback. Germany has the advantage, moreover, that it no longer possesses its own currency, giving it plausible deniability. If its exchange rate is low, then this can be conveniently dismissed as reflecting the circumstances of its euro-area partners, not self-interested manipulation by German policymakers.[21] And if Germany is running a trade surplus, any discomfort in the rest of the world is partially offset by the deficits of other less competitive euro-area countries.

But the single most devastating retort is that the share of manufacturing jobs in relation to total employment has been falling in Germany for half a century, just like in the United States. Having reached 40 percent in 1970, that share is now less than 20 percent. (Compare Figure 9.2 here with Figure 8.2 in Chapter 8, and try to detect a significant difference.)

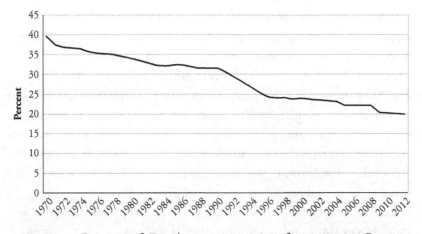

FIGURE 9.2 Percent of Employment in Manufacturing in Germany Since 1970

Source: U.S. Bureau of Labor Statistics, Percent of Employment in Manufacturing in Germany, retrieved from FRED, Federal Reserve Bank of St. Louis; https://fred. stlouisfed.org/series/DEUPEFANA.

Whatever its other merits, even the German system offers only limited protection from the decline of manufacturing employment.

If the problem is secular rather than cyclical, the result of technology rather than trade, and specifically due to the automation of routine tasks in manufacturing, then the solution is to better equip workers to undertake non-routine tasks, not just in manufacturing but also in the service sector. Restaurant chefs, home health care workers, security guards, and spiritual advisors require situational adaptability, interpersonal skills, and oral communication ability, but not always higher education. The importance of adaptability, collegiality, and communication make these jobs relatively safe from automation.[22] To be sure, a San Francisco start-up called Momentum Machines has developed a robot that not only flips hamburgers but makes them from scratch. But the mass production of burgers is the epitome of a routine task; it's hard to imagine the high-end Napa Valley restaurant French Laundry mechanizing the production of its tasting menu. In Japan, where a declining birth rate and a rapidly aging population make the problem of home health care especially acute, Honda has developed an autonomous humanoid robot, Asimo, to get food for the elderly and turn lights off and on. But in an age when robots still can't turn doorknobs or fold napkins, whether robotics can help with more complicated needs, provide emotional succor, and cope with the ethical dilemmas of elder care is uncertain. Another Silicon Valley company, Knightscope, is developing wheeled automatons equipped with sensors, microphones, and lasers to act as security guards. Its K5 model, however, is known mainly for knocking over a child and running over one of his feet at the Stanford Shopping Center. The company's website revealingly touts robots as appropriate for "boring and monotonous" patrols and acknowledges that "decision-making is best left to real people."[23]

Educators argue that the situational adaptability, ease of interpersonal interaction, and communication skills needed for non-routine tasks are heavily influenced by education, starting in early childhood. Interpersonal, collaborative, and communication skills are shaped when children are young, pointing to a high-return area in which to invest.[24] But it will take time, even in the best-case scenario, for such investments to pay off, the time from when a child receives early education to when she enters the labor force. That the problem of declining manufacturing employment due to the automation of routine tasks developed over a period of decades means, unavoidably, that it will similarly take decades to address.

Be this as it may, these were not directions in which the United States, following its startling 2016 election, was prepared to go. The new Congress and administration, critical of federal bureaucracy and mandates, were more inclined to cut early childhood education than to expand it. Skeptical of the ability of the federal government to solve problems, they had little appetite for place-based policies. The very notion of the federal government negotiating occupational profiles and dictating training curricula was anathema to the politicians brought to power in 2016.

And if the promise of bringing back good manufacturing jobs through restrictive trade policies and deregulation was false, it was unclear where those disappointed by that broken promise would turn next: back to the political center or, instead, to an even more radical alternative at one of the extremes.

10

Breaking Point

EUROPE'S DISTINCTIVE BRAND of populism has evident similarities but also important differences from its American counterpart. Both the similarities and the differences were apparent in the UK referendum on EU membership in 2016. The Leave campaign, personified by Nigel Farage, was fundamentally anti-elite, anti-immigrant, and nativist. Farage, the son of a stockbroker, hardly came from a disadvantaged background. He may not have attended Oxford, as did Prime Minister David Cameron and London mayor Boris Johnson, but his career as a commodities trader did not recommend him as a spokesman for the working class. (One might, of course, say the same of Donald Trump.) Be that as it may, none of this deterred Farage, as leader of the United Kingdom Independence Party (UKIP), from positioning himself as an outsider aligned with the disenfranchised masses. He encouraged media coverage of his addiction to cigarettes and beer as a way of playing up his image as a man of the people, much as hamburgers and junk food became media staples of Trump.

Farage, like Trump, embraced positions that were beyond the pale for mainstream politicians, first and foremost on immigration. His rhetoric and visuals, like Trump's, were designed to provoke. Farage was photographed with an incendiary poster headed "Breaking Point: The EU Has Failed Us All," depicting a flood of nonwhite migrants and refugees headed for British shores. Pro- and anti-EU Conservative Party and Labour Party activists alike denounced the image as xenophobic and racist.[1] Farage defended it by invoking terrorism. "In the last two weeks, the Dusseldorf bomb plot has been uncovered—a very, very worrying plan for mass attacks along the style of Paris or Brussels," he elaborated. "All those people came into Germany last year posing as refugees. When Isis say they will use the migrant crisis to flood the continent with their jihadi terrorists, they probably mean it."[2] Other material of Farage's Leave.EU organization was even more inflammatory, including a notorious photo of jihadist fighters captioned "Islamist Extremism Is a Real Threat to Our Way of Life: Act Now Before We See an Orlando-Style Atrocity Here Before Too Long."[3]

The mainstream media dismissed Farage as a buffoon, but there was nothing buffoonish about his message. In a 2015 radio interview he acknowledged inspiration from a visit to his childhood school by Enoch Powell, the 1960s nationalist firebrand notorious for invoking Virgil, no less, when denouncing immigration. The referendum result suggests that the intelligentsia, put off by Farage's clownish persona, should not have dismissed him or his anti-immigrant message so lightly.

That result, with 52 percent voting Leave, was as surprising as Trump's Electoral College victory. The majority of polls got it wrong, just as they did the 2016 U.S. presidential result, because respectable voters hesitated to acknowledge their support for an unrespectable position. Remain supporters complained that the outcome was a minority opinion, much as blue-state voters repeated ad nauseam that Trump lost the popular vote. Since only 72 percent of registered UK voters turned out, Leave's 52 percent meant that just 37 percent of eligible voters endorsed exiting the EU. The problem was that Remain supporters were not as easily mobilized. Sterile economic arguments for EU membership did not excite them in the same way opponents were galvanized by Farage's apocalyptic vision of Britain overrun. Leave had a simple narrative, while Remain did not. That tipped the balance.

The difference in the United Kingdom was that a politician with anti-elite, anti-immigrant, and authoritarian tendencies did not become the leader of one of the major parties. Farage himself stepped down as UKIP leader, citing personal circumstances. Cameron, the Conservative prime minister who called the referendum in a failed effort to unify his party, was replaced by another mainstream Conservative, Theresa May, who had supported Remain (although she embraced the result of the referendum on taking office). This contrast with the United States reflected differences in political institutions. Conservative Party members decide by majority vote between two candidates for party leader, but the two finalists are first nominated by Conservative members of Parliament, not by the party as a whole. This makes it hard for a political renegade to mount a hostile takeover.[4]

But if there were differences in institutions and outcomes, the underlying grievances were fundamentally the same. Economic disquiet was in the air, not surprisingly, in a country whose growth record can most charitably be described as uneven. Growth was slow in the golden age after World War II. Performance improved relative to the European average once Edward Heath made that most un-British of British decisions, taking the country into the European Community, and Margaret Thatcher spearheaded the removal of stifling regulation and agreed to UK participation in the Single Market. EU membership exposed producers to foreign competition, shattering the cozy environment created by tariffs and restrictive regulation. Competition weeded out weak firms and forced the survivors to shape up.[5] To preserve jobs, unions were compelled to agree to productivity-enhancing changes in work rules and shop-floor organization.

Analysts dispute the relative importance of EU membership and Thatcher-era reforms, but there is no disputing the results.[6] GDP per head in the United Kingdom rose by barely 50 percent between 1958 and 1973 while doubling in France, Germany, and Italy. But from the mid-1980s—that is, post-EU entry and post-Thatcher—output per person grew faster in the United Kingdom than in any of the big three continental European economies.[7]

In the United States the rise in inequality was a long-term trend, reflecting mainly labor-saving technical change. In the United Kingdom, in contrast, that rise occurred all at once, in the 1980s. There the Gini coefficient of income inequality rose from 0.25 in 1979 to 0.34 in 1992, after which it leveled off. That this took place in a few years suggests that the increase was not due mainly to a gradual, ongoing process of labor-saving technical change. Rather, it was linked to Thatcher's policies eviscerating the unions, privatizing state assets, and limiting social spending. The sudden Thatcher-era decline in the bargaining power of unions reduced their ability to exercise a moderating influence on CEO pay and to pressure employers to share their revenues with their workers.[8] There was also some impact from Thatcher's welfare-state cuts, which reduced public support for the poor, as described in Chapter 8, and from the privatization of council housing and other factors creating housing-affordability challenges.[9]

But after this surge in the 1980s, the extent of inequality remained roughly unchanged. There were even signs of it falling in the run-up to the referendum.[10] Why, then, was inequality, or at least the perception of inequality, so concerning to British voters?

One answer is that inequality, even if stable in the aggregate, had a prominent regional dimension. Like the United States, the United Kingdom experienced a decline in manufacturing jobs. Between 1978 and 2008 some 4 million U.K. manufacturing jobs were lost, proportionally the largest such fall in any OECD country.[11] There was a commensurate increase, meanwhile, in service-sector jobs, notably in finance and other business services, of a sufficient quality to keep aggregate inequality from rising. But the new service-sector jobs were in different places than the manufacturing jobs they replaced. Manufacturing had been concentrated in the Midlands and other traditionally industrial regions, while well-paying jobs in finance and business services were disproportionately in London and other metropolitan centers.

As a result, regional differences in U.K. living standards were among the highest in Europe. Median hourly pay was more than 50 percent higher in London than in the East Midlands.[12] Londoners enjoyed not just more consumption but also greater life expectancy. Given how their income growth was driven by finance and other services, Londoners were reasonably content with the status quo, while residents of the East Midlands were convinced that something had gone badly wrong.[13]

As for why it took until 2016 for these chickens to come home to roost, the existence of these problems was papered over by an enormous lending boom. Households whose incomes lagged were able to borrow, as in the United States, to purchase housing and finance their other spending. Household debt rose to 160 percent of household income in 2008, up from 100 percent a decade earlier.[14] The now notorious "Together Mortgages" extended by the swashbuckling onetime building society Northern Rock, which allowed borrowers to purchase houses without a deposit, take loans 25 percent more than the value of their property, and borrow up to six times their income, were only the most egregious examples of more general practice. Together Mortgages were only viable, for self-evident reasons, so long as home prices were rising. Thus, when they peaked in 2007 and then started to fall off, the less than solid Northern Rock became the first British bank to suffer a run in 150 years.

The Conservative-Liberal coalition formed in 2010 sought to restore confidence by buttressing the public finances. Its spending cuts severely impacted the public and social services on which residents of depressed regions relied. Meanwhile, recovery from the financial crisis was sluggish, whether due to the drag from those self-same policies or because recovery from financial crises is always sluggish.

The growth that did occur was too little to make up for losses from the financial crisis for those at the bottom of the income scale. In April 2016 the annual income of the typical working class household was still £345 below that prior to the crisis, mirroring the situation in the United States. In the absence of a high tide lifting all boats, resentment of inequality came to a boil. Financial crises that cause income losses for the middle and working classes regularly spur a turn away from the political establishment, typically in nationalist directions. Unsurprisingly, this was the case in 2016, when people in households with incomes below £20,000 were twice as likely to support Leave as those in households with incomes above £60,000 (62 versus 35 percent).

Just as in the United States, this nationalist reaction was also rooted in identity politics. It was stoked by anti-immigration sentiment, as Farage and the Leave campaign understood perfectly well. Brexiteers were uncomfortable with multiculturalism, social liberalism, feminism, globalization, and environmentalism, which they viewed as cosmopolitan, European, and un-British. Populism is a reaction against the challenge to a long-standing, homogeneous social grouping from outsiders. Outsiders in this case meant feminists, gays, lesbians, "alien" cultures, and, most especially, immigrants and Europeans.

Specifically, the populist reaction reflected the wish on the part of traditionally dominant groups in British society to regain control, socially from minority religions and races, practically from "faceless bureaucrats in Brussels." Half of Leave voters agreed that the most important consideration was that "decisions about the UK should be taken in the UK." Another third asserted that the main motivation for their vote was to enable "the UK to regain control over immigration and its own borders."[15] Fifty-three percent of white voters opted for Leave, as did nearly six in ten voters describing themselves as Christian. Other instances of populism suggest that an incumbent group will react most violently—that its members will be most inclined to feel that their core values are threatened—when they are falling behind economically. So it was in this case, where a majority of those working full- or part-time voted Remain, while most of those not working voted Leave.

Brexit voters were hostile above all to immigration. Fifty-four percent of all voters, according to Ashcroft Polls, acknowledged a dislike for immigration, and 80 percent of those hostile to immigration voted to leave the EU. Although that same 80 percent propensity to vote Leave was evident among voters who expressed a dislike for multiculturalism and social liberalism, aversion to these values was less prevalent.[16] Anti-immigrant sentiment was thus the determining factor on the Leave side.[17]

This anti-immigrant sentiment had a long history. Recall the rise of anti-Irish discrimination after the famine, with the mass arrival of Irish immigrants in Liverpool. In the 1960s Conservative MP Enoch Powell, Lafarge's inspiration, denounced Indian and Pakistani immigrants as inimical to the British way of life while using phobia of immigrants as a device for mobilizing opposition to the United Kingdom's entry into the European Community, which he saw as threatening British sovereignty. The critics of immigration, multiculturalism, and Europe now pointing to surging inflows followed in this not-so-proud tradition.

But the timing takes some explaining. Immigration overtook domestic population growth in England and Wales in 1994–1995. By 1998–1999 net inward migration, at some 200,000 per annum, was more than twice natural population growth.[18] At this point most immigrants came from outside the European Union, many from the onetime Commonwealth and Empire. This changed, however, with Tony Blair's decision in 2004 to allow unrestricted access to the U.K. labor market for citizens of the EU's eight new Central and Eastern European member states. The U.K. labor market was tight, and Blair had the backing of business. The policy was part of his strategy to reposition the Labour Party as business friendly and pro-globalization.[19] The decision to open the doors to the new EU8 was, in fact, part of a broader set of government initiatives that included also more permits and visas for young people seeking work in the tourist trade and for seasonal agricultural labor.[20]

Experts forecast as few as five thousand immigrants annually from the new EU countries, thirteen thousand tops.[21] These projections were predicated on the existence of little prior immigration from Eastern Europe, together with the fact that new migrants tend to follow their predecessors. They assumed that Eastern Europeans were more likely to want to work in Germany and Austria. But these studies did not anticipate that only Ireland and Sweden would join the United Kingdom in throwing open their doors to the new EU states, whereas other countries would invoke the seven-year escape clause permitted by EU rules. Immigrants who might have preferred to work in Germany were therefore diverted to the United Kingdom. And where early immigrants flowed, later immigrants followed. Nor did these studies account for the fact that Central and Eastern European workers were relatively well educated, education enhancing adaptability and encouraging mobility.

In the event, more than 50,000 immigrants from the EU8 arrived in the United Kingdom annually from 2004 through 2006; 112,000 then arrived in 2007 alone. This was decidedly not to the liking of Labour Party members already rendered anxious about their job security by globalization and automation. The enthusiasm with which New Labour's cosmopolitan leaders sought to establish their business-friendly bona fides and the readiness with which they dismissed these rank-and-file concerns drove disaffected workers into the arms of UKIP.

David Cameron, as leader of the opposition Conservatives, also sought to capitalize on these worries. He promised to reduce immigration "to the levels of the 1990s—meaning tens of thousands a year, instead of the hundreds of thousands a year under Labour."[22] But Cameron's limp efforts lacked business backing, and he failed to deliver on his promises: net migration in 2015 was even higher, at 333,000. Voters unhappy with these numbers were drawn to other options, where the obvious option was leaving the EU and "regaining control of the country's borders," as the goal was described by UKIP's immigration spokesman Steven Woolfe.

To be sure, not all the evidence supported this diagnosis of working-class problems. Since immigrants from Eastern Europe were relatively well educated, many of them did not compete for low-wage manual jobs.[23] Nor does the share of foreign-born residents help to explain voting patterns. The foreign-born share and the proportion of a region's voters supporting Leave were in fact negatively correlated.[24] It is as if regions where knowledge of immigrants was least, fear of immigrants was greatest.

The English regions with largest percentage increases in foreign-born residents after 1995 were the East Midlands, Merseyside, and Tyne and Wear (loosely, the area around Newcastle). Since these regions had few foreign-born residents at the start of the period, a modest amount of immigration could make a visible difference, fanning identity concerns. The presence of few foreign-born residents at the outset meant that even limited immigration could create the impression of radical change. Already these manufacturing-heavy regions were suffering a variety of ills, from job loss to inadequate public housing and health care, problems that could be blamed on immigrants who were conveniently not present in significant numbers to defend themselves. And neither Labour nor the Conservatives could contend that they had a credible strategy for addressing these concerns within the European Union, given the track records of Blair and Cameron.

Had observers paid closer attention to the fortunes of populist parties elsewhere, they might have been less surprised by the salience of immigration in the Brexit debate. A core feature of radical populist parties across Europe, as Matthew Goodwin noted in 2011, was hostility to immigration.[25] This is most commonly true of populists of the Right, who staked out violently anti-immigration positions in 2015 when more than 900,000 asylum seekers and refugees, mainly from Syria, Iraq, and Afghanistan, arrived on European shores. But the pattern was already evident earlier. As Goodwin wrote four full years ahead of the refugee crisis, "Across Europe, there is now a large body of evidence that the most powerful predictor of who will support populist extremists is whether they are hostile to immigration. Citizens who endorse [these parties] ... are profoundly concerned about immigration and its effects: they either want it halted completely or the number of immigrants to be reduced drastically."[26]

In 2008, Jens Rydgren had used the European Social Survey to establish that 93 percent of voters for the far-right Austrian Freedom Party preferred a policy of few or no immigrants (as opposed to accepting some or all who wished to come), compared to 64 percent of other voters.[27] The same disparity was evident between supporters of the far right and other voters in Denmark (89 versus 44 percent), France (82 versus 44 percent), Belgium (76 versus 41 percent), Norway (70 versus 39 percent), and the Netherlands (63 versus 39 percent). The association between this desire to limit immigration and support for far right parties long predated the refugee crisis, in other words. The flood of refugees simply increased the number of voters expressing that preference.

Making the case that hostility to immigration in Europe reflects mainly concerns about jobs and inequality is an uphill task, since economic conditions differ sharply across countries. The same association of anti-immigrant sentiment with far right political support is evident in prosperous, low-unemployment Sweden and more economically troubled France. It is hard to argue that the reaction against immigration is fueled by those left behind by technical change and globalization, because the rise in inequality since the 1980s was less in continental Europe than in the United States and United Kingdom, and because early twenty-first-century levels of inequality were lower. There was no obvious association between the extent of inequality and strength of support for right-wing nationalist, anti-immigration parties: the Northern League and Golden Dawn polled only in the single digits in Italy and Greece, two countries with high inequality by European standards, while the True Finns, the Austrian Freedom Party and the Swiss People's Party, competing in three relatively egalitarian countries, polled in excess of 20 percent.[28]

It is tempting to point to cross-country differences in the severity of the Great Recession, since Germany was the West European country that most successfully skated through the crisis (GDP per person in Germany was 3 percent higher in 2011 than at the end of 2007) and the nationalist, anti-EU Alternativ für Deutschland (AfD) made only limited electoral gains. But by 2017, capitalizing on the backlash against the refugee influx, AfD had broadened its appeal from anti-euro to anti-immigrant and anti-Muslim voters, becoming the third-leading party in Germany and attracting nearly 13 percent of the vote in September's parliamentary elections. Conversely, in Ireland, Greece, Italy, and Spain, the four continental European countries that suffered the largest declines in GDP per capita, right-wing populist parties failed to gain significant traction.

All this suggests that the salience of economic grievances was shaped by other factors, namely, identity politics. Radical right parties tend to be skeptical or outright hostile to liberal democracy, pluralism, and minority rights. Opinion polls reveal particular opposition to immigration by people of a different race or ethnicity. They indicate special resistance to immigrants from non-European countries. They show particular hostility to Muslim people.[29] These patterns may reflect the challenge of assimilating immigrants from North Africa and the Middle East and the perceived threat to the dominant culture. Consistent with this view, surveys suggest less concern over time with the impact of immigration on jobs, taxes, and public services but more concern with the effect on "cultural life," as the identity issue is framed by survey takers. One thinks of France, which bars Muslim women in head scarves from working in private day care centers and accompanying school outings, and where Parliament in 2010 passed a law banning women from wearing the burka and other face-covering headgear in public. One can stretch one's imagination and suggest that face coverings hinder the identification of potential terrorists, but it is more plausible that the burka is a visible reminder of the presence of a large religious minority and therefore a challenge to *laïcité*, the notion enshrined in the constitution of France as an indivisible secular republic.

In fact, immigration to France, Belgium, the Netherlands, and Germany from Turkey and North Africa has a long history. In the 1950s and 1960s, when labor was scarce, Western Europe actively sought to attract guest workers from these countries. Again this points up the question of why the impact of these immigrants on "cultural life" was now more of an issue. One answer is that the number of Moroccans and Turks in the Netherlands rose tenfold between the early 1970s and 2010, while the number of Turks living in Germany rose fourfold. Another is that the rise of religious fundamentalism made assimilation more difficult. Tradition-minded Muslims (head scarves making traditional Muslims more visible) challenged Dutch notions of "open-mindedness" and French conceptions of *laïcité*. A third explanation is that the presence of immigrants created security concerns, real or imagined, after 9/11.

In addition, there was the shift from temporary migration to permanent residency. In the 1950s and 1960s, guest workers in Germany had typically stayed for a limited period before returning home. They complied with what German bureaucrats called the *Rotationprinzip* (rotation principle), which authorized them to work for only a limited time. Returning to one's country of origin was attractive so long as Europe was booming and there was always the option of moving back.[30] But in the 1970s, with growth slowing, the prospects for reentry and reemployment dimmed. And as unemployment rose, Western European governments hardened their barriers to immigration.

Temporary migration thus became permanent. Permanent migrants not unreasonably sought to bring their families, as they were permitted to do by their host countries' reunification laws. Guest workers once had been single men shunted into company housing. Now they took up residence in working-class neighborhoods. Their children attended school. Their wives did what housewives do. As they became more visible, European societies were forced to grapple with diversity and assimilation.[31] This was a clear instance of the interaction of economic factors with identity politics, where slower growth led to the hardening of borders, which in turn caused a change in immigration from temporary to permanent, raising issues of cultural life on which populist parties subsequently pounced.

Greece too had its immigrants from Albania, Bulgaria, Romania, Georgia, and Russia even before the refugee crisis, which Golden Dawn had sought to exploit. By some estimates, as much as 10 percent of the Greek population is foreign born, or at least was before the country's crisis.[32] This was another unintended consequence of the hardening of borders in Northern Europe: immigration was diverted toward Southern Europe, where border enforcement was lax.

In Greece, however, the populist shift was to the left, not the right, and the dominant factor was external circumstances, namely, the country's need for a financial lifeline in order to stay in the euro area and the European Union. The European Commission, the European Central Bank, and the International Monetary Fund, the members of the so-called Troika, demanded harsh austerity as a condition of assistance. So when the mainstream parties were implicated in the crisis and surrendered to the Troika's terms, the populist backlash turned to the Left as the credible opponent of austerity. The reaction was not so much the people against foreigners, the split that makes for right-wing populism—although the Troika was unmistakably foreign—as much as it was the people against the elites, both the domestic elites blamed for creating the mess and the foreign technocrats seen as aggravating it, the split that makes for left-wing populism.

Greece's history of dictatorship also militated against the authoritarian Right, something that was similarly true in Portugal and Spain. Few disaffected voters wished to return to a brutal authoritarian regime like the military junta of 1967–1974. Syriza thus benefited from having descended from the independent Greek Communist Party with its anti-fascist, anti-dictatorial roots.

Still, the corruption and incompetence of earlier governments, the burden of Troika-imposed austerity, and the suspicion that wealthy individuals with assets abroad were getting off scot-free were more than enough to elicit a populist reaction. In the October 2009 elections Syriza had won barely 5 percent of the vote. In January 2015 it won 36 percent and was asked to form a government. Such is the power of a crisis.

Where Greece's history of military dictatorship limited support for Golden Dawn, Eastern Europe's history of Soviet domination shaped political reactions differently. In Eastern Europe the "others" opposed to the people were left-wing politicians and parties identified with now-discredited socialism. Politicians with leftist leanings were associated with the corrupt Communist elite of the period before 1990 by right-of-center figures seeking to define themselves in opposition. Because the elite was on the Left, politicians seeking to play up the division between the elite and people today are on the Right.

Under Communism these countries felt little pressure to come to terms with historical persecution of minorities, since such behavior could be ascribed to the contradictions of capitalism, following standard Marxist-Leninist logic. Not coming to terms meant that racism and anti-Semitism remained more prevalent, or at least more overtly prevalent, than in Western Europe. Starting in 2015 these attitudes and prejudices were redirected at refugees and asylum seekers by right-wing politicians seeking to mobilize nationalist support. And the fact that the nation-state had been subsumed by the international socialist order and dominated by the Soviet Union meant that aggressive nationalism could now be portrayed as a reassertion of what was just and right.

This historical connection was visible even in Germany. The dangers of nationalism and prejudice featured in public school curricula in the Federal Republic (West Germany) but not in the German Democratic Republic (East Germany), where the rise of the Nazis was ascribed not to a heritage of anti-Semitism or to a resurgent nationalism, base instincts now to be avoided, but to the contradictions of the market system.[33] Germans educated in the East were not instilled with the same intellectual and emotional aversion to nationalism and anti-minority sentiment. Forty-four percent of West Germans polled in 2015 opposed Chancellor Angela Merkel's policy of welcoming asylum seekers, while fully 56 percent of Easterners opposed the policy.[34] The far-right anti-Muslim movement Pegida (Patriotic Europeans Against the Islamization of the West) was founded, not incidentally, by an advertising executive and professional chef, Lutz Bachmann, born and bred in Dresden.

And it was not just in the United Kingdom that nationalist, anti-immigrant, anti-Muslim sentiment was channeled into EU-skepticism. The Single Market with its four freedoms, including freedom of labor mobility, makes it hard for individual member states to unilaterally secure their borders.[35] The EU's core values of pluralism and tolerance are clear in the *acquis communautaire*, the body of EU law that member states are required to follow. The *acquis* includes chapters on justice, freedom, and fundamental human rights. Governments that abridge minority rights or limit freedom of the press can be sanctioned by the European Commission, the EU's proto–executive branch, and the European Court of Justice, its judicial authority. In 2015 the Commission launched an investigation, cosmetically known as a "dialogue," of Polish legislation voted through by the right-wing Law and Justice Party that compromised the independence of the Constitutional Tribunal, the country's supreme court, and that subjected Poland's public broadcasters to state control, limiting freedom of the press and media. At roughly the same time, the commission launched an infringement case against the Hungarian government of Viktor Orbán for a restrictive refugee settlement law that conflicted with the Common European Asylum System and for erecting a steel fence along the country's southern border. Successful prosecution of such cases would require the country to change its national law in order to remain an EU member in good standing or else lose its voting rights in the Council of Ministers, where decisions on the EU budget and other such matters are taken, and be subject to financial penalties.[36]

It is thus unsurprising that right-wing, anti-elite, anti-establishment, nativist movements make the EU a target. The EU is an elite project, having been pushed on reluctant publics by intellectuals and high officials since the days of Jean Monnet. It is inadequately democratic, since important decisions are taken by technocrats of the European Commission who are not directly accountable to national parliaments or the voting public. Staffed by people from twenty-eight member states, it is dominated by foreigners, whatever the country in question. Its Rule of Law Framework, under which the 2015 Polish investigation was launched, is expressly designed to constrain illiberal, nationalist actions.

There is no consensus on how the EU should address these strains. The elites have responded, predictably, that the best way of containing discontent is by streamlining the Commission and other European institutions to enable them to operate more efficiently.[37] The problem is that nationalist critics of the EU are likely to oppose the "efficiently" part insofar as they already oppose the "more." Europhiles such as the economist Thomas Piketty suggest that the best way of beating back the nationalist threat is by correcting the democratic deficit, strengthening the decision-making powers of the European Parliament, and supplementing it for euro-related matters with a Eurozone Assembly.[38] But doing so implies sharing decision-making with foreigners, which is antithetical to those with nationalistic instincts. Still others suggest that faster economic growth is the best way of fostering support for the EU and for the ideas of Piketty et alia.[39] No doubt faster growth would help. Too bad that there is no agreement about how to best achieve it.

II

Containment

THE POPULIST TEMPTATION is greatest when economic concerns fuse with identity politics and when the two are inadequately addressed by mainstream parties. In some cases the political establishment has responded with policies that address voters' concerns about living standards, equity, economic security, and the sense that their voice is not being heard. The Populist Revolt in nineteenth-century America was defused by freight rate regulation, interest rate regulation, and changes to the gold standard, limited reforms that went some way toward addressing the complaints of farmers and others, together with political reforms such as the referendum processes and direct election of senators advocated by the Populist Party. These steps took the wind out of the populists' sails. Mainstream politicians also appropriated certain less savory elements of the populist agenda, restricting immigration from Asia and taxing imported manufactures, for example. But these and other questionable tactics were more limited than they would have been in the absence of constructive responses.

Those constructive responses and their positive reception were favored by good luck and good institutions. Growth accelerated in the 1890s, creating new opportunities and diminishing the sense that change was a zero-sum game. Not just more favorable U.S. monetary conditions but also a more benign global environment helped to banish deflation. This was good luck at the best possible time. But the decentralized nature of the country's political institutions also helped in this period of limited federal powers. Rather than having to organize a successful national movement, as the Populists ultimately failed to do, reformers in Oregon and California organized locally, using referenda to enhance the voice of the people and address the concern that legislators were beholden to moneyed interests. Oregon and Nebraska could push ahead with the direct election of senators, again bypassing suspect state legislators, until the requisite three-quarters of states finally agreed to amend the Constitution in 1913.

Time will tell whether we are as lucky this time and whether the political establishment is as capable of mounting a constructive response. The ultimate good luck would be a better economy. Productivity growth fell sharply across the advanced countries in the 1970s, as we saw in Chapter 8. It then recovered during the 1995–2005 period before declining again. One can imagine that the years after 2005 were the anomaly and that growth is now poised to accelerate. Just as it took time to figure out how to apply new information technologies to retail trade, wholesale trade, and financial services, the sectors that led the recovery of productivity growth in 1995–2005, it may simply be taking time to figure out how to apply the cloud, quantum computing, artificial intelligence, and other recent IT advances outside the IT sector. Firms throughout the economy must first reorganize how they interact with their customers and how they recruit and deploy their workers.[1] If we're lucky, the results will materialize quickly.[2] Growth will accelerate, obviating the need for hard choices and blunting political extremism. Or not.

For those willing to be patient, there is a plain-vanilla recipe for fostering faster growth. It starts with investing in basic literacy and numeracy but also in vocational training, university education, and lifelong learning. It includes relaxing excessive regulation, but also retaining regulations that correct market failures. It requires sound and stable economic policies making for a favorable investment climate. This means not boosting demand in unsustainable ways, as before 2007, but also avoiding policies that actively depress spending, as in Europe after 2010.

But one thing these policies have in common is that they take time to work their effects. It takes time to train a more skilled and productive labor force. It takes time to renew the capital stock. It takes time to translate principles into policies and to develop a consensus around their implementation. The plain-vanilla recipe for fostering growth is like the dietician's advice to "eat healthy." Enhancing the environment for growth, like changing one's diet, takes discipline, attention to detail, and time to see the effects. And time doesn't favor those seeking to head off a populist reaction.

If faster growth fails to materialize, then it is all the more pressing to address distributional concerns. This will require new thinking, since the forces that made for greater equality in the third quarter of the twentieth century are unlikely to return. Trade unions, which advocate for factory workers, will find it more difficult to organize people working remotely from home. They will be less able to extract rents in a world of internationally integrated markets, where emerging economies with lower wages welcome employers with open arms. Capital mobility makes it harder for governments to use tax policy to level the income distribution as they did after World War II, since the wealthy and the corporations in which they invest can now shift their assets to lower-tax jurisdictions. The ethnic, racial, and religious diversity of Western societies, reflecting the cumulative effects of immigration, limits political support for governmental transfers. And the bias of technological change no longer favors blue-collar workers; it is the routine jobs of less skilled workers that are being disproportionately automated, while more-skilled workers oversee the automatons.

Insofar as offshoring of the labor-intensive component of manufacturing supply chains in the advanced countries has raised capital's share of GDP, one way of addressing inequality is by ensuring that capital is held more widely.[3] Anthony Atkinson suggested strengthened inheritance taxes to prevent concentrated claims on capital from passing down to the fortunate few and using the revenues to provide every citizen with a capital grant at the age of majority.[4] But if the dead are in no position to lobby or flee to lower tax jurisdictions, wealthy parents can do both. Moreover, Atkinson's proposal centers on redistribution, which is politically fraught. It implies transfers from more to less fortunate ethnic, religious, and racial groups, which clashes with identity politics.

Subtler approaches would start with giving firms tax incentives to adopt employee stock option plans. Workers can be given tax incentives to invest in them. Individuals can be required to opt out of retirement and other payroll-linked savings plans instead of being given the choice to opt in. These policies won't redistribute capital ownership at a stroke. But they can give capital-poor individuals hope that the distribution of holdings will evolve in more equitable directions. And hope is what it's all about.[5]

Insofar as inequality reflects the very different labor incomes of top earners and others, societies again have the choice of whether to address this directly. In 2013 Switzerland voted on a referendum that would have limited executive pay to twelve times that of a company's lowest-paid employees. Voters rejected the proposal as too radical and too easily circumvented by non-salary compensation and perks. In the United States such regulation would likely be regarded as beyond the pale. Still, absent other measures to curb excesses, one can imagine more such proposals from left-wing populists in a variety of countries, including even the United States, where the average ratio of the pay of CEOs of big firms to that of their workers is a staggering 200 to 1.

Curbing those excesses should start with making corporate boards and compensation committees subject to stronger legal and administrative sanctions if they too readily acquiesce to CEO requests for higher pay, neglecting their fiduciary responsibility to other stakeholders. Regulators should require companies to disclose the existence of executive stock option plans. Only independent directors should be allowed to sit on compensation committees. Shareholders should be entitled to vote on—and veto—pay packages for top executives, as U.S. investors were empowered to do by the Dodd-Frank Wall Street Reform and Consumer Protection Act, put in place in 2010 in response to the financial crisis.[6] The fact that the increase in the share of labor income accruing to the top 1 percent has been heavily concentrated among employees in the financial sector, not just top executives but also others, suggests that restraining the growth of the financial industry, another intended effect of Dodd-Frank, can help to limit pay inequality in addition to limiting stability risks.[7] Whether Dodd-Frank will survive the backlash against post-crisis regulatory reform is uncertain. These are arguments for why it, or at least something like it, should.

In the United States, high rates of social mobility are traditionally cited as a reason not to be fixated on inequality. Even those at the bottom, the argument goes, have a chance of rising to the top. It follows that declining social mobility is part of the explanation for why inequality has become more of a concern. The economists Michael Carr and Emily Wiemers found evidence of a significant decline in lifetime earnings mobility in the United States since the early

1980s. The probability of an individual remaining in the same decile of the earnings distribution over his or her working lifetime went up for every decile of the distribution in the post-1980s period. Meanwhile, the chance that someone who starts in the bottom 10 percent of the earnings distribution will move above the 40th percentile dropped by 16 percent. The likelihood of workers who started their careers in the middle of the earnings distribution moving to the top deciles similarly declined by 20 percent.[8]

And what is true over an individual's working lifetime is true across generations as well. Fully 50 percent of a parent's earnings advantage, recent studies suggest, is passed on to the next generation. The intergenerational elasticity of earnings, the technical name for this form of persistence, is as much as two-thirds for those in the top half of the distribution.[9] Current estimates of intergenerational persistence are noticeably higher than those in the second half of the twentieth century.

Raj Chetty and his coauthors have shown further that the probability of a child from a family in the bottom fifth of the income distribution reaching the top fifth varies greatly across the United States. Areas with high earnings mobility have better primary and secondary schools; they better prepare children to succeed economically. Those areas have less residential segregation, enabling children from poor families to interact with people from different economic backgrounds and to acquire the social skills needed for getting ahead in the labor market. They have fewer single parents, a larger middle class, and more civic and religious organizations. Some of these variables are easier to influence with public policy than others, but these findings are at least suggestive that investing in primary and secondary education and legislating against residential segregation, using anti-discrimination and appropriate zoning laws, can enhance economic mobility and thereby ameliorate inequality concerns.[10]

When comparing regions, Chetty and colleagues do not find that people in places with better access to higher education, in the sense of sheer physical proximity, display higher earnings mobility. Physical access is less of an issue today than after World War II, given the proliferation of public, private, and for-profit institutions.[11] The University of California, to pick an example not entirely at random, added four general campuses in the 1950s, five in the 1960s, and a further one in the twenty-first century. Those campuses were situated where they were precisely in order to serve neglected communities.

Access to elite education still matters, however. The higher education that most affects the probability of an individual moving from the lower or middle part of the income distribution to the top 1 percent is attending an Ivy League–type school. This is a problem for those concerned with inequality of income and opportunity, since, as another Chetty-coauthored study shows, children from families in the top 1 percent of the income distribution are seventy-seven times more likely to attend an Ivy League–type school than children of families in the bottom fifth of the income distribution.[12]

This suggests eliminating favorable treatment by admissions committees of children of alumni, so-called legacy admissions.[13] It points to limiting the tax advantages of private universities with large endowments that cater to the children of the wealthy. It is an argument for providing additional funding to middle-tier public institutions like the City University of New York and California's system of state and community colleges (as opposed to the university) that enroll disproportionate numbers of lower-income students who, after graduation, have high rates of earnings mobility.[14]

All this can better equip young people preparing to enter the workforce, but there remains the question of what to do for those well into their working years. In a variety of times and places, from Bismarckian Germany and Edwardian Britain to the United States in the 1930s, a populist reaction against economic change has been contained by public programs that compensate the displaced and comfort others who fear the same fate. Unemployment insurance, health insurance, and old-age insurance address this need, as does assistance with retraining, job search, and relocation. These programs help workers cope with circumstances that they are less than fully capable of handling themselves, thereby addressing the anxieties of creative destruction. In some countries administration of these programs is top-down, while in others, like the United States, it is heavily decentralized—essentially for historical reasons, as we have seen. In Canada, the United Kingdom, and many European countries, health care provision and insurance are directly administered by the government, while in the United States, again for historical reasons, the direct role of government is limited to those with special needs—namely, the elderly (Medicare), the poor (Medicaid), and the military (the Veterans Administration)—to providing subsidies for people for whom health coverage is prohibitively costly, and to providing tax deductions for large medical expenses.[15]

It is not coincidental that the United States, where for historical and ideological reasons the role of government in providing social insurance is most limited, is also where the backlash against free trade and concern with the decline of manufacturing employment have been especially intense. Americans understand that they will not receive much help from publicly provided unemployment insurance, health insurance, and old-age insurance and little assistance with retraining and relocation if they lose their jobs to globalization and automation. Ethnic, racial, and religious heterogeneity has worked against the extensive provision of social assistance, with each group resisting calls to fund programs they believe benefit mainly others.

What is true of racial divides is true equally of socioeconomic divides. Insurance is not provided under a veil of ignorance. Skilled workers whose jobs are secure understand that they are being asked to finance insurance and income maintenance for less skilled workers whose livelihoods are at risk from globalization and technology. But this very observation suggests a bargain. Whereas less skilled workers are disproportionately on the receiving end of social insurance benefits, more skilled workers in the advanced economies benefit disproportionately from globalization, since their countries export mainly skill-intensive goods. Skilled workers also benefit disproportionately from new technologies that complement their skills. The high-wage workers in question may be funding transfers to others, but in return they are getting a social consensus favoring economic openness and technical change.

In other words, globalization and technological progress may be good things, as economists argue, but even good things are rarely free. Otto von Bismarck understood this when he advanced health, disability, and old-age insurance to reassure Silesian weavers displaced by technical change and imports that the German Empire had their backs. David Lloyd George and the New Liberals understood this when they adopted unemployment insurance to fend off pressure for tariff reform from workers in the shipbuilding, engineering, and iron-founding trades. Franklin Delano Roosevelt understood this when, at the same time as he sought to walk back the import restrictions of the 1920s and 1930s under authority granted him in 1934 by the Reciprocal Trade Agreements Act, he spearheaded a historic expansion of the welfare state.[16] John F. Kennedy understood this when he signed the Trade Expansion Act of 1962, which authorized the president to cut tariffs by 50 percent but also created programs to provide job training, job search assistance, and exceptional income support to workers displaced by foreign trade, enlisting the support of union leaders for the trade expansion bill.[17] The failure of twenty-first-century politicians, specifically in the United States, to make this connection is either a failure of courage, to the extent they are intimidated by hardcore ideological opponents of government action, or a simple failure of logic.

There are also more ambitious ideas. If jobs for unskilled workers are gone for good and not everyone can acquire the necessary skills, then there is a solidarity argument for a basic income for all. This was another idea the Swiss considered in a referendum, this one in June 2016. Although the ballot measure didn't specify the amount, campaigners suggested that it would be some 2,500 Swiss francs per month per adult, or roughly $2,500—almost exactly the same in 2016 dollars, as fate would have it, as the allowance proposed under the Townsend Plan, described in Chapter 5, or under Huey Long's "Share Our Wealth" plan, as described in Chapter 9.[18] The Swiss proposal was defeated, with 77 percent voting against, on grounds of cost (the measure would have cost 4 to 5 percent of GDP) and also for fear that an unconditional scheme would encourage indolence. It's not hard to anticipate the same reaction elsewhere.[19]

Better would be to question the presumption that there is a large class of citizens unable to acquire the skills to make them employable and to reject the proposition that jobs for humans are gone for good.[20] Also better would be to redesign education and training to prepare workers for non-routine jobs that are difficult to automate—to impart the adaptability, interpersonal skills, and oral communication ability required for twenty-first-century work. This suggests focusing from an early age not just on literacy and numeracy but also on cultivating empathy, compassion, and other human instincts that machines find it difficult to emulate (so far) but which the elderly, ill, infants, and others value in interactions.

But if there are limits on the ability of society, through education and training, to raise the productivity of workers to the point where employers who have the option of using robots are willing to pay those workers a socially acceptable wage, then the solution is subsidizing wages and work. This would be cheaper and more socially acceptable than an unconditional basic income. It would enable workers to learn on the job. It would give people the satisfaction of having work. Wage subsidies could be extended to the worker or employer through the tax code. Even countries traditionally as suspicious of social engineering as the United States have experience with such programs. The U.S. federal government provides an Earned Income Tax Credit, for example, which reduces the taxes of low-income families so long as they work and which may even give them a refund (a negative tax liability). This tax credit scheme is in fact the country's third-largest social welfare program after Medicaid and food stamps. The United States similarly provides a Work Opportunity Tax Credit to firms that hire certain types of low-skilled workers, thereby making it more economical for employers to take them on.[21]

Also fashionable, since it has been suggested by no less than Bill Gates, is taxing robots to level the playing field.[22] Why should people pay taxes while robots get off scot-free? The resulting revenues could then be used to fund socially worthwhile programs.

But where, one might ask, do we draw the line between robots and ordinary machines? Is an ATM a robotic bank teller, and if so, should ATMs be taxed? Should all machines be taxed?

Definitional problems aside, a moment's reflection reveals that the owners of robots don't, in fact, get off scot-free. If robots are a source of profits, then their corporate owners pay tax. To the extent that those profits end up as dividends and capital gains, the recipients of these forms of income pay tax as well. And if they don't, then the fix is to reform corporate profits and personal income taxation.

Consumers, meanwhile, benefit from the cheaper goods and services provided by the new technology embodied in robots. From this vantage point, taxing robots is ultimately no different from taxing technological progress. It is also no different from taxing international trade. Taxing international trade limits the ability of a country to transform the goods it can produce most cheaply and efficiently into goods that can be produced more cheaply abroad. Taxing trade therefore reduces the purchasing power and living standards of residents overall. A tax on robots is no different.[23]

Not just these ambitious schemes but also more traditional interventions such as unemployment insurance and job training must confront the erosion of social solidarity in ethnically, religiously, racially, and economically diverse societies. The mechanical ties of kinship and the shared values emphasized by Emile Durkheim as sources of social solidarity no longer bind as tightly in countries whose residents lack the hegemonic belief system, the basis in community, the equality of incomes, and the access to opportunity of a fabled past. The organic ties of economic interdependence—the solidarity rooted in mutual economic interest also emphasized by Durkheim—no longer bind now that high- and low-tech industries are located in different places, out of sight of one another, and now that people of different political persuasions cluster in red and blue states.[24] This problem is, in a sense, even worse in the European Union, insofar as the majority of residents stubbornly self-identify as Spanish or Italian rather than European, notwithstanding the fact that "solidarity" is one of the six pillars of the European Union's Charter of Fundamental Rights.

In this setting, inequality and lack of social cohesion feed on one another. If income disparities result less from individual merit than from inheritance, family connections, and access to elite education, then those disparities will rightly be seen as unfair. This perception will in turn undermine trust in fellow citizens and in society generally.[25] As a result, government will not be trusted to undertake programs that reduce inequality, in turn making disparities worse and eroding trust and solidarity still further.

What's a heterogeneous society to do? One answer is federalism. Americans with a high level of trust in government and in one another can congregate in blue states, while the less trusting congregate in red states, and both can pursue their preferred policies. Blue states can offer higher minimum wages and more public support for education, training, and relocation, while red states do the opposite. If Californians want to organize a single-payer health plan and finance it with a wealth tax on residents with assets of more than, say, $20 million, and with a tax on the global profits of companies levied on the basis of the share of their sales occurring in California, then the U.S. Constitution allows them to proceed.[26] This would be not unlike the response to economic change and inadequate political voice that motivated reformers in Oregon and California to push for direct democracy at the state level in the early twentieth century. No less an authority than Mick Mulvaney, Donald Trump's budget director, said as much when Congress was debating repeal of the Affordable Health Care Act in 2017: "If you live in a state that wants to mandate maternity coverage for everybody, including 60-year-old women, that's fine." And if you don't, "then you can figure out a way to change the state that you live in ... Change ... state legislatures and state laws. Why do we look to the federal government to try and fix our local problems?"[27]

But the federal solution has limits. Some things, like providing a strong national defense, securing the nation's borders, and regulating immigration, can be done only at the national level, and in Europe's case at the European level. This is true of trade policy, so long as a country has free interstate commerce (in European terms, as long as the EU is a single market). Different trade policies are feasible only with restrictions on interstate commerce, since otherwise goods will enter through the state with the most liberal policy, which will then become the de facto standard. Decentralization therefore doesn't solve the problem of displacement of labor by import competition. And it doesn't reconcile different attitudes toward immigration.

Different states can still pursue different approaches to displacement, providing more or less ambitious retraining programs. But there are limits, since workers receiving retraining in one state can seek employment in another that doesn't share the cost of imparting the new skills. The same is true of environmental policy. California can follow its own ambitious environmental policy, since it's a big state and the wind blows off the ocean. But smaller states that are downwind will find adopting a stringent environmental policy more costly.

Clustering by taste will also limit interaction between individuals with different attitudes, thereby eroding trust and solidarity still further. This will make it even harder to agree on the provision of collective goods and services at the federal level. Familiarity breeds trust, not contempt, as James Coleman famously put it.[28] Communities with high levels of ethnolinguistic diversity spend less on collective goods like health, education, and infrastructure, as we saw in Chapter 1. But the more those different groups mix—the greater the extent to which they are co-located geographically—the more those effects are attenuated.[29] Also consistent with this view is the observation in Chapters 9 and 10 that natives of regions that are home to the fewest foreign-born residents display the least trust of immigrants.

This brings us finally to the vexed question of immigration. The narrowly economic case for more immigration in the advanced countries is impeccable. The immigrants themselves benefit enormously: both un-skilled and skilled workers in developing countries see the purchasing power of their earnings rise by a factor of ten when they move to an advanced country where better infrastructure, technology, and contract enforcement render them more productive.[30] It's hard to point to an-other way that income gains of this magnitude can be conjured up overnight. The advanced countries on the receiving end benefit as well. They are capital abundant and labor scarce. Their dependency ratios are high. The labor force is growing slowly or, in some cases like those of Japan and Italy, not at all.[31]

The narrowly economic objections and alternatives to more immi-gration are not compelling. Although immigrants consume public ser-vices, they also pay taxes, on balance contributing more than they take.[32] Foreign aid might seem like an alternative to immigration: aid that fosters economic development can reduce the incentive to move and, not incidentally, make the donors feel less guilty about closing their borders. Both motives were apparent in the so-called Marshall Plan for Africa unveiled by the German Development Ministry in 2017. But even the most optimistic assessments do not suggest that development assis-tance can raise living standards tenfold overnight.[33] Additional trade pref-erences can be extended to poor countries, but access to export markets is not enough to bring incomes up to advanced-country levels when local institutions are the problem and, for historical reasons, remain difficult to change.

It can be objected that immigrants bring with them not just their manpower but also the culture and experience that lie behind the low productivity of their native country.[34] But the literature warning of such adverse effects is entirely evidence free.[35] It runs counter to his-torical experience with successful assimilation, and specifically to the historical experience of the United States, which has successfully assimilated successive waves of immigrants, raising their productivity to the level of natives rather than the other way around. It runs counter to the observation that immigrants are not randomly selected, it being the industrious and hardworking who have the get-up-and-go to migrate.

Maybe assimilation is harder now because the religion, race, or ethnicity of the current wave of immigrants is so different from that of natives. But every generation argues that assimilation is harder now. In the United States, the same argument was made about Irish and Italian immigrants in the nineteenth century, and then about Eastern Europeans and Asians. It could be that assimilation is harder when immigration reaches high levels. Immigrants then cluster in their own communities, reinforcing traditional values, and have less contact with natives. But this argument, if valid, is an argument against unlimited immigration, not against current levels of immigration, which have not obviously disrupted assimilation in this economic sense.[36] And insofar as residential and economic segregation make it difficult for immigrants to adapt to host country practices, it is in the interest of the host country to pursue housing policies that allow immigrants to interact more with natives, job training and nondiscriminatory employment policies that give immigrants more contact with other workers, and education policies that allow the children of immigrants to mix with the children of natives and be exposed to host country mores.

And apart from these economic arguments, there is also a humanitarian argument for admitting more refugees from impoverished, strifetorn countries.

These economic and humanitarian arguments of course run headlong into distributional and identity concerns—they run headlong, in other words, into populist politics. Where immigrants are unskilled, their arrival in large numbers is likely to have some impact, or at least to create fears of some impact, on the wages of less skilled natives.[37] This effect is especially problematic in advanced countries where import competition from low-wage countries and skill-biased technical change similarly disadvantage the less skilled and widen inequality.[38] And it is easier to point the finger of blame at immigrants and shut the door on new arrivals than it is to blame inventors and investors and turn back the clock on technology.

More education and training is an obvious policy response to pressure on the wages of less skilled natives. This is the same formula economists regularly recommend for addressing the negative impact on unskilled labor of skill-biased technical change and globalization. This observation is a reminder that simply shutting the door on immigration will not relieve the pressure on working-class living standards or reverse the rise in inequality that has fanned nativist sentiment, since shutting the door to foreign labor will not eliminate the unequalizing effects of technology and trade. It is a reminder that additional immigration creates a dilemma for those seeking to increase funding for education and training, insofar as ethnically, religiously, and racially heterogeneous societies find it harder to cultivate the trust in government and in others needed to maintain popular support for such programs. Again, this suggests that policies countering residential and economic segregation should be a priority, since they facilitate interaction between groups, building trust and thereby neutralizing the negative impact of increased diversity on society's willingness to provide education, training, and other services collectively.[39]

Some have suggested reforming the immigration system to deal with economic and identity concerns. U.S. immigration policy could move away from family unification and toward a Canadian-style point system that rewards education and training, as Donald Trump proposed in 2017. Since immigrants will be more skilled, they will not drive down wages for unskilled work. But this change, which downgrades humanitarian motives, would not be universally embraced. It would not be helping the poorest but rather favoring the relatively advantaged possessing advanced degrees. Alternatively, countries could move to a fixed-term guest worker system, like the Bracero Program implemented by the United States and Mexico in 1942 to alleviate wartime labor shortages and the German *Gastarbeiter* system of the 1950s and 1960s.[40] Since temporary workers won't set down roots, they won't be perceived as posing a threat to identity. Since they will be in the country for a limited period, they won't be inclined to bring their families, establish their own houses of worship, and found their own civic organizations. Since there is a large pool of farmworkers and software engineers in the developing world, the advanced countries can easily meet their labor force needs through a system of rotating fixed-term contracts.

But there are good reasons to doubt the feasibility of such schemes. The *Gastarbeiter* system broke down because German employers objected to the costs of training new workers every two years and pressured the authorities to let the incumbents stay. The Bracero Program was abolished in 1964 because of complaints that farmers were providing substandard wages and housing, problems that neither the Department of Labor nor the Department of Agriculture saw as priorities to solve, while Mexican farmworkers for their part lacked the civic and economic organizations, starting with unions, through which they could insist that these deficiencies be corrected.[41] Such systems can be made to work, it is said, if the authorities are sufficiently vigorous about enforcing fixed-term contracts and holding employers to the same wage and safety standards that apply to other workers. But the fact that guest workers lack a path to citizenship and are wards of the state for only a limited period suggests that their treatment will not be seen as a priority and that they would have few advocates and channels through which to press their case.

Lastly, there is the question of what kind of political system is best placed to respond to the populist threat. The traditional answer is a presidential system like that in the United States, where winner takes all. In this system, populist movements find it hard to make political headway against the established parties. Nominees appealing to the median voter have an incentive to move to the political center in the general election and to shun divisive, us-against-them policies.

But however sensible these rules of the road, recent experience suggests that the U.S. system is also dangerously accident prone. Against a backdrop of economic insecurity and contested identity and with his rivals at one another's throats, it is not impossible for an unconventional politician to capitalize on anti-elite, nativist sentiment and capture a major party nomination. Faced with a weak opponent and benefiting from a bit of foreign meddling, it is not impossible for that nominee to win an election without moving to the political center.

In the American winner-takes-all system, the 49 percent of the electorate that voted for the other party may then be left with no political voice. Indeed, under the U.S. Electoral College system, which apportions electors mostly on a state-level winner-take-all basis, it is possible for an absolute majority of voters to be left without voice in the executive branch, as happened in 2016. Because the Electoral College was designed to enhance the representation of sparsely populated rural states—the number of electors equals the size of each state's congressional delegation, one for each member in the House of Representatives plus two senators for each and every state—the system aggravates the urban-rural divide that is regularly a feature of populist politics and was a feature of the 2016 U.S. campaign. It may be fun to imagine Electoral College reform, but it's hard to envisage three-fourths of state legislatures, necessarily including a number of smaller rural states, agreeing to amend this provision of the Constitution.[42]

Then there's the problem of buyer's remorse. Even if mainstream Republicans develop deep reservations about the actions of President Trump, they will hesitate to impeach him, because doing so would call into question the process through which he secured his party's nomination and therefore the integrity of the party itself. In the U.S. system, populist leaders are hard to remove once in office. A robust political system, like a driverless car, must be capable of course correction. In the United States, midterm elections that regularly produce divided government are the main course-correction mechanism. But because the president is able to appoint Federal Reserve Board members for fourteen years and Supreme Court justices for life, the course set previously may be impossible to correct.

Recent experience suggests that systems of proportional representation, as in the Netherlands, and two-stage general elections, as in France, are more robust when it comes to coping with populist insurgencies. In the Dutch system, parties are represented in parliament roughly in proportion to their share of the popular vote, ensuring a hearing for different religious and regional voices. Government is by coalition, and other parties can refuse to ally with an extremist party. The knowledge that this party will not be part of the policy-making coalition will discourage some voters from throwing away their ballots by supporting what will almost certainly be the opposition. These were the incentives that limited electoral support for Geert Wilders, his Freedom Party, and their racist, anti-Muslim message in 2017. In the French system, a large number of candidates compete in the first round, but only the two leading vote-getters proceed to the second. Even if an extremist wins a plurality in the first round, supporters of the other mainstream candidates have an incentive to unify around her rival in the second, allowing the center to hold. This was the system that hobbled Marine Le Pen in 2017.[43]

The French system isn't perfect. If the non-populist survivor is too far to the left or the right, voters from the other end of the political spectrum, whose preferred candidate doesn't make it to the second round, may fail to unite behind the non-populist alternative. Proportional representation systems similarly have drawbacks. Coalitions are fragile. Governmental turnover is high, and if elections are frequent, officials may devote more energy to campaigning than to governing. Government instability and the difficulty of making progress on policy when parliament includes many splinter groups can breed dissatisfaction with mainstream parties and leaders, and this frustration may feed support for more extreme alternatives, as in Italy in the 1920s. Minimum thresholds for parliamentary representation and hurdles to no-confidence votes, as in Germany, while helpful, do not eliminate these problems entirely.

In the end, all political systems are imperfect. But some are more imperfect than others.

12

Au Revoir Europe?

THAT THE EUROPEAN Union is a regular target of populist ire will hardly come as a surprise. The EU lacks what political theorists refer to as "output legitimacy."[1] It was unable to deliver the economic goods following the global financial crisis and thus failed to amass support on the basis of results. Growth was anemic, and the deregulation and austerity endorsed by the technocrats of the European Commission, the EU's executive branch, only worsened the problem. Its commitment to light-touch regulation and construction of an integrated financial market helped set the stage for the financial crisis. Budget cuts in countries like Greece, insisted on by the Commission and European Central Bank (ECB) as a condition for their assistance, visibly aggravated inequality. The EU's failure to secure its external borders and then to enforce its rules requiring member states to share the refugee resettlement burden made the EU seem complicit in the immigration problem.

Thus, if economic hard times, inequality, and immigration are key triggers of populist reaction, then the EU is implicated in all three. Populists of the Right, like Hungarian prime minister Viktor Orbán, seeking to capitalize on authoritarian and nativist tendencies, could accuse the Commission and the governments of member states like Germany of weakness in the face of immigration. Orbán could inflame his followers by attacking "elite European politicians" for "deliberately bring[ing] millions of migrants to Europe," in a not very veiled attack on German chancellor Angela Merkel, among others.[2] Populists of the Left, such as Alexis Tsipras in Greece, could accuse the institutions of Europe, meaning the Commission, the ECB, and other member states, again prominently including Germany, of insisting on policies that destroy growth while placing the adjustment burden squarely on the shoulders of the working class. The result has been that "social inequalities...soared—Greece places first on the social inequality index in Europe—unemployment tripled, wages s[a]nk, pensions suffered dramatic cuts and the welfare state literally collapsed. The only ones who did not sustain damage during this five-year period were the wealthy Greeks."[3] All this, Tsipras could allege, was the fault of the Commission, the ECB, the International Monetary Fund, and the memorandum of understanding that set out their conditions for financial assistance to Greece.

It is no coincidence, then, that these organizations, officials, and governments became the subjects of populist wrath. The ECB and the Commission are technocratic institutions staffed by experts with advanced degrees from elite institutions. The German Federal Republic has championed the European Union's fundamental values of liberal democracy, pluralism, and rule of law, making it a target for politicians with authoritarian, nativist, and nationalist tendencies. Berlin is also an advocate, for reasons rooted in German history, of conservative monetary and budget policies, rendering German officials temperamentally critical of budget-busting populist leaders—and vice versa.

The EU is equally lacking in "input legitimacy," that is, in legitimacy rooted in the process by which decisions are reached. The ECB is the least politically accountable central bank in the world. Its president regularly refuses to appear before national parliaments, whether on principle or because he would have to attend hearings of all nineteen.[4] Decisions on bailouts and debt restructuring are made through inter-governmental negotiations in which the big countries caucus beforehand and present the others with a fait accompli. Decisions by the European Commission are ratified by the European Council, the assembly of heads of state, by a two-thirds majority, where votes are weighted by country size, leaving small countries feeling that they have no voice. An example was the decision in 2016 on posted workers, which tightened rules allowing a company to send (or "post") its employees to work in other EU countries while continuing to make social security contributions in the country of origin. The parliaments of twelve smaller member states objected, but the Commission, with the support of big countries possessing two-thirds of the votes in the Council, barreled ahead.

It doesn't help that European integration has always been an elite project designed by technocrats and only then ratified by national parliaments and occasionally publics. The Single Market was an elite project. The euro was an elite project. There was broad public support, to be sure, for economic integration as a way of fostering political cooperation, with the goal of ultimately making another war unthinkable. Members of the former Soviet bloc displayed a strong desire to join the EU as a way of becoming normal European countries. That said, none of the specific economic projects of the EU bubbled up from below. None was the product of spontaneous public support. There was no mass movement to create a Single Market with free internal mobility of labor. There was no popular groundswell for replacing national currencies with the euro. In only a few cases were there referenda once leaders decided to take the plunge. When it turned out that not all Europeans benefited equally, and when some drew the conclusion that they benefited not at all, these initiatives were vulnerable to populist criticism as elite projects foisted on the people.

The elite in question, moreover, was foreign, necessarily so since it was made up of technocrats drawn from more than two dozen countries. The regulations of the Commission, promulgated in the name of Europe, could thus be attacked as ill-suited to domestic conditions. If the monetary policies of the ECB produced too little stringency for German taste but too much for that of Italians, this, it could be claimed, was because those policies were dictated by the national self-interest of officials from the other country. If their policies failed to deliver positive results, then they were construed as trampling on the will of the people.

In practice, the will of the people meant the will of the nation. Most Europeans continue to identify as French, German, or Italian nationals first and Europeans second if at all. A Eurobarometer survey in the spring of 2015 showed that 52 percent of EU residents defined themselves primarily by their nationality. Just 6 percent defined themselves first as European and second by their nationality, and just 2 percent defined themselves as European only.[5] The remaining 40 percent identified themselves exclusively by their nationality.

Common European culture, history, and economic interests are the most frequently cited factors making for a feeling of community or shared identity across EU countries. Awareness of these common cultural, economic, and historical factors is most prevalent among the well-educated and the middle and upper classes. Not only does education impart knowledge of that common history and culture, but more educated, prosperous individuals are best able to capitalize on the opportunities afforded by European integration (hence their belief in the existence of shared economic interests). The well-educated are in the best position to move in response to opportunities in other countries. They disproportionately benefit from free intra-European trade for the same reasons they disproportionately benefit from globalization. At the same time, those with less education and lower incomes are disproportionately hurt by the welfare-state cuts and austerity with which the EU is associated.

Inevitably, then, the solidarity required for effective EU policies runs up against the fact that Europeans continue to identify by nationality—they feel solidarity mainly or exclusively with their fellow countrymen. Recent events, the euro crisis and the refugee crisis in particular, only made the consequences worse. They sharpened antagonisms between member states, deepening international divisions and resuscitating old stereotypes. Greeks were irresponsible children, Germans heartless paymasters. Dutch finance minister Jeroen Dijsselbloem, in an unusual fit of candor, accused spendthrift Southern Europeans of frittering away their money on women and drink.[6]

At the same time, Europe's crises heightened divisions within countries, given the different attitudes the cosmopolitan elite and the working class hold toward the euro and toward refugees, and given the uneven impact of crisis policies. Recall Tsipras's remarks about how the response to the Greek crisis prescribed by "the institutions" (meaning the Commission, the ECB, and the IMF) hurt the average citizen of his country while sparing the wealthy.

Faced with these tensions within and between countries, European leaders have been unable to decide whether to go forward, go back, or stand still. Going forward would mean deeper integration. It would entail common economic and foreign policies implemented by officials elected at the European level and held accountable by a European Parliament with teeth. Going back, on the other hand, would entail abandoning the European dream and renationalizing politics and policies. It would mean following Britain's path. Standing still would mean gritting one's teeth and hoping for the best, a strategy that history suggests doesn't have high odds of success. In the spring of 2017, Jean-Claude Juncker, wearing his hat as Commission president, offered up all these scenarios and more, but, indicative of the pervasive confusion of the political class, refused to hang that hat on any one.

If there is a solution, it lies in rejecting the argument favored by populist politicians like Orbán that "more Europe" and "less Europe" are in fact the alternatives. In some cases, for example securing the EU's external borders, actions taken—or not taken—by one country can have powerful repercussions for others. Here the choice is not between more Europe and less Europe but between more Europe and no Europe. If Greece can't secure its borders, then Hungary will build a razor-wire fence and other countries will reinstate passport controls. Trucks will be delayed at border crossings. Trains will be stopped for passport checks. There will be no Schengen Agreement, no Single Market, and, ultimately, no Europe.

This argument, that European policy needs to be centralized or at least very strongly coordinated, can be made not just for border security but also for bank regulation, where the spillovers of one country's policies to its neighbors are powerful. It can be made for foreign and security policy, where individual European countries are too small to go it alone. Most Europeans, with the exception of the British, see the EU not so much as an engine of economic growth as a vehicle for maintaining Europe's geopolitical relevance in a twenty-first-century world where individual European countries are too small to matter.[7]

But this is another area where the EU lacks "output legitimacy," since it has failed to reassert Europe's geopolitical relevance or guarantee the security of its citizens. This last failure is especially galling to populist politicians for whom the forceful assertion of power and protection from foreign threats are the essence of politics. It thus provides an especially effective talking point for the EU's populist detractors.

In other areas, however, it is not at all clear that more Europe is needed. There's no reason why, for example, all EU member states should be required to adopt the euro. The cross-border spillovers of national monetary policies, especially those of small countries, are simply not that large. A Danish central bank that allows the krone to depreciate against the euro can make life slightly more difficult for German and French companies that compete with Danish exporters, but only slightly. We don't hear loud complaints from Berlin and Paris about Danish monetary policy, in other words. Similarly, each and every EU member state doesn't have to join the Schengen Area for the passport-free zone to function. Countries can opt in or out.

None of these points is controversial. Where there is controversy is on fiscal and refugee policies. The EU in its wisdom has decreed that there should be strong central oversight of the fiscal policies of its member states, those of euro-area states in particular. It has adopted a Stability and Growth Pact and a raft of ancillary procedures to give that surveillance teeth. Governments must submit their draft budgets to the Commission before presenting them to their national parliaments. They are subject to fines and sanctions for missing agreed fiscal targets. This approach is all but guaranteed to incite a populist reaction. Nothing is socially and politically more sensitive than whom to tax, how to tax, and how much to tax, unless it's the corresponding decisions of on whom and what to spend the money. These are national prerogatives, since it is only at the national level that the solidarity exists to raise taxes for collective purposes. EU oversight of national budgets by technocrats in Brussels is thus a chronic sore point.

This insistence on centralized oversight of budgets was adopted at German behest. It was Germany's condition for abandoning the deutschmark for the euro. Germans believe in their bones that fiscal profligacy leads to inflation. Infringing on the national fiscal sovereignty of euro countries is therefore necessary to ensure the stability of the euro and protect the ECB from pressure to inflate.

This argument, while straightforward, is shot through with holes. The ECB is governed by independent central bankers appointed to long terms in office and chosen precisely because they are more economically conservative than the average politician. For nearly two decades now, the ECB, under the guidance of these conservative central bankers, has demonstrated its price-stability bona fides, national budget deficits notwithstanding. Moreover, the aftermath of the global financial crisis was a reminder, if one was needed, that there is no one-to-one relationship between budget deficits and inflation. To the contrary, when deficits went up, inflation came down. And there was no sign of inflation exploding subsequently.

Moreover, the evidence for large cross-border spillovers of national fiscal policies is weak. The logic is straightforward. Excessive deficits in, say, France will raise spending and suck in more imports from Germany, stimulating the German economy and stoking inflation there. At the same time, however, deficits in France will drive up interest rates both at home and abroad, since the euro zone is an integrated monetary and financial area; those higher interest rates will tend to moderate German spending and inflation. Since these two offsetting effects on Germany work in opposite directions, their net effect on growth and inflation is no more than marginal. Indeed, German officials have made precisely this point when resisting calls for more expansionary fiscal policies in Germany, arguing that any positive spillovers to other euro-area countries—that is, any stimulus to spending and economic growth elsewhere—would be vanishingly small. None other than the European Central Bank has acknowledged as much.[8]

When cross-country spillovers are small but national preferences differ, the best approach is to leave decision-making at the country level. For fiscal policy, then, the appropriate reform is less Europe, not more. National parliaments and their constituents should be allowed to choose their preferred fiscal policies. Arguments from which populist politicians make hay—that the EU is the agent of austerity, that it is preventing the government from compensating the losers from technological change and globalization, and that it is violating society's inalienable right to tax and spend as it wishes—will then be off the table.

The objection to this argument is that when things go wrong, as they can when governments mismanage their finances, the results are catastrophic. Trusting each European government with its own budgetary policy is like trusting it with its own nuclear bomb. Countries like Greece and Italy have heavy debts already, leaving them little margin for error. Their banks hold government bonds, so when governments default on their debt obligations, the banking system comes crashing down. And because banks do cross-border business, what happens in Greece or Italy doesn't stay in Greece or Italy. We saw the power of this contagion and the depth of the its damage in the global financial crisis in 2008, and again when debt and banking problems erupted in Greece in 2010.[9]

But this only means that there are preconditions for repatriating fiscal policy. If the danger is that fiscal irresponsibility that culminates in debt default will topple the banking system, then banks should be bulletproofed. Specifically, they should be prevented from holding dangerous numbers of government bonds. For years, European policymakers did precisely the opposite. They maintained the fiction that government bonds were risk free. Those bonds were given zero risk weights, freeing the banks from the requirement of holding capital against them. Astonishingly, Greek government bonds received this preferential treatment even after the 2012 restructuring, when private investors were stripped of more than half the value of their holdings.[10] Banks resisted changing this rule because they would have had to hold more capital. Governments resisted because if they lost this captive market, they would have to pay more to finance and service their deficits.

But those governments would be getting something in return, namely, more control over their fiscal affairs, since this key objection to repatriating fiscal policy would be no more. Greece would no longer be subject to oppressive fiscal oversight from Brussels. Populist politicians, for their part, would no longer be able to blame foreigners for the country's dire straits.

This change should appeal to Germany as well, since surveillance by the European Commission creates an obligation to help if that surveillance goes wrong, help that ends up being footed, more often than not, by the German government and the long-suffering German taxpayer.[11] If Europe disconnects its banks from its sovereign debt market, it will finally be able to enforce its "no-bailout rule," the clause in the European Treaty specifying that member states should not be liable for the debts of other member states.[12] With banks no longer holding significant numbers of government bonds, applying this rule—which will require a government with an unsustainable debt to restructure it, instead of that government receiving an emergency bailout from other EU member states—will no longer endanger the financial system, neither the Greek financial system nor the German financial system. And then the likes of Alternative für Deutschland will no longer be able to attack the EU as a "transfer union" that exploits hardworking German taxpayers.

If responsibility for fiscal policy belongs at the national level, then a solution to the refugee problem, in strong contrast, can only be found at the EU level. Securing the EU's external borders can only work if that border security encompasses Europe's entire perimeter, and only if countries with exposed coastlines, including Greece and Italy, receive adequate financial and logistical support. The Dublin Regulation (so called because it was signed in Dublin in 1990) requires that applications for asylum be processed in the country in which a refugee first lands, making this a national responsibility and a national financial burden. Such a system may have been workable when refugee numbers were small, but this is no longer true. And the resettlement of large numbers of refugees will not be feasible, politically or economically, so long as only Germany and Sweden take them.

These are arguments for a coordinated response. But the reality and the constraint are that different European countries, with their different histories and identities, perceive the refugee problem differently. In the middle of the twentieth century Germany and Austria absorbed roughly 14 million refugees, mainly ethnic Germans (so-called *Volksdeutsche*) who fled or were expelled from the countries of Central and Eastern Europe in the late stages of World War II and after. This is an episode of which Germans of a certain age have firsthand recollection and about which young people learn at school. The result is a different attitude toward the refugee crisis than in countries on the other side of the postwar divide, such as Hungary, whose president has asserted, "We want no more people to come. Those who are here, go home!" and "We do not want to see among us significant minorities that possess different cultural characteristics and background to us. We would like to preserve Hungary as Hungary."[13]

This is not to claim that there is no resistance in Germany to refugee resettlement. Nor does it imply that resettling refugees from the Middle East and North Africa will be as easy as resettling native German-speakers. But it is a reminder of how differences in history, culture, and policy preferences complicate efforts to mount a coordinated response.

The European Commission's initial attempt to organize that response, the European Agenda on Migration in September 2015, was not well received. It created a mandatory distribution formula based on the population of member states (with a weight of 40 percent), their GDP (40 percent), their unemployment rate (10 percent), and their number of past asylum applications (10 percent). Members were promised lump-sum transfers of €6,000 from the EU budget for each refugee taken. Only under exceptional circumstances like natural disaster could a country opt out, in which case it was required to make a contribution to the EU budget of 0.002 percent of its GDP.[14] Orbán, it is fair to say, was not pleased. It's comforting to imagine, as the Commission apparently does, that all European countries will adopt the same welcoming posture toward refugees. But the reality is that attitudes rooted in national histories will continue to differ.

Rather than abandoning the effort to mount a European response to a European problem, better would be to strengthen incentives. If countries want to limit resettlement, they should be required to pay generously. If other countries absorb a larger share of the refugee population, then they should receive significantly more than the measly €6,000 of the Commission's action agenda.

Agreeing on a formula won't be easy. But in a Europe of member states whose preferences differ, there has to be a formula that is superior for all concerned to the Commission's one-size-fits-all policy. Critics may regard bargaining over refugee resettlement as unsavory and insist that countries should display the solidarity to accept refugees according to their capacity purely on humanitarian grounds. That, unfortunately, isn't the actual, existing Europe.

Viewing the issues this way leads, then, neither to more Europe nor to less Europe but to a different Europe. On some issues, such as the Single Market and securing Europe's external borders, all member states will have to work together to achieve acceptable results, and their efforts must be coordinated. On other issues, including the euro and the passport-free Schengen zone, some countries will be in while others can remain out, both to their mutual satisfaction. And on still other issues, like fiscal policy, the relevant competency can reside entirely with the nation-state.

Note that this is not the two-tier Europe advocated by Eurofederalists like now former German finance minister Wolfgang Schäuble, in which an inner core of committed countries speeds ahead to deep economic, financial, and political integration while an outer ring of more cautious countries, still jealous of their national prerogatives, initially remains behind. Once upon a time there may have been a logic for this two-speed Europe. When Schäuble originally advanced this idea in a white paper written for Germany's Christian Democratic Union in 1994, it was possible to imagine that Europe would consist of a deeply integrated inner core centered on France and Germany, surrounded by the rest.[15] But today Schäuble's vision lacks a functional logic. Degrees of integration overlap: they do not break down into an inner core and outer ring. Not everything must be deeply integrated: the logic for a single fiscal policy run from Brussels is no more compelling than the logic for a single European language. This vision of a two-tier Europe also elicits strong opposition from Eastern European countries and other reluctant integrationists, which fear becoming second-class members.

Fortunately, there is no need to divide Europe into "ins" and "outs." Groupings for different areas may overlap, but they need not coincide. In fact, this is already the case: Denmark is in the Schengen Area but outside the euro zone, while Ireland is in the euro area but outside of Schengen. All countries that have adopted the euro participate in the EU's banking union, since monetary union without banking union will not work, but not all countries that are party to the banking union have adopted the euro or will necessarily do so. This may not be the forced march to economic, financial, and political union envisaged by dyed-in-the-wool Eurofederalists, but it is a way of preserving the fruits of European integration while acknowledging that national identities exist and preferences continue to differ.

Once upon a time, this model of overlapping groupings was sufficiently fashionable to have a name: it was called "flexible integration." That phrase, curiously, seems to have fallen from fashion: Google's Ngram Viewer, which tracks mentions in books, shows that references to the term peaked in 2000, around the time of the euro's creation, but declined subsequently.[16]

That the concept fell by the wayside is not coincidental. Its champions couldn't figure out how to structure a political system to hold those responsible for formulating these different policies accountable for their actions. They couldn't figure out how to ensure the legitimacy of the policymaking process and satisfy citizens in different countries that their voices were being heard. If, for example, residents of the Schengen Area were unhappy with the operation of their passport-free zone, because some participating members were not adequately securing their borders, then it was not clear to whom exactly they should complain and how to get satisfaction. And the more overlapping clubs the EU created, the more opaque and complicated this process became, and the less satisfactory the results.

One conceivable mechanism for accountability is the European Parliament, and there have been many calls over the years for strengthening its powers. The Parliament could be given the power to initiate legislation, an agenda-setting prerogative that currently resides with the Commission. The range of Commission proposals and directives requiring approval by the European Parliament could be expanded; presently, most EU legislation is adopted via a procedure under which the Commission must only consult with the Parliament, and the latter has only the power of delay.[17] In the limit, all directives issued by the Commission could be required to receive the support of two-thirds of members of Parliament, or of the members of the relevant subcommittee, as opposed to just the support of the heads of state and government of countries holding two-thirds of the votes in the Council.[18] All Europeans would then have a voice in EU decision-making, insofar as all significant parties have members in the European Parliament—as opposed to the current situation, where only voters who supported the national head of state, or the coalition standing behind her, have a voice.

But strengthening the Parliament is harder when the policy domain is made up of a crazy quilt of countries that have agreed to pool their national prerogatives in some areas but not others. Why should the representatives of countries that have not adopted the euro vote on the appointment of the president of the ECB, for example? Why should countries that are not party to the Schengen Agreement have the right to approve decisions on how much additional intelligence and security information is shared by its members?

Thomas Piketty has suggested creating a second parliament—call it an assembly—made up of the representatives of countries adopting the euro.[19] That euro-area assembly would vote whether to restructure Greece's debt, extend a bailout loan, or attach specific conditions to financial assistance, decisions currently taken behind closed doors by the finance ministers and heads of state of the principal European countries. Members could be drawn from the European Parliament, directly from national parliaments, or, as Piketty suggests, from a combination of the two.

This is at best a partial solution, since it harks back to the antiquated vision of a two-tier Europe with a deeply integrated inner core, whose members are represented in the assembly and Parliament both, and the rest, whose representatives sit only in the Parliament. It equates deep integration with the euro, when in fact deep integration means different things to different people in different countries. To many Europeans, it means a common security and foreign policy, not a common monetary and fiscal policy.[20] And this approach assumes that national parliamentarians, who are generally preoccupied by other things, have the bandwidth to participate in this euro-area assembly. It imagines that national parliaments will reorganize their deliberations to enable their delegated members to attend.

In fact, the EU tried this before, in its first quarter century of existence, and the shortcomings of an assembly of national parliamentarians were what led to the creation of a separately elected parliament in 1979.[21] Going back to a European Parliament of appointed or nominated national representatives would ignore this history. It would be like the United States going back to the system of state legislative appointments under which the U.S. Senate was constituted before 1913. Returning the power to select members to national parliamentarians rather than giving this right to the voters is the opposite of what is needed.

Better would be to work within the framework of the already existing European Parliament. The Parliament could be given enhanced powers over, say, euro-related matters, but only parliamentarians from euro-zone countries would have the right to deliberate and vote on that subset of questions. A different subset of members, again from the participating countries, would have the power to vote on Schengen-related matters, and so forth. The Parliament would channel the voice of the people, rendering the technocrats of the Commission, the ECB, and other EU institutions democratically accountable, but only the voice of the relevant people—citizens of those countries that agreed to cede national prerogatives on the issue in question.

Critics of the European Parliament will object that it isn't capable of providing the democratic accountability for which Europeans hanker. Voters don't pay attention to the Parliament; turnout in European elections is rarely above 50 percent. Members do their business far removed from their constituents and are known mainly for their lavish expenses and for shuttling between their legislative homes in Brussels and Strasbourg. But if the Parliament had more power to initiate legislation and approve or reject directives and other decisions directly affecting the people, voters would have more reason to pay attention. They would have an incentive to elect members who more effectively represent their interests.[22]

A more radical step would be direct popular election of the head of the Commission. Under the provisions of the Lisbon Treaty, adopted in 2009, a candidate for president of the Commission is selected by heads of state from a slate of candidates put forward by the major political groupings, after which he is confirmed by the European Parliament.[23] This process puts two layers of separation between the people and their president. The distance between the Commission and the people would be less if its president was chosen by the voting public. If border security, national defense, and foreign policy become important EU competencies, these being the areas where European citizens, when polled, think the EU can make a difference, then the Commission will necessarily acquire additional decision-making power, since defense and security decisions have to be made quickly by an executive. With increased powers, it will then be important for that executive to be directly accountable to the voting public.

Skeptics will contend that no candidate can campaign in twenty-seven member states (although candidates for the American presidency campaign in most or all of the fifty U.S. states). They will object that linguistic obstacles make it difficult for such candidates to effectively communicate with their constituents (although translators both human and mechanical exist).[24] But the fact that Europeans expect the EU to deliver on border security, defense, and foreign policy means that in order to recapture and maintain widespread public support, the EU is going to have to create the more powerful executive that will be needed to effectively carry out these policies and act decisively when needed. And with power must come accountability. If EU members are serious about narrowing the gulf between their executive and the people, they will have to move to direct election of that executive.

Will this political reengineering be enough to beat back the populist insurgency threatening Europe? In politics there are no certainties. But an important prerequisite is to reject the vision of a one-size-fits-all Europe and, equally, the idea that two sizes fit all. Countries that are especially jealous of specific national prerogatives will be reassured by their ability to opt out of European policies in those delicate issue areas. Voters in those countries will then be less inclined to lend their support to a party or leader critical of the European project. It can only help to give the European Parliament strengthened powers to hold the EU's technocrats democratically accountable. Those who complain that the elites take key policy decisions behind closed doors, without due regard for the wishes of the people, should be assuaged.

Will this be enough? Maybe not. But it's a start.

13

Prospects

THIS COMPARISON OF populism in the United States and Europe leads inevitably to the question of which countries are most immediately at risk. At one level the answer is clear: the United States. The United States glorifies income disparities. With a culture that celebrates the entrepreneur and decries government intervention, it does little to restrain market forces. But at the same time as it encourages creative destruction, it provides little assistance to the casualties of what is destroyed. It insists that workers displaced by globalization and technical change should fend for themselves and leave government out of it. When times are tough, this mix of policies and attitudes is all but guaranteed to produce high anxiety about income security, discomfort about prevailing levels of inequality, and anger at the political class.

In part these attitudes are a product of the distinctive American ideology of individualism and market fundamentalism. As the *New York Times* observed midway through the first year of the Trump administration, candidate Trump cited Ayn Rand, the objectivist avatar of individualism and market fundamentalism, as his favorite author, and her 1943 book, *The Fountainhead*, as his favorite novel.[1] Howard Roark, Rand's protagonist in *The Fountainhead*, is a determined individualist, one of the "exceptional men, the innovators, the intellectual giants... not held down by the majority."[2] The last six words are key. As Rand once put it, "Man exists for his own sake" and "must not sacrifice himself to others, nor sacrifice others to himself." So much, one might say, for helping one's brother. So much for collective goods. So much for trade adjustment assistance and social insurance.

Ideology doesn't exist in a vacuum, of course. This distinctively American antipathy to government and championing of individualism have material roots. The hostility of early Americans toward government was a reaction against the Navigation Acts and other economic impositions by the English on their North American colonies. Their exaltation of individualism stemmed from an abundance of natural resources and the safety valve of the frontier, which made it possible, in actual fact, for many Americans to lift themselves up by their bootstraps. Doubts about the efficacy of public programs reflected the limited bureaucratic capacity of a federal government that, after the War of 1812, never faced an existential threat from abroad and was never confronted with a national-defense imperative to develop its administrative competency. They reflected the corruption and patronage that grew up in the absence of that bureaucratic capacity, against which late nineteenth- and early twentieth-century Progressives inveighed and which fed popular skepticism about the ability of public policy initiatives, however well intentioned, to solve social problems.

Resistance to federal government intervention also reflected the country's historic division between black and white and between North and South. From Reconstruction through the civil rights movement, southern businessmen and farmers opposed federal government involvement in the economy for fear that it would compromise control of their black labor force. In the 1930s they opposed New Deal programs out of concern that these would interfere with their established way of doing business and the prevailing social order. White southerners were not opposed to the decentralization of social programs or to receiving federal matching funds so long as the design or at least the administration of those programs devolved to the states. Such devolution was consequently a legacy of the New Deal, one that endures even today, for example in the power of states to decide whether to expand Medicaid to cover low-income households under the Affordable Care Act, or Obamacare.

In practice, those individual states, acting on their own, can go some way toward addressing their residents' concerns over economic insecurity and inequality, but only some way. Smaller states, especially, find it hard to independently organize and fund retraining and relocation schemes for displaced workers or to impose additional taxes on high earners with the goal of leveling the income distribution, since such states constitute only a small part of a larger national market. Meanwhile, suspicion of and therefore opposition to federal social programs remain intense. For an America with this inheritance, the challenge of organizing adjustment assistance and compensating the casualties of globalization and technical change is daunting.

This same history of division works in still other ways to limit the willingness of Americans to fund collective goods, including social and economic insurance, as emphasized in Chapter 1 and elsewhere in this book. As the sociologist William Julius Wilson put it, "Many white Americans have turned against a strategy that emphasizes programs they perceive as benefiting only racial minorities.... [W]hite taxpayers saw themselves as being forced, through taxes, to pay for medical and legal services that many of them could not afford."[3] And what is true of racial diversity is true also of the ethnic and religious diversity that, in other respects, is a strength of the United States but which makes it more difficult to contemplate income redistribution, to provide public goods, and specifically to organize social insurance against economic insecurity, given lack of solidarity and the belief that the benefits of such programs accrue to others.

From this perspective, the contradictory nature of populism in the United States is no anomaly. People displaced by globalization and technical change are distressed about not sharing in the benefits of an expanding economy and by their government's failure to do more about it, leaving them susceptible to the siren song of populism. But their views are also informed by an ideology that tells them government is the problem, not the solution. One can't help but think of the constituent who allegedly warned Representative Robert Inglis of South Carolina, at a town hall meeting, to "keep your government hands off my Medicare," not realizing that Medicare was a government program. Herein lies the appeal of Donald Trump, who gives voice to the anger of the masses over their economic condition and the failure of government to address their problems, all in the manner of a populist, but who also opposes more spending on social insurance, more trade adjustment assistance, and higher taxes on the rich, all in the manner of a committed Randian. This is not a combination that bodes a happy ending.

Viewed through this lens, Europe has a number of advantages in seeking to beat back the populist threat. From Jean-Baptiste Colbert to

Otto von Bismarck, Europeans have more freely acknowledged the role of the state in managing the economy. Industrial policy (*planisme* in French) is not a dirty word. Public policies to address issues of distribution have always been regarded as legitimate instruments of the state. Hostility to government intervention in the economy is not intrinsic to the European psyche. For all these reasons, Western Europe went further than the United States in the direction of the mixed or managed economy after World War II. To be sure, Europe is far from immune to neoliberalism. It has deregulated its markets. It has opened its economy to trade with the rest of the world. It has encouraged technical change and, in some cases at least, has allowed leading domestic firms to go under. But it has always gone further than the United States in acknowledging the role of government in managing economic change. As a result, most Europeans do not share the instinctual aversion of Americans to public programs offering trade adjustment assistance to displaced workers and training to the technologically unemployed.

Again, these are attitudes in which ideology plays a role. Social Democracy as an economic, social, and political philosophy stretches back to the foundation of the German Workingmen's Union and the Social Democratic Workers' Party in the 1860s, as described in Chapter 4. While social democracy means different things to different people, one definition is an ideology that supports economic and social policy interventions intended to promote equality and social justice, including active labor market policies and redistribution, to be implemented by the state within a framework of market economy and representative democracy.[4] This idea that the fundamental goal of policy is to regulate the economy in order to correct its visible defects and alter the distribution of income in ways that make for solidarity and social justice is not something that is spoken out loud by the leaders of either U.S. political party, much less by their more Randian followers. It developed in Europe as an alternative to more radical working-class movements hostile to the market economy and to representative democracy, notably revolutionary Marxism—movements that never gained the same foothold in the United States. It was an effort to get European societies to pull together in order to avoid splintering apart.

Christian Democracy, also with origins in the mid-nineteenth century, is more fiscally and socially conservative and less enamored of an expansive economic role for the state.[5] But it also rejects individualism—again, contrast the United States—while privileging social consensus and, consistent with Catholic theology, solidarity with the weak. It thus supports state intervention to advance economic justice.[6] Again, this is not exactly a core philosophy of either U.S. political party.

In Europe too, these ideologies have material roots. The European continent is made up of a patchwork of small and medium-sized economies, not even the largest of which, Germany, approaches the continental reach of the United States. Small countries exposed to world markets are by their nature vulnerable to economic (and other) shocks from outside. They need government to buffer the effects, which is why they typically have large and active public sectors.[7] They face the imperative of having to adjust quickly—they need different social groups to pull together—which is why they have a history of national solidarity pacts, some stretching back to the 1930s, as described in Chapter 7.[8] In parts of Europe, like the Nordic countries, they have the advantage of relatively high levels of ethnic and religious homogeneity, limiting us-versus-them politics and easing agreement on the provision of social insurance and adjustment assistance. In other cases they have developed institutions and understandings, like the so-called Polder Model of political decision-making in the Netherlands, that acknowledge ethnic and religious differences but emphasize the importance of compromise and consensus.[9]

Finally it can be argued, as in Chapter 11, that European political systems are less susceptible to capture by populists and other dangerously out-of-the-mainstream politicians. This having happened in the 1920s and 1930s, electoral systems were restructured to prevent it from happening again. The United States avoided the shock of extremist capture, which was good, but it also avoided the subsequent process of political and electoral reform, a consequence that is not so happy.

To all these generalizations there are, of course, exceptions. Eastern European countries are in many respects exceptions. Collectivism and certain forms of government intervention have a serious taint in the region as a result of its half-century-long experience with Communism. The exposure of these countries to democratic political systems and their checks and balances is relatively recent. Their parliaments and courts, being young, and their media, being new, do not always restrain leaders with autocratic and authoritarian tendencies. Respect for individual rights, for different ethnicities, and for religious minorities is not always strongly informed by the lessons of the 1930s, insofar as successive post–World War II generations enjoyed an intellectual holiday from that history in the years of communist rule. Nor do dim recollections of that history delegitimize aggressive nationalism and hostility toward foreigners and minorities when these are used as rallying points by populist leaders, at least not to the same extent as in, say, Germany. Here we have Viktor Orbán's Hungary and Jaroslaw Kaczyński's Poland in a nutshell.

The United Kingdom is another exception. Britain never developed social democracy in the classic European mold.[10] To be sure, like other European countries it moved a long way in the direction of the welfare state and the managed economy after World War II. But starting in the 1980s, in response to a long period of singularly poor economic performance widely blamed on those same governance arrangements, it moved sharply back the other way. Under the leadership of Margaret Thatcher, it moved faster and further in the direction of deregulation, privatization, and welfare state retrenchment than other European countries. It responded similarly, with exceptional public spending cuts, to the financial crisis of 2008–2009, to the point where it now has one of the lowest levels of general government expenditure as a proportion of GDP of any advanced economy, limiting the scope for funding social insurance programs. It has a history of adversarial labor relations and is a kingdom of English, Welsh, Scots, and Irish, facts that complicate efforts to reach a consensus on social issues.

Finally, the United Kingdom, it can be said without threat of contradiction, displays more than the usual level of ambivalence toward the European Union. This reflects its position as an island, its historical status as a global power, and its supposed special relationship with the United States. This ambivalence means that when anti-elite, anti-immigrant, and nativist sentiment—that is to say, populism—rears its head, the resulting rancor is likely to be directed at the EU. But while Brexit satisfies these base instincts, it doesn't obviously provide a way to simultaneously control immigration, maintain the country's privileged access to European markets, achieve a faster rate of growth, and attack problems of economic insecurity (by, for example, magically increasing funding for the National Health Service, as the Brexiteers promised). Again, this is not a combination of circumstances that looks to end well.

More generally, Brexit points to Europe's gravest populist vulnerability, namely, lack of trust in the European Union. When asked by the European Social Survey in 2014 to rate their trust in the European Parliament on a scale of 0 to 10 (where 0 meant no trust at all and 10 meant complete trust), 12 percent of European respondents answered 0, and more than two-thirds returned a rating of 5 or below, which does not exactly indicate a favorable reaction. There is a strong correlation between lack of trust in the European Parliament and negative views of European integration, on the one hand, and support for populist parties in national elections, on the other.[11] The EU is, inevitably, a rich populist target. European integration has always been an elite project. The EU's most consequential institutions, the European Commission and the European Central Bank, are directed by technocrats. As a union of many countries, it is necessarily dominated by foreigners. It champions political freedom, transparency, and human and minority rights. Having started life as a customs union, it is inextricably linked to free trade and foreign competition. Because of the Single Market, it is associated with the right to immigrate in order to work, and therefore with all the economic and cultural concerns posed by immigrants. It is seen as subjecting national economies to a vast array of regulations not well suited to local circumstances, regulations that typify the loss of control felt by residents of once but no longer powerful nations.

In all these respects, then, the EU is readily portrayed as riding roughshod over national values, and over the national sovereignty needed for those values to be upheld. It is seen as a champion of globalization and cosmopolitanism and the enemy of national control. Here we have the platform of Marine Le Pen, steely leader of France's National Front, in short compass. "The EU world is ultra-liberalism, savage globalization, artificially created across nations," as she put it a BBC interview in February 2017, concluding, "I believe this world is dead."[12] Her party's 144-point election manifesto centered on a vow to restore "monetary, legislative, territorial and economic sovereignty," code for beating back interference by the EU and limiting the presence and influence of foreigners.[13] Le Pen vowed to pull out of the Schengen Agreement and create a 6,000-person-strong border control unit, and proposed in addition a phalanx of new rules affecting immigrants, foreigners, and followers of Islam, all at odds with EU norms. These would have limited legal immigration to ten thousand people a year and insisted on the immediate and obligatory deportation of illegals. They would have prohibited companies in other EU countries from sending their employees to work in France while paying social charges at home. They would have eliminated automatic naturalization for spouses and required French citizenship to be either inherited or "merited," a thinly disguised purity test if there ever was one. Le Pen vowed to end free education for the children of undocumented immigrants. "Playtime is over" was how she winningly described the idea. Her National Front's election manifesto would have restricted the use of foreign languages in schools. It would have banned radical Islamic groups and closed extremist mosques. It would have prohibited all wearing of veils in public.

While Le Pen did everything she could to distance herself from her father, Jean-Marie Le Pen, the founder of the National Front, and from his history of racist, anti-Semitic remarks, it was not hard to see the true targets of her proposed directives. These were the "external menaces" that had featured so prominently over the years in National Front rhetoric. They were immigrants from other continents, specifically immigrants of different races and religions who could be portrayed as not suitably French. They were the nationals of other EU countries, primarily the nationals of Eastern European countries, where wages and social charges were low. And they were the fundamental values of the European Union.

Le Pen's other economic proposals attacked the EU and its integrationist project directly. She promised to repudiate EU laws banning national preference in public procurement, while prohibiting foreign investment in strategic industries and protecting French companies damaged by "unfair foreign competition." She proposed replacing the EU's Common Agricultural Policy with a new French agricultural policy and "supplementing" the euro, whatever that meant, with a new French currency. She advocated adding to the French constitution a formal "national preference" for French citizens in hiring, housing, and social benefits, thereby institutionalizing discrimination against foreign nationals, including those of other EU member states. As the capstone, she proposed a referendum on EU membership within six months of taking office, raising the question of France's continued participation in the European project.

In the end, Le Pen failed to carry the day in France's 2017 presidential campaign. The opponents of her extreme brand of populism rallied around the other finalist, the pro-EU Emmanuel Macron, who rode to victory in the second round of the election. Reassured, many so-called experts declared that the wave of anti-EU populism in Europe had crested. One may ask whether their happy conclusion was premature. In a Europe where national histories differ and continue to shape national attitudes—and politics—in distinct ways, and where the majority of citizens identify first by their nationality and only secondarily, if at all, as European, tension between these mixed allegiances is unavoidable. While the EU is not going away, neither are populist attacks on its policies and its legitimacy.

Where, then, is vulnerability to a populist reaction most acute, in Europe or in the United States? The answer, unavoidably, is both. In both places, that vulnerability has deep historical roots. The individualism and the antipathy toward government that complicate efforts on the part of Americans to formulate public policy responses to problems of insecurity and inequality, giving populists fodder, have origins in the nineteenth century and earlier. In Europe, three wars in a century have made the EU and some pooling of sovereign functions an established fact, one that, Brexit notwithstanding, is not going to be undone. But that fact coexists uneasily with durable national identities and therefore with the desire for a significant degree of national policy autonomy, something that in turn will continue to empower anti-establishment, anti-EU politicians, including those of an extreme, Islamophobic, Marine Le Pen–like bent.

In neither case do the resulting problems admit of easy solutions. But understanding the problem is at least a start.

NOTES

Preface

1. Max Weber, "Die drei reinen Typen der legitimen Herrschaft," *Preussische Jahrbücher* 187 (1922): 1–12. Republished as "The Three Types of Legitimate Rule," in *Berkeley Publications in Society and Institutions* 4 (1958): 1–11.

Chapter 1

1. Peter Wiles, "A Syndrome, Not a Doctrine," in *Populism: Its Meaning and National Characteristics*, ed. Ghita Ionescu and Ernest Gellner (Macmillan, 1969), 166.
2. This distinction follows John Judis, *The Populist Explosion: How the Great Recession Transformed American and European Politics* (Columbia Global Reports, 2016). A similar formulation is Jan-Werner Müller, *What Is Populism?* (University of Pennsylvania Press, 2016).
3. See Cas Mudde, "The Populist Zeitgeist," *Government and Opposition* 39 (2004): 541–563. Associating the elites and the people with capital and labor, as Marxists may be inclined to do, doesn't work given how populist leaders are often wealthy businessmen. The dimension of populism that emphasizes charisma and personal success means that populist leaders can claim their authority on the basis of business achievement.
4. Wiles, "A Syndrome, Not a Doctrine," 166.
5. The classic history here is Lawrence Goodwyn, *Democratic Promise: The Populist Moment in America* (Oxford University Press, 1976). See also Charles Postel, *The Populist Vision* (Oxford University Press, 2007).

6. The *Oxford English Dictionary* defines a technocrat as "a member of a technically skilled *elite*" (emphasis added). See https://en.oxforddictionaries.com/definition/technocrat.

7. See Robert Johnston, *The Radical Middle Class: Populist Democracy and the Question of Capitalism in Progressive Era Portland, Oregon* (Princeton University Press, 2003), chs. 8–9. U'Ren's California counterpart, Dr. John Haynes, a physician and real estate speculator, took longer to drive his campaign to fruition, having to wait on the election of Progressive Party candidate Hiram Johnson as governor. See Steven Piott, *Giving Voters a Voice: The Origins of the Initiative and Referendum in America* (University of Missouri Press, 2003).

8. The words here are those of Trump's senior policy advisor Stephen Miller, quoted in Laura King, "Top Trump Aid Again Asserts Widespread Vote Fraud, Cites No Evidence," *Los Angeles Times*, February 12, 2017.

9. As in "Brexit Secretary David Davis Warns MPs: Don't Obstruct the 'Will of the People,'" *Sunday Herald* (Scotland), January 24, 2017.

10. Ninety-one percent of members of the Royal Economic Society who responded to a Ipsos MORI survey agreed that Brexit would have a negative impact on the United Kingdom's GDP in the medium to long run. See "Economists' Views on Brexit," Ipsos MORI, May 28, 2016, https://www.ipsos-mori.com/researchpublications/researcharchive/3739/Economists-Views-on-Brexit.aspx.

11. Henry Mance, "Britain Has Had Enough of Experts, Says Gove," *Financial Times*, June 3, 2016.

12. See the discussion in Benjamin Moffitt and Simon Tormey, "Rethinking Populism: Politics, Mediatisation and Political Style," *Political Studies* 62 (2014): 381–397.

13. See Michael Conniff, "Introduction," in *Populism in Latin America*, ed. Michael Conniff (University of Alabama Press, 1999), 9.

14. There is also Germany in the 1930s, although this case is complicated by the fact that radio was controlled prior to 1932 by the political establishment, slowing the rise of the Nazis, but thereafter by the Reich Propaganda Ministry. See Maja Adena, Ruben Enikolopov, Maria Petrova, Veronica Santarosa, and Ekaterina Zhuravskaya, "Radio and the Rise of the Nazis in Prewar Germany," *Quarterly Journal of Economics* 130 (2015): 1885–1939. Radio was by no means the exclusive preserve of populists: Franklin Delano Roosevelt famously made use of it in his fireside chats as a way of taking his message directly to the people.

15. R. Hal Williams, *Realigning America: McKinley, Bryan, and the Remarkable Election of 1896* (University Press of Kansas, 2010), 91.

16. Rudiger Dornbusch and Sebastian Edwards, "Macroeconomic Populism," *Journal of Development Economics* 32 (1990): 247–277, quote from 247.

17. One perhaps might better say populism's "resurgence" in the advanced countries, given the historical precursors considered below.

18. More recently Google Translate has turned to artificial intelligence, but no matter.

19. When their attempt to catalyze a peasant revolt failed, the Narodniks turned to assassination of state officials, a strategy with no analog in nineteenth-century American populism. See Ronald Seth, *The Russian Terrorists: The Story of the Narodniki* (Barrie & Rockliff, 1967). Seth, aka "John de Witt" and "Agent Blunderhead," served as professor of literature at the University of Tallinn in the 1930s. In 1942, with Estonia under German occupation, he was parachuted in by British intelligence, which tasked him with destroying the country's shale oil plants. When captured, he went to work as a German double agent, although his new allegiance was quickly uncovered by the British security services. Seth had a successful postwar career writing popular books on terrorism and espionage. Under the pseudonym Robert Chartham, he also published such self-help books as *Sex Manners for Advanced Lovers* (1969) and *The Sensuous Couple* (1971).

20. One scholar, Margaret Canovan, in *Populism* (Harcourt Brace Jovanovich, 1981), 17, describes Bryan as "semipopulist." For more on Bryan's attitude toward foreigners and minorities, see Chapter 2.

21. This did not prevent opponents of FDR's efforts to expand government and pack the Supreme Court in 1937 from accusing him of fomenting a plan for "one-man rule" and "authoritarian government." See William Leuchtenburg, *The FDR Years: On Roosevelt and His Legacy* (Columbia University Press, 1997). On FDR's attitude toward foreigners and religious minorities (Jews in particular), see Richard Breitman and Allan Lichtman, *FDR and the Jews* (Belknap Press of Harvard University Press, 2013).

22. An example is Ray Dalio, Steven Kryger, Jason Rogers, and Gardner Davis, "Populism: The Phenomenon," *Bridgewater Daily Observations*, March 22, 2017.

23. See Alan Murray, "The Pro-Business Populist," *Fortune*, February 26, 2017.

24. This definition is from Giovanni Capoccia, *Defending Democracy: Reactions to Extremism in Interwar Europe* (Johns Hopkins University Press, 2005), 11. Thus, the Narodniks, by turning to the assassination of state officials, exposed themselves as anti-system rather than populist (see note 19, above).

25. Postel, *Populist Vision*, 4.

26. Thus it can be argued that right-wing populism, which emphasizes the opposition of the people to immigrants and minorities, is more conducive to this authoritarian, anti-system tendency than left-wing populism, which juxtaposes "the people" and the elites—a distinction drawn by Judis, *Populist Explosion*, and Müller, *What Is Populism?*

27. These are classic tactics of anti-system politicians as described by Juan Linz in *The Breakdown of Democratic Regimes*, vol. 1, *Crisis, Breakdown, and Reequilibration* (Johns Hopkins University Press, 1978).

28. An analysis of these patterns is Luigi Guiso, Helios Herrera, Massimo Morelli, and Tommaso Sonno, "Demand and Supply of Populism," unpublished manuscript, Einaudi Institute, Warwick University, Bocconi University, and Catholic University of Leuven, February 2017.

29. See Manuel Funke, Moritz Schularick, and Christoph Trebesch, "Going to Extremes: Politics After Financial Crises 1870–2014," *European Economic Review* 88 (2016): 227–260.

30. The tendency toward this reaction in low-trust societies is documented in Nathan Nunn, Nancy Qian, and Jaya Wen, "Trust, Growth and Political Stability," unpublished manuscript, Harvard University, April 2016.

31. Fareed Zakaria, "It's No Longer the Economy, Stupid: Our Identity Politics Are Polarizing Us," *Washington Post*, September 15, 2016.

32. Some see those gold discoveries and their timing as chance events, while others see them as the result of the prior deflation that raised the real price of gold and the attractions of prospecting. See Hugh Rockoff, "Some Evidence on the Real Price of Gold, Its Costs of Production, and Commodity Prices," in *A Retrospective on the Classical Gold Standard, 1821–1931*, ed. Michael Bordo and Anna Schwartz (University of Chicago Press, 1992), and Barry Eichengreen and Ian McLean, "The Supply of Gold Under the Pre-1914 Gold Standard," *Economic History Review* 47 (1994): 288–309. An additional bit of good luck was a series of poor harvests abroad starting in 1895, which raised prices for American grain growers and muted their complaints about globalization.

33. These connections among deflation, real interest rates, investment, and growth are explored in Barry Eichengreen, "The Proximate Determinants of Domestic Investment in Victorian Britain," *Journal of Economic History* 42 (1982): 87–95. While my focus there is the United Kingdom, the British and U.S. economies experienced the same deflationary and inflationary trends, their respective price levels being tied together by the gold standard. An analysis showing that a further deterioration of economic conditions could have tipped the Electoral College in Bryan's favor is Barry Eichengreen, Michael Haines, Matthew Jaremski, and David Leblang, "Populists at the Polls: Economic, Political and Social Factors in the 1896 Presidential Election," NBER Working Paper no. 23932, National Bureau of Economic Research, October 2017.

34. Leo Wolman, "Wages and Hours Under the Codes of Fair Competition," National Bureau of Economic Research *Bulletin* 54 (1935): 1–10.

35. The Bryan quote is from a letter to Carter Glass, reprinted in the *Commercial and Financial Chronicle*, August 30, 1913, 569. This comment might seem to rest uneasily with traditional populist skepticism about central banking, but this observation neglects the fact that the Federal Reserve was structured precisely in order to reassure the populists (more on this below).

36. There was of course the American Recovery and Reinvestment Act, or Obama stimulus, signed into law in the president's first month in office.

I compare it with the New Deal in Barry Eichengreen, *Hall of Mirrors: The Great Depression, the Great Recession, and the Uses—and Misuses—of History* (Oxford University Press, 2015).

37. See David Cameron, "The Expansion of the Public Economy: A Comparative Analysis," *American Political Science Review* 72 (1978): 1243–1261, and John Ruggie, "International Regimes, Transactions and Change: Embedded Liberalism in the Postwar Economic Order," *International Organization* 36 (1982): 379–415. On the connections between economic volatility and social insurance, specifically with respect to external shocks and globalization, see Dani Rodrik, "Why Do More Open Economies Have Bigger Governments?," *Journal of Political Economy* 106 (1998): 997–1022, and Alberto Alesina and Romain Wacziarg, "Openness, Country Size and Government," *Journal of Public Economics* 69 (1998): 305–321. Later in the book we will encounter trade unions and other organizations through which workers, at various points, were able to self-insure against unemployment. But some such groups had restrictions on membership (skilled workers only, for example) that created barriers to joining (and even then they required public subsidies; see the discussion of the Ghent system in Chapter 6) or else provided a very limited level of benefits (as in the case of the English friendly societies; see Chapter 3). It is obviously difficult for displaced workers seeking retraining to borrow against their future earnings, recent "innovations" in the market for student loans notwithstanding.

38. Alberto Alesina, Reza Baqir, and William Easterly document the point by comparing U.S. cities, metropolitan areas, and urban counties. They suggest that different ethnic groups may have different preferences for public goods (in the present context, they may be subject to different risks of displacement by economic change). Alternatively, each group's perceived benefit from public-good provision may be reduced if other groups also benefit (the majority group may support government-subsidized health insurance exchanges less, for example, if it sees minorities also benefiting from them). See Alberto Alesina, Reza Baqir, and William Easterly, "Public Goods and Ethnic Divisions," *Quarterly Journal of Economics* 114 (1999): 1243–1284.

39. This aspect is emphasized by Alberto Alesina, Edward Glaeser, and Bruce Sacerdote, "Why Doesn't the United States Have a European-Style Welfare State?," *Brookings Papers on Economic Activity* (2001): 187–278. But there is also the possibility that the negative effects of these differences diminish when groups interact with one another and build trust through contact (see Chapter 11).

Chapter 2

1. The phrase in quotes is the title of the classic study by John D. Hicks, *The Populist Revolt: A History of the Farmers' Alliance and the People's Party* (University of Minnesota Press, 1931).

2. Examples of this revisionist view are Anne Mayhew, "A Reappraisal of the Causes of Farm Protest in the U.S., 1870–1900," *Journal of Economic History* 32 (1972): 464–475; Steven Hahn, *The Roots of Southern Populism: Yeoman Farmers and the Transformation of the Georgia Upcountry, 1850–1890* (Oxford University Press, 1985); and Adam Rome, "American Farmers as Entrepreneurs," *Agricultural History* 56 (1982): 37–49.

3. See Hugh Rockoff, "The 'Wizard of Oz' as a Monetary Allegory," *Journal of Political Economy* 98 (1990): 739–760. This is not a universally accepted interpretation; see also the discussion in Quentin Taylor, "Money and Politics in the Land of Oz," *Independent Review* 9 (2005): 413–426.

4. See Leon Fink, *Workingmen's Democracy: The Knights of Labor and American Politics* (University of Illinois Press, 1983), and Matthew Hild, *Greenbackers, Knights of Labor and Populists: Farmer-Labor Insurgency in the Late-Nineteenth-Century South* (University of Georgia Press, 2007).

5. Gompers was of course the influential leader of the American Federation of Labor.

6. John Commons et al., *History of Labor in the United States* (Macmillan, 1935–1936).

7. Fink, the historian of the Knights, writes of "an unprecedented wave of strikes and boycotts that carried on into the renewed depression in 1884–85 and spread to thousands of previously unorganized semiskilled and unskilled laborers." Fink, *Workingmen's Democracy*, xii–xiii.

8. Peter Lindert and Jeffrey Williamson, *Unequal Gains: American Growth and Inequality Since 1700* (Princeton University Press, 2016).

9. Alexis de Tocqueville, *Democracy in America* (A. S. Barnes, 1851).

10. T. J. Stiles, *The First Tycoon: The Epic Life of Cornelius Vanderbilt* (Knopf, 2009).

11. Bryan's own views of racial matters were complex and continue to be disputed; see Willard Smith, "William Jennings Bryan and Racism," *Journal of Negro History* 54 (1969): 127–149.

12. Mary Elizabeth Lease, *The Problem of Civilization Solved* (Laird and Lee, 1895).

13. See C. Vann Woodward, *Tom Watson: Agrarian Rebel* (Macmillan, 1938).

14. Elliott Young, *Alien Nation: Chinese Migration in the Americas from the Coolie Era Through World War II* (University of North Carolina Press, 2014), 103.

15. Though Roosevelt started the Progressive or Bull Moose Party in 1912 as a result of his dissatisfaction with the mainstream parties, he went out on his own only as a result of his inability to secure the Republican nomination.

16. Woodrow Wilson, "Inaugural Address, March 4, 1913," American Presidency Project, http://www.presidency.ucsb.edu/ws/index.php?pid=25831. Similarly, Wilson's emphasis on the advantages of American neutrality during World War I on the grounds that "there are many things still be done at home" echoed populist themes.

See Woodrow Wilson, "Inaugural Address, March 5, 1917," American Presidency Project, http://www.presidency.ucsb.edu/ws/?pid=25832.

17. The phrase "elastic currency" is from the official title of the Federal Reserve Act.

18. Leonard Moore, "Historical Interpretations of the 1920's Klan: The Traditional View and the Populist Revision," *Journal of Social History* 24 (1990): 353. See also Leonard Moore, *Citizen Klansmen: The Ku Klux Klan in Indiana, 1921–1928* (University of North Carolina Press, 1991).

19. The Klan was more prominently associated with the Democrats because of its opposition, at the party's 1924 convention, to the nomination of New York governor Al Smith on the grounds that he was Catholic.

20. See Thomas Piketty and Emmanuel Saez, "Income Inequality in the United States, 1913–1998," *Quarterly Journal of Economics* 118 (2003): 1–41.

21. My own analysis of the political economy and the consequences is Barry Eichengreen, "The Political Economy of the Smoot-Hawley Tariff," *Research in Economic History* (1989): 1–35.

22. See Francisco Balderrama and Raymond Rodríguez, *Decade of Betrayal: Mexican Repatriation in the 1930s*, rev. ed. (University of New Mexico Press, 1996).

23. The first generic use of the term "populist" to refer to anti-establishment, authoritarian, nativist political figures (as opposed to its use in referring to the American Populist Party of the 1890s) was apparently in a *New York Times Magazine* article in 1935 discussing Long and the radio evangelist Father Thomas Coughlin (more on whom below). See Francis Brown, "The Drums of Populism Are Heard Anew," *New York Times Magazine*, June 23, 1935. The observation is from John Emerson, "A Short History of Populism in America," *Counterpunch*, November 5, 2013.

24. Quoted in William Ivy Hair, *The Kingfish and His Realm: The Life and Times of Huey P. Long* (Louisiana State University Press, 1991), 188.

25. These are the words of the midcentury scholar of southern politics V. O. Key in *Southern Politics in State and Nation* (Knopf/Vintage, 1949).

26. Quoted in Richard Cortner, *The Kingfish and the Constitution: Huey Long, the First Amendment, and the Emergence of Modern Press Freedom in America* (Greenwood Press, 1996), 29.

27. The tax was ultimately overturned by the Supreme Court in 1936 as an abridgement of freedom of the press.

28. These were in fact loans, which were fully collateralized, but for Long this was bureaucratic hairsplitting. For him, that plutocrats like Charles Dawes, formerly U.S. vice president and head of the Reconstruction Finance Corporation, were on the receiving end of those loans underscored the point.

29. As noted in Chapter 1, it was not the New Deal but an assassin's bullet, fired shortly after he announced his candidacy for the presidency, that brought Long's national ambitions to an end.

30. See Donald Warren, *Radio Priest: Charles Coughlin, the Father of Hate Radio* (Free Press, 1996).

31. Respondents were even more inclined to answer "no difference." Only third-party supporters answered that they would be more inclined to vote for a candidate on the basis of Coughlin's endorsement.

32. Ira Katznelson, *Fear Itself: The New Deal and the Origins of Our Time* (Liveright, 2013). More generally, one can view FDR's response as illustrating the importance of incumbent leaders seizing the public and political high ground, addressing the concerns fueling anti-system political sentiment, and beating back the populist challenge. See the related discussion in Giovanni Capoccia, *Defending Democracy: Reactions to Extremism in Interwar Europe* (Johns Hopkins University Press, 2005).

33. FERA had been created in 1932 by President Herbert Hoover as the Emergency Relief Administration but was reorganized and expanded under FDR; in 1935 it was replaced by the Works Progress Administration.

34. The quote is from Raymond Moley, one of FDR's advisors. Raymond Moley, *After Seven Years* (Harper, 1939), 305. Moley's interpretation has not gone undisputed; see the discussion in Edwin Amenta, Kathleen Dunleavy, and Mary Bernstein, "Stolen Thunder? Huey Long's 'Share Our Wealth,' Political Mediation and the Second New Deal," *American Sociological Review* 59 (1994): 678–702.

35. See Claudia Goldin and Robert Margo, "The Great Compression: The U.S. Wage Structure at Mid-Century," *Quarterly Journal of Economics* 107 (1992): 1–34.

36. For more detail see Chapter 7.

37. The Trump-McCarthy parallel is fully drawn by James Risen and Tom Risen, "Donald Trump Does His Best Joe McCarthy Impression," *New York Times*, June 22, 2017.

38. Michael Rogin, *The Intellectuals and McCarthy: The Radical Specter* (MIT Press, 1967); David Oshinsky, *A Conspiracy So Immense: The World of Joe McCarthy* (Oxford University Press, 2005).

Chapter 3

1. Observe that technical change disadvantaged relatively skilled workers in industry in this period—in contrast to the situation in recent decades, where less skilled workers have been put at a disadvantage. This point and explanations for the contrast are discussed in Chapter 8.

2. The modern estimates are those of N. F. R. Crafts, *British Economic Growth During the Industrial Revolution* (Clarendon Press, 1985), and C. Knick Harley, "British Industrialization Before 1841: Evidence of Slower Growth During the Industrial Revolution," *Journal of Economic History* 42 (1982): 267–289.

3. Specifically, these acts coincided with the most restrictive phase of Napoleon's Continental System and disruption of Britain's trade with the United States, which made cotton imports temporarily unavailable. The Luddites were named after Ned Ludd, or Edward Ludlam, a weaver from greater Leicester said to have smashed two knitting frames in a fit of rage in 1779. Starting in 1812, protesting handloom weavers adopted this moniker, using it to sign their letters and proclamations.

4. Recent scholars argue that nineteenth-century critics of Parliamentary enclosure, including Karl Marx, exaggerated its impact in this period, since access to open land had already declined by the mid-eighteenth century. Gregory Clark and Anthony Clark, "Common Rights to Land in England, 1475–1839," *Journal of Economic History* 61 (2001): 1009–1036. That said, earlier enclosures could have contributed to farmworkers' sense of insecurity and, in addition, had symbolic importance.

5. See Toke Aidt, Gabriel Leon, and Max Satchell, "The Social Dynamics of Riots:Evidence from the Captain Swing Riots 1830–1831," unpublished manuscript, Cambridge University and King's College London, 2017; Bruno Caprettini and Hans-Joachim Voth, "Rage Against the Machines: Labour-Saving Technology and Unrest in England, 1830–32," CEPR Discussion Paper no. 11800, Centre for Economic Policy Research, London, January 2017.

6. The quotation, a paraphrase, is in J. L. and Barbara Hammond's *The Village Labourer 1760–1832: A Study in the Government of England Before the Reform Bill*, new ed. (Longmans, Green, 1913), 240.

7. See E. P. Thompson, *The Making of the English Working Class* (Pantheon Books, 1963); J. R. Dinwiddy, "Luddism and Politics in the Northern Counties," in *Radicalism and Reform in Britain, 1880–1850* (Hambledon Press, 1992), 371–402.

8. See Maxine Berg, *The Machinery Question and the Making of Political Economy 1815–1848* (Cambridge University Press, 1982) and Haim Barkai, "Ricardo's Volte-Face on Machinery," *Journal of Political Economy* 94 (1986): 593–613.

9. Malcolm Chase, *Chartism: A New History* (Manchester University Press, 2007), 7.

10. Gaston Rimlinger, *Welfare Policy and Industrialization in Europe, America and Russia* (John Wiley & Sons, 1971), 89.

11. Nor can one dismiss the influence of Thomas Malthus's *Essay on the Principle of Population* (especially the sixth edition, 1826), where Malthus argued that income support encouraged procreation, aggravating the imbalance between population and agriculture.

12. Parishes had been responsible for collecting voluntary weekly sums for supporting the poor since the sixteenth century and were required to participate in a compulsory system by acts of 1597–1598 and 1601.

Parliamentary action was prompted by a series of economic shocks leading to the erosion of real wages and decline of other sources of charitable support, due to inter alia dissolution of the monasteries. See George Boyer, *An Economic History of the English Poor Law, 1750–1850* (Cambridge University Press, 1990).

13. As with many measures intended to limit migration, this one proved easier to enact than to enforce. The Settlement Act was amended repeatedly and gave rise to legal disputes between parishes removing nonresidents and parishes to which those nonresidents were removed, not unlike disputes between EU member states over the settlement of extra-European refugees. See Michael Rose, "Settlement, Removal, and the New Poor Law," in *The New Poor Law in the Nineteenth Century*, ed. Derek Fraser (Macmillan, 1976), 25–44.

14. In this connection, friendly societies, dominated by well-paid, regularly employed manual workers but including also regularly employed agricultural workers, were more important than unions with more than four times the membership at the turn of the century. See Pat Thane, "The Working Class and State 'Welfare' in Britain, 1880–1914," *Historical Journal* 27 (1984): 877–900.

15. This refers to the percentage gap in wages, as in Jeffrey Williamson, *Did British Capitalism Breed Inequality?* (Unwin Hyman, 1985). But see also R. V. Jackson, "The Structure of Pay in Nineteenth-Century Britain," *Economic History Review* 11 (1987): 561–570.

16. Benjamin Brown, *The Tariff Movement in Great Britain, 1881–1895* (Columbia University Press, 1943), 35. "More or less" because some of the delegates disqualified on these grounds reentered the meeting hall the next day, leading the organizers to summon the police.

17. A number of countries taxed imports of refined sugar for revenue-raising purposes. Where refiners were a powerful lobby, their governments responded with export subsidies or bounties to neutralize the impact.

18. In the absence of this connection one would have expected the dockworkers, whose livelihood depended on import and export trade, to be the least likely supporters of protection. Brown, *Tariff Reform Movement*, 37.

19. Ibid., 45.

20. Quoted in Peter Fraser, *Joseph Chamberlain: Radicalism and Empire, 1868–1914* (Cassell, 1968), 230.

21. Chamberlain at this time was a member of the Liberal Unionist Party, which allied with the Conservatives to form a government following the 1895 general election. The Liberal Unionists split off from the Liberal Party in 1886 over Irish Home Rule, unionists believing in a unified United Kingdom and in Chamberlain's case in a larger all-British federation (more on which below). See Fraser, *Joseph Chamberlain*.

22. Here too there is a parallel with Bismarck's strategy, as described in Chapter 4.

23. This was especially so once the central Poor Law authority relaunched its attack on outdoor relief, including now even for the infirm elderly. See E. P. Hennock, *The Origin of the Welfare State in England and Germany, 1850–1914: Social Policies Compared* (Cambridge University Press, 2007), 214. On the parallel with imperial Germany, see also Chapter 4.

24. Bruce Murray, *The People's Budget 1909/10: Lloyd George and Liberal Politics* (Clarendon Press, 1980), 27. Earlier, as mayor of Birmingham, Chamberlain had championed a similarly expansive role for municipal government, introducing publicly owned gas, water, and sewer works. Sydney Zebel, "Joseph Chamberlain and the Genesis of Tariff Reform," *Journal of British Studies* 7 (1967): 131–157.

25. Fraser, *Joseph Chamberlain*, 231.

26. The quote is from Travis Crosby, *Joseph Chamberlain: A Most Radical Imperialist* (I. B. Tauris, 2011), 1.

27. Indicative of the importance he attached to the rise of Germany, Chamberlain described his vision as an "All-British Zollverein" in a speech to the Chambers of Commerce of the Empire in 1896. Zebel, "Joseph Chamberlain," esp. 140.

28. The comparison was to indigenous Americans, Australian Aboriginals, and New Zealand Maori. To be fair, Dilke also had some sympathy for native peoples dispossessed by English colonists. See Bill Schwartz, *Memories of Empire*, vol. 1, *The White Man's World* (Oxford University Press, 2011).

29. In the priority it attached to this combination of industrial prowess and national identity, Chamberlain's campaign thus resonated with classic populist themes. The quote is from Crosby, *Joseph Chamberlain*, 122.

30. Julian Amery, *Joseph Chamberlain and the Tariff Reform Campaign*, vol. 5 of *The Life of Joseph Chamberlain* (Macmillan/St. Martin's, 1969), 184–195. The speech in question was in May 1903.

31. Crosby, *Joseph Chamberlain*, 163, 167.

32. Lloyd George had been attracted to Chamberlain's earlier proposals for social reform, traveling to Birmingham for the first meeting of his National Radical Union. See Bentley Brinkerhoff Gilbert, "David Lloyd George: Land, the Budget, and Social Reform," *American Historical Review* 81 (1976): 1058–1066.

33. See J. M. Winter, "Military Fitness and Civilian Health in Britain During the First World War," *Journal of Contemporary History* 15 (1980): 211–244.

34. This is similarly argued by Noel Whiteside, "L'assurance sociale en Grand-Bretagne, 1900–1950: La genèse de l'État-providence," in *Les assurances sociales en Europe*, ed. Michel Dreyfus (Presses Universitaires de Rennes, 2009), 127–158.

35. These health insurance subsidiaries were intended to prevent friendly societies, which otherwise would have been the sole recipients of government subsidies, from capturing the business. Lloyd George's bill

had limited provision to approved friendly societies but was criticized by commercial insurance companies. Ultimately, the insurance companies and their armies of door-to-door premium collectors carried the day.

36. On these obstacles to a universal contributory pension scheme, see Leslie Hannah, *Inventing Retirement: The Development of Occupational Pensions in Britain* (Cambridge University Press, 1986) and John Macnicol, *The Politics of Retirement in Britain, 1878–1948* (Cambridge University Press, 1998).

Chapter 4

1. That growth was unusually rapid once it began in this, a late-developing catch-up economy, was a point emphasized by the economic historian Alexander Gerschenkron in *Economic Backwardness in Historical Perspective* (Harvard University Press, 1962), who also highlighted the unusually active role of the German government in the process (see below).

2. Lorenz Stein, *Proletariat und Gesellschaft* (W. Fink, 1971; orig. 1848). See also Christopher Clark, *Iron Kingdom: The Rise and Downfall of Prussia 1600–1947* (Belknap Press of Harvard University Press, 2006), 615–616. Stein's views of the roles of the monarchy and the state in advancing social welfare extended as far as Japan, where he advised the government of Prime Minister Itō Hirobumi on that country's constitution.

3. The writings of these reformers in turn influenced the views of public intellectuals such as Hermann Wagener, editor of the *Neue Preussische Zeitung* and Bismarck's confidant. See Erik Grimmer-Solem, *The Rise of Historical Economics and Social Reform in Germany, 1864–1894* (Clarendon Press, 2003).

4. The North German Confederation under Bismarck had already adopted universal male suffrage in 1867.

5. There were parallels in Chamberlainian support for protection and social reform in Britain, as discussed in Chapter 3, and in Republican Party support for tariffs and Civil War veterans' pensions, as discussed by Theda Skocpol in "The Politics of American Social Policy, Past and Future," in *Individual and Social Responsibility: Child Care, Education, Medical Care and Long-Term Care in America*, ed. Victor Fuchs (University of Chicago Press, 1996), 309–340, and in Chapter 5. But the German "marriage of iron and rye" was more durable, and its social insurance state was more precocious.

6. The quotation in the text is from Gaston Rimlinger, *Welfare Policy and Industrialization in Europe, America and Russia* (Wiley, 1971), 95.

7. Towns were not permitted, however, to deny residence to individuals currently with means who might become destitute in the future.

8. E. P. Hennock, *The Origin of the Welfare State in England and Germany, 1850–1914: Social Policies Compared* (Cambridge University Press, 2007), 23–24.

9. Peter Baldwin, *The Politics of Social Solidarity: Class Bases of the European Welfare State, 1875–1975* (Cambridge University Press, 1990), 97–98.

10. See James Brophy, *Popular Culture and the Public Sphere in the Rhineland, 1800–1850* (Cambridge University Press, 2007), 87.

11. Friedrich Engels, "Rapid Progress of Communism in Germany," *New Moral World* 25 (December 13, 1844).

12. The constitution ultimately adopted is more accurately described as drafted by the Crown and its aristocratic allies subject to agreement by the assembly. Suffrage was universal although subject to a voting system under which representation was proportional to taxes paid, thereby favoring the wealthy.

13. Rimlinger, *Welfare Policy*, 100.

14. Ibid., 105.

15. Early formation of the Social Democratic Party, in contrast with Britain, where the Labour Party was only founded at the turn of the century, is sometimes cited as a factor in Germany's pioneering development of social insurance. This is argued by Stein Kuhnle and Anne Sander, "The Emergence of the Western Welfare State," in *The Oxford Handbook of the Welfare State*, ed. Francis Castles, Stephan Leibfried, Jane Lewis, Herbert Obinger, and Christopher Pierson (Oxford University Press, 2010), 61–80.

16. Rimlinger, *Welfare Policy*, 116.

17. The quote is from Volker Hentschel, "German Economic and Social Policy, 1815–1939," in *The Cambridge Economic History of Europe*, vol. 8, *The Industrial Economies: The Development of Economic and Social Policies*, ed. Peter Mathias and Sidney Pollard (Cambridge University Press, 1989), 793.

18. Analogous U.S. legislation came even later, in the second decade of the twentieth century, as we will see in Chapter 5.

19. Falk and others note how the term "anti-Semitism" was coined by the German journalist Wilhelm Marr in this period. Avner Falk, *Anti-Semitism: A History and Psychoanalysis of Contemporary Hatred* (Praeger, 2008), 41–42.

20. German iron producers suffered further from the slowdown in railway construction following the 1873 crash. By 1878, the prices of most iron products had fallen to less than half 1873 levels. In addition, the phosphorus-rich ore deposits of Alsace, under German control following the Franco-Prussian War, were not usable prior to the development of the Thomas-Gilchrist process for eliminating impurities toward the end of the decade. Prior to that, German producers were forced to import non-phosphoric ore from Spain and North Africa. Ivo Lambi, *Free Trade and Protection in Germany, 1868–1879* (Franz Steiner Verlag, 1963), 76.

21. See Steven Webb, "Tariffs, Cartels, Technology and Growth in the German Steel Industry, 1879 to 1914," *Journal of Economic History* 40 (1980): 309–329.

22. Gordon Craig, *Germany 1866–1945* (Oxford University Press, 1978), 86.

23. In 1877, the Liberal Party, Bismarck's post-1863 power base, had won 27 percent of the vote, the Center Party 25 percent, and the Conservative Party 10 percent.

24. Grimmer-Solem, *Rise of Historical Economics*, 200.

25. Under Bismarck's initial proposal, workers with annual incomes below 750 marks, who were mainly employees of small enterprises, would have made no contributions, while those with incomes between 750 and 1,200 marks would pay a third, and workers with incomes above 1,200 marks would pay half. The Saar-based coal and iron magnate Carl Ferdinand Stumm favored compulsory insurance as a way of limiting the risk of labor disputes that might shut down his capital-intensive operation. As a member of the Reichstag in 1878, Stumm submitted a plan to the government for compulsory old-age and disability insurance. Hennock, *Origin*, 182.

26. Those regional insurance offices in turn operated under the supervision of the imperial insurance office. In addition, Bismarck's state subsidies were eliminated, consistent with the preferences of large industrial enterprises. Rimlinger, *Welfare Policy*, 119.

27. The entitlement period was extended to twenty-six weeks in the event of treatment in hospitals. In case of the death of an insured worker, his family received a lump-sum "death grant." where the employer or other workers were liable.

28. Hennock, *Origin*, 196.

29. Hentschel, "German Economic and Social Policy," 794–795.

30. See Steven Webb, "Agricultural Protection in Wilhelminian Germany: Forging an Empire with Pork and Rye," in *Selected Cliometric Studies on German Economic History*, ed. John Komlos and Scott Eddie (Franz Steiner Verlag, 1997), 66–82.

Chapter 5

1. In 1924 Congress had voted a bonus of $1.25 for each day served overseas and $1.00 for each day served in the United States, but provided veterans entitled to these payments with certificates that could not be redeemed until 1945.

2. This floating underclass is described by Alexander Keyssar, *Out of Work: The First Century of Unemployment in Massachusetts* (Cambridge University Press, 1986).

3. This was the situation as of 1910.

4. Edwin Amenta, *Bold Relief: Institutional Politics and the Origins of Modern American Social Policy* (Princeton University Press, 1998), 60.

5. The quote is from an 1884 edition of the reformist magazine *Century*, cited in Anne Shola Orloff, *The Politics of Pensions: A Comparative Analysis*

of Britain, Canada, and the United States, 1880–1940 (University of Wisconsin Press, 1993), 234.

6. This argument is elaborated by Amenta, *Bold Relief*, 57.

7. Harry Hopkins, who was intimately involved in the administration of AFDC under the Roosevelt administration, had worked from 1912 to 1915 for the Association for Improving the Condition of the Working Poor, a charitable organization in New York concerned with widows' and children's welfare.

8. U.S. Congress, Senate, Conference on Care of Dependent Children, *Proceedings*, 60th Cong., 2nd sess., 1909, S. Doc 721, 9.

9. See Theda Skocpol, Marjorie Abend-Wein, Christopher Howard, and Susan Goodrich Lehmann, "Women's Associations and the Enactment of Mothers' Pensions in the United States," *American Political Science Review* 87 (1993): 686–701. Opposition came mainly from private social agencies that did not welcome state-sponsored competition. See Mark Leff, "Consensus for Reform: The Mothers'-Pension Movement in the Progressive Era," *Social Service Review* 47 (1973): 397–417.

10. Select states also extended eligibility to divorced or deserted women and, in a few cases, to unwed mothers. Carolyn Moehling shows that eligibility requirements and other provisions varied across states as a function of local conditions (whether state or local government was responsible for providing the funding, for example). See Carolyn Moehling, "Mothers' Pension Legislation and the Politics of Welfare Generosity," unpublished manuscript, Rutgers University, January 2014.

11. Employers tempered their opposition further when state legislatures, under Progressive influence, modified liability laws to enhance the ability of injured workers to sue. See Price Fishback and Shawn Kantor, *A Prelude to the Welfare State: The Origins of Workers' Compensation* (University of Chicago Press, 2000).

12. A few states had broader coverage, but they were exceptions.

13. Theda Skocpol, "The Politics of American Social Policy, Past and Future," in *Individual and Social Responsibility: Child Care, Education, Medical Care, and Long-Term Care in America*, ed. Victor Fuchs (University of Chicago Press, 1996), 314.

14. Paolo Coletta, "William Jennings Bryan and Currency and Banking Reform," *Nebraska History* 45 (1964): 31–58. The quote in the text is from 41.

15. See Sanford Jacoby, *Employing Bureaucracy: Managers, Unions and the Transformation of Work in American Industry, 1900–1945* (Columbia University Press, 1985) on these other changes in labor-management practices.

16. The War Labor Board, which commenced operations in April 1918, arbitrated disputes between labor and management to minimize interruptions to labor supply and maintain war production. Its decisions

generally supported the right to organize and bargain collectively. Partly as a result, AFL membership rose by half in the course of the war.

17. Beth Stevens, "Blurring the Boundaries: How the Federal Government Has Influenced Welfare Benefits in the Private Sector," in *The Politics of Social Policy in the United States*, ed. Margaret Weir, Ann Shola Orloff, and Theda Skocpol (Princeton University Press, 1998), 126.

18. Orloff, *Politics of Pensions*, 277.

19. In addition, perhaps 75,000 government employees drew pensions to which they were entitled as a result of earlier civil service reforms.

20. See William Pratt, "Rethinking the Farm Revolt of the 1930s," *Great Plains Quarterly* 8 (1988): 131–144.

21. This is the traditional interpretation of the political aspect of the movement, as in Richard Neuberger and Kelley Loe, *An Army of the Aged* (Caldwell, 1936).

22. The scheme, as Townsend envisaged it, would be financed by a federal sales tax. Subsequent incarnations raised the monthly payment to $200 and substituted a transactions or value-added tax for the sales tax. When the plan was attacked as extravagant and underfunded, Townsend then proposed lowering the monthly allotment to $60 in 1935.

23. Smith had moved his family from the Midwest to Louisiana in 1928 because his wife suffered from tuberculosis and Shreveport had a well-regarded sanitarium. Like Charles Coughlin, he was a pioneer of radio evangelicalism, a technology that Long also employed to publicize his "Share Our Wealth" plan. Smith had previously organized Share Our Wealth clubs for Long along similar lines to the Townsend Clubs he now oversaw.

24. There are always predecessors: in this case there was the less well-known American Association for Old Age Security, founded in 1927.

25. As in other periods of high unemployment, the youngest and oldest workers were disproportionately affected by the downturn. See Linda Levine, "The Labor Market During the Great Depression and the Current Recession," Congressional Research Service Report no. R30655, June 19, 2009.

26. Frances Perkins, FDR's secretary of labor, who was involved in designing the legislation, later remarked that the Congress would have been unlikely to lavish the same attention on the bill that became the Social Security Act without pressure from the Townsendites. Frances Perkins, *The Roosevelt I Knew* (Viking, 1964), vi. A view questioning the effectiveness of the Townsendites while not entirely dismissing their influence is Edwin Amenta, *When Movements Matter: The Townsend Plan and the Rise of Social Security* (Princeton University Press, 2006).

27. See Richard Vedder and Lowell Gallaway, *Out of Work: Unemployment and Government in Twentieth-Century America* (New York University Press, 1997).

28. Factors adversely affecting consumer spending, on durables and in general, are emphasized by Peter Temin, *Did Monetary Forces Cause the*

Great Depression (Norton, 1976) and Christina Romer, "The Great Crash and the Onset of the Great Depression," *Quarterly Journal of Economics* 105 (1990): 597–625.

29. See Peter Lindert, "What Limits Social Spending?," *Explorations in Economic History* 33 (1996): 1–34, for variations on this theme.

30. Quoted in Charles Noble, *Welfare as We Knew It* (Oxford University Press, 1997), 77. Later, when business turned against him, Roosevelt sought to mobilize public support by campaigning against business and finance; recall his "I welcome their hatred" speech, cited in Chapter 2. But his goal in 1933 was to enlist business in his reform and recovery plans, not to alienate it.

31. See Sally Denton, *The Plots Against the President: FDR, A Nation in Crisis, and the Rise of the American Right* (Bloomsbury, 2012), ch. 28.

32. This decline was interrupted, but only temporarily, by an uptick in the number of relief jobs in the recession of 1937–1938.

33. Margaret Weir and Theda Skocpol, "State Structures and the Possibilities for 'Keynesian' Responses to the Great Depression in Sweden, Britain and the United States," in *Bringing the State Back In*, ed. Peter Evans, Theda Skocpol, and Dietrich Rueschemeyer (Cambridge University Press, 1985), 107–163. The post–World War II experience is discussed in Chapter 7.

34. The act was amended in 1939 to provide for partial benefits for the dependents and survivors of wage earners.

35. In addition, the Social Security Act appropriated funds for temporary provision of old-age assistance, again subject to states providing matching funds and submitting an acceptable plan.

36. The Social Security Act appropriated only modest sums for public health. Disability benefits were added to the Social Security Act in 1956.

37. Paul Starr, *The Social Transformation of American Medicine* (Basic Books, 1982), 273.

38. See Daniel Hirshfield, *The Lost Reform: The Campaign for Compulsory Health Insurance in the United States from 1932 to 1943* (Harvard University Press, 1970), 44–46.

39. Some, like Henry Kaiser, the West Coast steelmaker and shipbuilder, went further, contracting directly with doctors to provide medical care to his workers and their families.

40. When President Harry Truman proposed an optional national health insurance plan in 1945, the AMA characterized White House staff as "followers of the Moscow party line."

Chapter 6

1. Benito Mussolini, "Fundamental Ideas," in *Fascism: Doctrine and Institutions* (Ardita, 1935), 10. This article, though signed by Mussolini, is generally attributed to the Fascist philosopher Giovanni Gentile.

2. What started as the British Union of Fascists became the British Union of Fascists and National Socialists (known also as the British Union) in 1936.

3. Robert Skidelsky, *Oswald Mosley*, 3rd ed. (Macmillan Papermac, 1990), 1.

4. This argument has many sources; it is best made by Charles Maier, *Recasting Bourgeois Europe: Stabilization in France, Germany and Italy in the Decade After World War I* (Princeton University Press, 1975).

5. Nor was Italy so burdened, although Mussolini complained that the country, having belatedly sided with France and Britain, was not the recipient of larger payments itself.

6. See, for example, the international comparisons in Michael Kitson, "Slump and Recovery: The UK Experience," in *The World Economy and National Economies in the Interwar Slump*, ed. Theo Balderson (Palgrave Macmillan, 2003), 88–104.

7. This is similarly Skidelsky's conclusion. *Oswald Mosley*, 333.

8. Details on the debate are in Chapter 3.

9. An example of contemporary criticism was Edwin Cannan, *An Economist's Protest* (Adelphi, 1928).

10. As two historians of Italy summarize the situation, "The core of skilled urban industrial workers, who had irreversibly severed their links with agriculture, was relatively small." Gianni Toniolo and Francesco Piva, "Interwar Unemployment in Italy," in *Interwar Unemployment in International Perspective*, ed. Barry Eichengreen and Timothy Hatton (Kluwer Academic Publishers, 1989), 225. When Mussolini's government felt compelled to help the unemployed, it linked payment to employment on public works projects so as to discourage perceived problems of idleness and irresponsibility.

11. Robert Salais, "Why Was Unemployment So Low in France During the 1930s?," in *Interwar Unemployment in International Perspective*, ed. Barry Eichengreen and Timothy Hatton (Kluwer Academic Publishers, 1989), 255–256. Union schemes received subsidies from the state, as did municipal schemes approved by the Ministry of Labor. State subsidies were in proportion to the resources and expenditures of the schemes in question but were subject to a long list of prerequisites.

12. France only finally adopted compulsory unemployment insurance in 1958, in yet another example of how history casts a long shadow. Revealingly, not even the Blum government of 1936–1937, despite its socialist aspirations, was able to secure agreement on a national program of unemployment insurance.

13. In addition, there are actor-based explanations for the contrast, as emphasized by Linz and Stepan and also by Capoccia. These authors emphasize the agency and decisions taken (or not taken) by the executive and by leaders of pivotal parties. See Juan Linz and Alfred Stepan, eds., *The Breakdown of Democratic Regimes* (Johns Hopkins University Press, 1978) and Giovanni Capoccia, *Defending Democracy: Reactions to Extremism in Interwar Europe* (Johns Hopkins University Press, 2005).

14. As Skidelsky, *Oswald Mosley*, 333, writes, "British parliamentary institutions were … much more legitimate than many of their continental counterparts. … [T]he main British social groups were properly integrated into the political system through their political and industrial organisations: there were no atomistic 'masses' available for mobilization, except at the margins."

15. See Eric Waldman, *The Spartacist Uprising of 1919 and the Crisis of the German Socialist Movement* (Marquette University Press, 1958).

16. The parallel episode in Britain in 1931, the Invergordon Mutiny, was in fact little more an industrial action, again pointing up the difference between the two countries.

17. The Banca Italiana di Sconto affair bred support for Mussolini's Fascist alliance, in the manner that the backlash against banking crises regularly breeds support for extreme right-wing parties; see Manuel Funke, Moritz Schularick, and Christoph Trebesch, "Going to Extremes: Politics After Financial Crises, 1870–2014," *European Economic Review* 88 (2016): 227–260, sec. 4.1. On the banking crisis, see Vera Zamagni, *The Economic History of Italy 1860–1990* (Clarendon Press, 1993), Gianni Tonniolo, "Italian Banking, 1919–1936," in *Banking, Currency and Finance in Europe Between the Wars*, ed. Charles Feinstein (Oxford University Press, 1995), 296–314, and Douglas Forsyth, *The Crisis of Liberal Italy: Monetary and Financial Policy, 1914–1922* (Cambridge University Press, 1993).

18. Recent historians (e.g., Forsyth, *Crisis*) argue that most of the hard budgetary lifting had in fact already been done by previous governments, but no matter.

19. Bentley Gilbert, *British Social Policy 1914–1929* (Batsford, 1970), 66, quoted in Richard Garside, *British Unemployment 1919–1939* (Cambridge University Press, 1990), 36.

20. The exceptions were railway workers (who already had their own mutual insurance system), public employees (who were regarded as exempt from unemployment risk), white-collar workers with annual incomes above £250 (who presumably accumulated their own reserve), and domestic servants and farm workers (who, it was thought, could rely on personal contacts).

21. The Chancellor of the Exchequer, Philip Snowden, favored the May Committee's recommendations, but the cabinet could not agree. Prime Minister MacDonald proposed instead 10 percent cuts but secured the support of only eleven of twenty ministers. Foreign banks having made clear that their provision of emergency credits depended on fulsome cabinet support, the government fell.

22. The Import Duties Advisory Committee, under the chairmanship of the selfsame Sir George May, was authorized to adjust that initial 10 percent tariff; it quickly raised most rates to 15 to 35 percent. The exemption for the Commonwealth and Empire was also temporary; permanent

preferences were negotiated at the Ottawa Imperial Economic Conference in November 1932.

23. See Barry Eichengreen, "Keynes and Protection," *Journal of Economic History* 44 (1984): 363–373.

24. Moreover, to the extent that the tariff shifted spending toward British goods and strengthened the trade balance, its effect now was merely to cause the floating pound sterling to appreciate, eliminating the shift in demand and neutralizing any positive employment effects. Barry Eichengreen, "Sterling and the Tariff, 1929–31," Princeton Studies in International Finance no. 48, 1981, International Finance Section, Department of Economics, Princeton University.

25. That legacy is discussed in Chapter 3.

26. Evidence on this relationship is marshaled by Stephen Broadberry and Nicholas Crafts, "The Implications of British Macroeconomic Policy in the 1930s for Long-Run Growth Performance," *Rivista di Storia Economica* 7 (1990): 1–19.

27. See Thomas Paster, "German Employers and the Origins of Unemployment Insurance: Skills Interest or Strategic Accommodation?," MPIfG Discussion Paper no. 11/5, Max Planck Institute for the Study of Societies, Cologne, 2011; E. Peter Hennock, *The Origin of the Welfare State in England and Germany, 1850–1914: Social Policies Compared* (Cambridge University Press, 2007).

28. Union members who cared about the disposition of their contributions, moreover, could be expected to police their rank and file. This belief had encouraged a few municipalities to provide subsidies to union-run unemployment schemes from the turn of the century. Subsidizing efficiently run union funds was attractive to municipal governments where the alternative was spending on poor relief. These municipally subsidized funds were known as Ghent schemes, after the Belgian town that pioneered the approach in 1901. Only a limited number of German municipalities adopted this approach, however; see Hennock, *Origin*, 327.

29. This economic volatility, and especially the inflation of 1923, encouraged the centralization of union and municipal schemes by exhausting the resources of local entities and serving as a reminder that only the central government ultimately had the printing press as a mechanism for backstopping the system. Whether the government would now utilize the printing press for this purpose, given the lessons drawn from this earlier experience with inflation, was another question.

30. See Isabela Mares, "Is Unemployment Insurable? Employers and the Development of Unemployment Insurance," *Journal of Public Policy* 17 (1997): 299–327.

31. For instance, there was the question of whether reparations were senior to other credits—that is, whether the recipients had first call on available tax

revenues, leaving commercial creditors the scraps. See Albrecht Ritschl, "The German Transfer Problem 1920–1933: A Sovereign Debt Perspective," CEPR Discussion Paper no. 1155, Centre for Economic Policy Research, London, July 2012. Reparations also explain why Germany didn't adopt significant trade restrictions prior to 1932— although it certainly did subsequently: the ability to earn foreign exchange so as to make reparations payments dictated maintaining trade relations. The commercial clauses of the Treaty of Versailles stripped Germany of its tariff autonomy, but those clauses expired in 1925. As the Depression deepened, German governments responded with under-the-radar trade restrictions such as the quotas on wood products, pork, and fats introduced by the von Papen government in September 1932.

32. Only Austria, Poland, and Czechoslovakia, all German trading partners, did worse.

33. Employment Stabilization Research Institute of the University of Minnesota, *An Historical Basis for Unemployment Insurance* (University of Minnesota Press, 1934), 27. The same report (39) shows that there was little change in administrative costs as a share of expenditure over the period.

34. Calculations here are from Nicholas Dimsdale, Nicholas Horsewood, and Arthur van Riel, "Unemployment and Real Wages in Weimar Germany," Discussion Papers in Economic and Social History no. 56, University of Oxford, October 2004.

35. Compare Paul Omerod and G. D. N. Worswick, "Searching for an Explanation of Unemployment in Interwar Britain: A Comment," *Journal of Political Economy* 90 (1982): 400–409.

Chapter 7

1. These are not entirely unrelated cases: Powell's 1963 slogan "Trust the People," designed to signal the public's alienation from the political elite, was adopted by Wallace for his 1976 presidential campaign.

2. The periods in question, more precisely, are 1919–1939, 1950–1975, and 1976–2014. Extreme-right parties attracted 7, 2, and 6 percent of the popular vote in elections in twenty democracies in these three periods. Parties on the extreme left or right are defined as parties that advocate changing the system of government; this definition follows Giovanni Sartori, *Parties and Party Systems* (Cambridge University Press, 1976). The taxonomies used here are from de Bromhead et al. for the interwar period and Funke et al. since. See Alan de Bromhead, Barry Eichengreen, and Kevin O'Rourke, "Right-Wing Political Extremism in the Great Depression: Do the German Lessons Generalize?," *Journal of Economic History* 73 (2013): 371–406, and Manuel Funke, Moritz Schularick, and Christoph Trebesch, "Going to Extremes: Politics After Financial Crises 1870–2014," *European Economic Review* 88 (2016): 227–260.

3. See Sebastian Dullien and Ulrike Guérot, "The Long Shadow of Ordoliberalism: Germany's Approach to the Euro Crisis," European Council on Foreign Relations Policy Brief, 2012.

4. Specifically, the Basic Law permits German troops to be deployed abroad only on missions with an international mandate, and even this requires parliamentary approval.

5. See Stephen Fisher, *The Minor Parties of the Federal Republic of Germany: Toward a Comparative Theory of Minor Parties* (Martinus Nijhoff, 1974).

6. Best as can be determined, Baader-Meinhof members were reacting to their belief that the political system was dominated by ex-Nazis in cahoots with a conservative press. Japan had its equivalent, the Japanese Red Army, or Nihon Sekigun, a group of militant Communists responsible for the Lod Airport massacre in 1972.

7. See, e.g., Nicholas Crafts, "The Golden Age of Economic Growth in Western Europe, 1950–73," *Economic History Review* 48 (1995): 429–449. A recent treatment of the golden age that overlaps with my own is Marc Levinson, *An Extraordinary Time: The End of the Postwar Boom and the Return of the Ordinary Economy* (Basic Books, 2016).

8. Again, this is for the period from 1950 through 1973. Data on growth, here as elsewhere, are from the Groningen Growth Project, http://www.rug.nl/ggdc/historicaldevelopment.

9. For details, see Barry Eichengreen, *The European Economy Since 1945: Coordinated Capitalism and Beyond* (Princeton University Press, 2008).

10. Those pioneering developments in turn reflected the country's abundant natural resources (high-speed throughput methods of mass production being resource-using), large domestic market (those same methods requiring scale), and efficient transport system (to get inputs to the factory and outputs to the market). Alfred Chandler, *Scale and Scope: The Dynamics of Industrial Capitalism* (Belknap Press of Harvard University Press, 1990) is the classic statement.

11. Much of what is said about Europe in the remainder of this paragraph applies to Japan with equal force.

12. For details, with international comparisons, see William Form, *Blue-Collar Stratification: Autoworkers in Four Countries* (Princeton University Press, 1976).

13. This was the factor emphasized by the American economist and Marshall Plan strategist Charles Kindleberger in his account of the European growth miracle. See Charles Kindleberger, *Europe's Postwar Growth: The Role of Labor Supply* (Harvard University Press, 1967).

14. James Silberman and Charles Weiss, "Restructuring for Productivity," World Bank Industry and Energy Department Working Paper no. 64, 1992. A skeptical view is Jacqueline McGlade, "Americanization: Ideology or Process? The Case of the United States Technical Assistance and

Productivity Programme," in *Americanization and Its Limits: Reworking U.S. Technology and Management in Postwar Europe and Japan*, ed. Jonathan Zeitlin and Gary Herrigel (Oxford University Press, 2000), 53–75.

15. See Nick Tiratsoo and Jim Tomlinson, "Exporting the Gospel of Productivity: United States Technical Assistance and British Industry, 1945–1960," *Business History Review* 71 (1997): 41–81.

16. On educational attainment, see Claudia Goldin and Lawrence Katz, *The Race Between Education and Technology* (Belknap Press of Harvard University Press, 2008). The GI Bill also provided financial support to veterans pursuing a high school degree. For those who did not qualify for the GI Bill, public institutions financed by state governments competing for talent, and via that route for business investment, provided higher education at near zero tuition and opened their doors to the sons and daughters of immigrants as well as Brahmins.

17. Robert Gordon, *The Rise and Fall of American Growth: The U.S. Standard of Living Since the Civil War* (Princeton University Press, 2016), 544. As Gordon notes, the increase in educational attainment was relatively rapid in earlier decades as well, which could have contributed further to what followed.

18. There is no single set of criteria and therefore less than full agreement on business cycle dates. Here I employ, with adjustments, Economic Cycle Research Institute, "Business Cycle Peak and Trough Dates, 21 Countries, 1948–2015," 2016.

19. The contrast with the volatile 1920s and 1930s was even greater. Variability here is measured as the coefficient of variation of real GDP growth, aggregated by decade, for fifteen Western European countries.

20. The dean of U.S. business cycle analysts, Victor Zarnowitz, contrasted the "period of relatively high economic stability," 1948–1969, with "periods of relatively low economic stability," 1929–1948 and 1969–1980, and showed that the coefficient of variation of the rate of growth of real GDP was significantly lower in the former. See Victor Zarnowitz, "Business Cycles and Growth," in *Business Cycles: Theory, History, Indicators and Forecasting*, ed. Victor Zarnowitz (University of Chicago Press, 1992), 203–231.

21. This also enhanced the effectiveness of those limited countercyclical monetary and fiscal initiatives that central banks and governments undertook. Since the commitment to the par values of the Bretton Woods System meant that inflation could exceed U.S. levels only temporarily, measures to stimulate demand produced mainly higher spending, as intended, as opposed to higher wage demands, subduing any potential wage-price spiral.

22. This despite the fact that OPEC was created in 1960. Several Arab states declared an embargo on the United States, United Kingdom, and West

Germany in the belief that they provided Israel with air cover at the outset of the 1967 war, but the embargo was not effectively enforced, and the target countries continued to receive Arab oil.

23. GATT stands for the General Agreement on Tariffs and Trade. Similarly, exchange controls limiting access to foreign currency for purposes of purchasing merchandise imports were relaxed gradually, over more than a decade, under the Code of Liberalisation of the Organisation of European Economic Cooperation (subsequently the Organization for Economic Cooperation and Development, or OECD), the club of advanced, initially Western economies.

24. The contrast is detailed by David Autor, David Dorn, and Gordon Hanson, "The China Shock: Learning from Labor-Market Adjustment to Large Changes in Trade," *Annual Review of Economics* 8 (2016): 205–240, and discussed further in Chapter 8.

25. This follows the definition of banking and financial crises of Michael Bordo and Barry Eichengreen, "Crises Now and Then: What Lessons from the Last Era of Financial Globalization?," in *Monetary History, Exchange Rates and Financial Markets: Essays in Honour of Charles Goodhart*, ed. Paul Mizen (Edward Elgar, 2003), 2:52–91.

26. This is documented in Funke, Schularick, and Trebesch, "Going to Extremes."

27. The fall in the share of the top 1 percent of the income distribution around World War II is evident in all these places. After the war that share then stabilized at lower levels in Japan and some European countries, such as France, while continuing to fall in Germany, Sweden, Canada, and the United States. See Facundo Alvaredo, Anthony Atkinson, Thomas Piketty, and Emmanuel Saez, "The Top 1 Percent in International and Historical Perspective," *Journal of Economic Perspectives* 27 (2013): 3–20.

28. Gordon, *Rise and Fall*, 609.

29. Kenneth Scheve and David Stasavage, *Taxing the Rich: A History of Fiscal Fairness in the United States and Europe* (Princeton University Press, 2016). A similar argument pitched at a more general level is Walter Scheidel, *The Great Leveler: Violence and the History of Inequality from the Stone Age to the Twenty-First Century* (Princeton University Press, 2017).

30. This is as of the early 1960s. See Thomas Piketty and Emmanuel Saez, "How Progressive Is the U.S. Federal Tax System? A Historical and International Perspective," *Journal of Economic Perspectives* 21 (2007): 3–24, fig. 3. Rubolino and Waldenström reinforce the point, showing that more progressive tax systems in this period reduced even pre-tax income inequality, as if top earners had less incentive to stretch the income distribution. See Enrico Rubolino and Daniel Waldenström, "Tax Progressivity and Top Incomes: Evidence from Tax Reforms," CEPR Discussion Paper no. 11936, Centre for Economic Policy Research, London, March 2017.

31.   More generally, authors such as Titmuss and Wilenksy draw a causal connection between World War II and the subsequent growth of the welfare state. See Richard Titmuss, *Problems of Social Policy* (H.M. Stationery Office, 1950), and Harold Wilensky, *The Welfare State and Inequality* (University of California Press, 1975).

32.   These and other interpretations of the persistence of higher marginal rates on top incomes in the wake of World War II are analyzed in Juliana Londoño Vélez, "War and Progressive Income Taxation in the 20th Century," unpublished manuscript, University of California, Berkeley, September 2014.

33.   That is the story of the company in which the author's father was a partner.

34.   Moreover, these innovations only began to diffuse widely in the 1980s. Still later came the networked credit card reader, which approved use of a card in retail transactions without the need for human intervention or telephonic confirmation.

35.   As described by John Parsons, the father of numerical control, in Russ Olexa, "The Father of the Second Industrial Revolution," *Manufacturing Engineering* 127 (August 2001).

36.   See Marc Levinson, *The Box: How the Shipping Container Made the World Smaller and the World Economy Bigger* (Princeton University Press, 2006).

37.   An introduction to the issue is Lawrence Katz and Lawrence Summers, "Industry Rents: Evidence and Implications," *Brookings Papers on Economic Activity*, 1989, 209–275.

38.   Along with this came newfound strength in numbers: as a result of these same wartime trends, the unionized share of the nonagricultural labor force in the United States rose from 13 percent in 1935 to 33 percent in 1953. See Brantly Callaway and William Collins, "Unions, Workers and Wages at the Peak of the American Labor Movement," NBER Working Paper no. 23516, National Bureau of Economic Research, Cambridge, MA, June 2017.

39.   See Frank Levy and Peter Temin, "Inequality and Institutions in 20th Century America," Working Paper no. 07-18, Department of Economics, MIT, June 2007, and Samuel Bowles and Herbert Gintis, "The Crisis of Liberal Democratic Capitalism," *Politics and Society* 11 (1982): 51–93.

40.   It provided also for the appointment of an additional neutral member on whom both workers and the employer could agree. It is not a coincidence that the German law was passed immediately following threats of massive strikes against the coal and steel industry in 1950–1951. See Ewan McGaughey, "The Codetermination Bargains: The History of German Corporate and Labour Law," LSE Legal Studies Working Paper no. 10/2015, London School of Economics, March 2015.

41.   The last of these arrangements was abolished by the Nazis in 1934.

42.   That council had met from 1881 to 1884, when it was allowed to expire owing to parliamentary opposition to the existence of a rival power center.

43. See Gosta Edgren, Karl-Olof Faxen, and Clas-Erik Odhner, *Wage Formation and the Economy* (Allen & Unwin, 1973, orig. 1970 in Swedish).

44. The classic reference is Peter Katzenstein, *Small States in World Markets: Industrial Policy in Europe* (Cornell University Press, 1985). See also the same author's *Corporatism and Change: Austria, Switzerland, and the Politics of Industry* (Cornell University Press, 1984).

45. See the voting analysis in Douglas Schoen, *Enoch Powell and the Powellites* (Macmillan, 1977). For more on Powell's legacy, see Chapter 12.

46. This is true whether measured by the share of the population covered by unemployment, disability, health, and old-age insurance or by the share of national income devoted to those purposes. Flora and Heidenheimer construct an index of overall social insurance coverage. For European countries, their index rises by more than 50 percent between 1950 and 1975. Starting from lower initial levels, it rises even faster for Canada, but more slowly for the United States. See Peter Flora and Arnold Heidenheimer, *The Development of Welfare States in Europe and America* (Transaction, 1981).

47. Figures in this paragraph are from Christopher Pierson, *Beyond the Welfare State: The New Political Economy of Welfare*, 3rd ed. (Pennsylvania State University Press, 2007).

Chapter 8

1. These are annual figures. There was then something of an acceleration over the subsequent decade (discussed below), which is conventionally attributed to the boost from a new generation of information and communications technologies (the Internet, personal computers), after which productivity growth again fell back. Figures here are from Angus Maddison, *Monitoring the World Economy, 1820–1992* (OECD, 1995).

2. Ray Fair, "The Effect of Economic Events on Votes for President: 1980 Results," *Review of Economics and Statistics* 64 (1982): 322–325. There is no incompatibility between the two interpretations. As the political scientist Morris Fiorina described the 1980 election, "First, there was national frustration with the course of international affairs, especially with America's apparent helplessness in the face of terrorism. Second, there was deep dissatisfaction with the course of economic affairs." Morris Fiorina, "Elections and the Economy in the 1980s: Short- and Long-Term Effects," in *Politics and Economics in the Eighties*, ed. Alberto Alesina and Geoffrey Carliner (University of Chicago Press, 1991), 17–40. The quote is from 17.

3. Sidney Weintraub, "Carter's Hoover Syndrome," *New Leader*, March 24, 1980, 5–6.

4. See Charles Hulten, James Robertson, and Frank Wykoff, "Energy Obsolescence and the Productivity Slowdown," in *Technology and Capital Formation*, ed. Dale Jorgenson and Ralph Landau (MIT Press, 1989), 225–258.

5. See Assar Lindbeck, "The Recent Slowdown of Productivity Growth," *Economic Journal* 93 (1983): 13–34.

6. See Claudia Goldin and Lawrence Katz, *The Race Between Education and Technology* (Belknap Press of Harvard University Press, 2008).

7. The fact that overall educational attainment continued to rise after the onset of the productivity slowdown was true of the United States as well when one considers increases in the attainment of not just men but also women.

8. Not even the information and communications revolution has had comparable effects. This is the argument of Robert Gordon, *The Rise and Fall of American Growth: The U.S. Standard of Living Since the Civil War* (Princeton University Press, 2016).

9. Research and development spending as a share of GDP declined modestly in the advanced countries after 1973. See Elisa Arond and Martin Bell, "Trends in the Global Distribution of R&D Since the 1970s: Data, Their Interpretation and Limitations," Economic and Social Research Council, 2009, esp. fig. 2.

10. For a pre-financial-crisis discussion that anticipates subsequent analysis, see Edward Leamer, "Foreigners and Robots: Assistants of Some, Competitors of Others," in *Social Dimensions of U.S. Trade Policy*, ed. Alan Deardorff and Robert Stern (University of Michigan Press, 2000), 19–52.

11. The rise in inequality since the 1970s is most prominent in the English-speaking countries and Italy, less so in Germany and France. The United States looks worse if one considers all males, including those with zero earnings, better if one considers women as well as men (since female labor force participation and relative wages rose over the period). See Michael Greenstone and Adam Looney, "The Uncomfortable Truth About American Wages," *Economix* (blog), *New York Times*, October 22, 2012.

12. Germany is an exception—which points again to the role of the labor market institutions highlighted in Chapter 7. Clayton and Pontusson analyze the percentage change in the relative incomes of the top 10 and bottom 10 percent of the wage distribution in 1979 and 1995 (with small differences in dates for some countries), and show that inequality so measured increased everywhere except Germany and Belgium. See Richard Clayton and Jonas Pontusson, "Welfare-State Retrenchment Revisited: Entitlement Cuts, Public Sector Restructuring and Inegalitarian Trends in Advanced Capitalist Societies," *World Politics* 41 (1998): 67–98, tab. 1.

13. See the discussion in Chapter 3.

14. Henry Ford, *My Life and Work* (Doubleday, Page, 1922), 79. As Ford elaborated (110), "The length of time required to become proficient in the various occupations is about as follows: 43 per cent of all jobs require not over one day of training; 36 per cent require from one day to one week; 6

per cent require from one to two weeks, 14 per cent require from one
month to one year; one per cent require from one to six years."

15. The earnings gap then widened to 63 percent by 2013. Data are from Paul
Taylor, Kim Parker, Rich Morin, Rick Fry, Eileen Patten, and Anna
Brown, *The Rising Cost of Not Going to College* (Pew Research Center,
2014).

16. The situation differed, for example, because relatively high minimum
wages in European countries supported the relative earnings of
nongraduates. See Christian Dreger, Enrique López-Bazo, Raul Ramos
Vicente Royuela, and Jordi Suriñach, "Wage and Income Inequality in
the European Union," Directorate General for Internal Policies, European
Commission, January 2015.

17. Daron Acemoglu, "Changes in Unemployment and Wage Inequality: An
Alternative Theory and Some Evidence," *American Economic Review* 89
(1999): 1259–1278; Timothy Bresnahan, Erik Brynjolfsson, and Lorin
Hitt, "Information Technology, Workplace Organization, and the
Demand for Skilled Labor: Firm-Level Evidence," *Quarterly Journal of
Economics* 117 (2002): 339–376; Eve Caroli and John van Reenen, "Skill-
Biased Organizational Change? Evidence from a Panel of British and
French Establishments," *Quarterly Journal of Economics* 116 (2001):
1449–1492.

18. These observations can also be reconciled with the unskilled-labor-
favoring bias of technical change during the British Industrial Revolution,
when the release of labor from agriculture described in Chapter 3 freed
unskilled workers for employment in manufacturing, and in the United
States in the late nineteenth and early twentieth centuries, when the
country became the technological leader and was on the receiving end of
immigrants from Southern and Eastern Europe.

19. An IMF study using the share of information technology in the capital
stock as a measure of technology found a positive association with
inequality. See International Monetary Fund, "An Empirical Investigation
of Globalization and Inequality," *World Economic Outlook* (International
Monetary Fund, 2007), 31–65.

20. Nor can the skill bias of technical change adequately account for the
timing—why the growth of the return to college slowed in the 1990s,
limiting concerns about increasing inequality for a time, even though
computer adoption proceeded apace. See David Card and John DiNardo,
"Skill-Biased Technological Change and Rising Wage Inequality: Some
Problems and Puzzles," *Journal of Labor Economics* 20 (2002): 733–783.

21. David Autor, Frank Levy, and Richard Murnane, "The Skill Content of
Recent Technical Change: An Empirical Exploration," *Quarterly Journal
of Economics* 118 (2003): 1279–1333.

22. This is known as the Stolper-Samuelson theorem, after Wolfgang Stolper
and Paul Samuelson, "Protection and Real Wages," *Review of Economic
Studies* 9 (1941): 58–73.

23. See Elhanan Helpman, "Globalization and Wage Inequality," NBER Working Paper no. 22944, National Bureau of Economic Research, December 2016.

24. David Autor, David Dorn, and Gordon Hanson, "The China Shock: Learning from Labor-Market Adjustment to Large Changes in Trade," *Annual Review of Economics* 8 (2016): 205–240. Other work suggests that the firms in question responded by hiring more skilled labor and undertaking more R&D, engineering, and design. See Ildikó Magyari, "Firm Reorganization, Chinese Imports and US Manufacturing Employment," unpublished manuscript, Columbia University, January 2017. But this didn't help the unskilled workers displaced by foreign competition. A study of the impact of NAFTA on blue-collar workers reaches similar conclusions: Shushanik Hakobyan and John McLaren, "Looking for the Local Labor Market Effects of NAFTA," *Review of Economics and Statistics* 98 (2016): 728–741. And what was true of the United States was broadly true of the other advanced economies, with a few exceptions. The prominent exception, once again, was Germany, where manufacturing was composed not of unskilled-labor-intensive products but of capital goods, the demand for which rose with globalization. Wolfgang Dauth, Sebastian Findeisen, and Jens Suedekum, "Trade and Manufacturing Jobs in Germany," *American Economic Association Papers and Proceedings* 107 (2017): 337–342. It is revealing that Germany did not share the general trend toward greater wage inequality, as noted above.

25. There was also trade in oil and related commodities, but this was of a different sort.

26. The computer and semiconductor sector is an exception, but this is scant comfort to less-skilled workers. See Susan Houseman, "Is American Manufacturing in Decline?," unpublished manuscript, Upjohn Institute, October 2016.

27. Or at least most immigrants have been less skilled up to now, it being possible that U.S. immigration policy could change, as discussed in Chapter 11. On the evidence, see Lawrence Mishel, Josh Bivens, Elise Gould, and Heidi Shierholz, *The State of Working America*, 12th ed. (Cornell University Press, 2012).

28. Gianmarco Ottaviano and Giovanni Peri, "Rethinking the Effects of Immigration on Wages," *Journal of the European Economic Association* 10 (2012): 152–197, and Council of Economic Advisors, "Immigration's Economic Impact," Washington, DC, June 20, 2007. Larger negative effects are reported by George Borjas, *Heaven's Door: Immigration Policy and the American Economy* (Princeton University Press, 1999), but even there immigration accounts for only a portion of the decline in the earnings of unskilled workers and of the rise in inequality.

29. Martin Ruhs and Carlos Vargas-Silva, "The Labor Market Effects of Immigration," Migration Observatory of the University of Oxford, May 22, 2016.

30. For more on the composition of U.K. immigration—and whether it could change with Brexit—see Chapter 10.

31. The same absence of a correlation at the regional level is true of Canada, Australia, and nine European countries considered by Frédéric Docquier and his coauthors. Frédéric Docquier, Caglar Ozden, and Giovanni Peri, "The Labour Market Effects of Immigration and Emigration in OECD Countries," *Economic Journal* 124 (2014): 1106–1145.

32. See also David Card, "The Effect of Unions on the Structure of Wages: A Longitudinal Analysis," *Econometrica* 64 (1996): 957–979.

33. Stephen Machin and John Van Reenen, "Changes in Wage Inequality," Special Paper no. 18, London School of Economics, April 2007; Bruce Western and Jake Rosenfeld, "Unions, Norms and the Rise in U.S. Wage Inequality," *American Sociological Review* 76 (2011): 513–537.

34. Service-sector workers employed by government are an exception; see Bernhard Ebbinghaus and Jelle Visser, "When Institutions Matter: Union Growth and Decline in Western Europe, 1950–1995," *European Sociological Review* 15 (1999): 135–158.

35. See Daron Acemoglu, Philippe Aghion, and Giovanni Violante, "Deunionization, Technical Change and Inequality," *Carnegie-Rochester Conference Series on Public Policy* 55 (2001): 229–264.

36. See John DiNardo, Nicole Fortin, and Thomas Lemieux, "Labor Market Institutions and the Distribution of Wages, 1973–1992: A Semiparametric Approach," *Econometrica* 64 (1996): 1001–1044, and David Lee, "Wage Inequality in the United States During the 1980s: Rising Dispersion or Falling Minimum Wage?," *Quarterly Journal of Economics* 114 (1999): 977–1023. David Autor, Alan Manning, and Christopher Smith, "The Contribution of the Minimum Wage to U.S. Wage Inequality over Three Decades: A Reassessment," *American Economic Journal: Applied Economics* 8 (2016): 58–99, find smaller effects without changing the basic conclusion.

37. The association between progressive taxation and lower inequality is evident also in the data. See OECD, "Income Inequality and Growth: The Role of Taxes and Transfers," OECD Economics Department Policy Note no. 9, January 2012.

38. On the role of slowing growth in welfare-state retrenchment, see Torben Iversen, "The Dynamics of Welfare State Expansion: Trade Openness, De-Industrialization, and Partisan Politics," in *The New Politics of the Welfare State*, ed. Paul Pierson (Oxford University Press, 2001), 45–79. The idea of welfare state overshooting is associated with Assar Lindbeck, "Overshooting, Reform and Retreat of the Welfare State," *De Economist* 142 (1994): 1–19.

39. There were exceptions to the general pattern, such as cuts in replacement rates in Canada and Japan and sick pay in Denmark. See Evelyne Huber and John Stephens, *Development and Crisis of the Welfare State* (University of Chicago Press, 2001).

40. "Sickness and Disability Schemes in the Netherlands," OECD, November 2007.

41. This is the logic used in Chapter 1 to explain the relatively low level of welfare-state spending in the United States. See also Roland Bénabou, "Human Capital, Technical Change, and the Welfare State," *Journal of the European Economic Association* 1 (2003): 522–532.

42. There is a positive correlation between unionization rates and welfare spending, across countries and over time, although in order to pick out that correlation it is important to control for other factors influencing welfare spending. See *The New Politics of the Welfare State*, ed. Paul Pierson (Oxford University Press, 2001), and Torsten Persson and Guido Tabellini, *Political Economics: Explaining Economic Policy* (MIT Press, 2002).

43. Pay-as-you-go pension systems are where contributions by the currently working are used to pay benefits to the retired.

44. This refers again to trends in the 1980s. Huber and Stephens, *Development and Crisis*, 209–210.

45. James Allen and Lyle Scruggs, "Political Partisanship and Welfare State Reform in Advanced Industrial Countries," *American Journal of Political Science* 48 (2004): 496–512. These authors construct replacement rates on a net basis (subtracting income taxes and the like), not on a gross basis as in Huber and Stephens, *Development and Crisis*. There are seventeen rather than eighteen countries in the case of sick pay because the United States has no national program.

46. This is argued by Paul Pierson, *Dismantling the Welfare State? Reagan, Thatcher, and the Politics of Retrenchment* (Cambridge University Press, 1994).

47. The phrase in quotes is from a speech by Federal Reserve governor Ben Bernanke, "The Great Moderation," Remarks at the Meetings of the Eastern Economic Association, February 20, 2004, https://www.federalreserve.gov/boarddocs/speeches/2004/20040220. Influential analyses documenting the decline in volatility were Chang-Jin Kim and Charles Nelson, "Has the US Economy Become More Stable? A Bayesian Approach Based on a Markov-Switching Model of the Business Cycle," *Review of Economics and Statistics* 81 (1999): 608–616, and James Stock and Mark Watson, "Has the Business Cycle Changed and Why?," *NBER Macroeconomics Annual* 17 (2003): 159–230.

48. See Karen Dynan, Douglas Elmendorf, and Daniel Sichel, "Can Financial Innovation Help to Explain the Reduced Volatility of Economic Activity?," *Journal of Monetary Economics* 53 (2006): 123–150.

Chapter 9

1. The quotes here are from "Donald J. Trump: Address on Immigration," August 31, 2016, https://www.donaldjtrump.com/press-releases/donald-j.-trump-address-on-immigration.

2. "New Television Ad: 'Donald Trump's Argument for America,'"
November 4, 2016, https://www.donaldjtrump.com/press-releases/new-
television-ad-donald-trumps-argument-for-america.

3. Jeremy Diamond, "'Common Sense,' Trump's Campaign Strategy from
the Get-Go," *CNN Politics*, November 18, 2016.

4. This is the argument of Robert Baldwin, "The Changing Nature of U.S.
Trade Policy Since World War II," in *The Structure and Evolution of Recent
U.S. Trade Policy*, ed. Robert Baldwin and Anne Krueger (University of
Chicago Press, 1984), 5–30.

5. The bank's first president, the less than exemplary William Jones, a
speculator in bank stock himself, had encouraged state banks to
oversupply currency and credit. Jones was succeeded by Langdon Cheves,
former U.S. representative from South Carolina and onetime opponent
of the Bank. On replacing Jones, Cheves called in the Bank's loans and
drastically tightened credit, triggering the Panic of 1819. See Robert
Remini, *Andrew Jackson and the Bank War* (W. W. Norton, 1967) and
Paul Kahan, *The Bank War: Andrew Jackson, Nicholas Biddle, and the Fight
for American Finance* (Westholme, 2015).

6. This episode was discussed at more length in Chapter 2.

7. Yian Mui, "Donald Trump Says Federal Reserve Chair Janet Yellen
'Should Be Ashamed of Herself,'" *Washington Post*, September 12, 2016.
Or as Trump put it in July 2017, "I do like low interest rates. I mean, you
know, I'm not making that a big secret. I think low interest rates are
good." Josh Dawsey and Hadas Gold, "Full Transcript: Trump's *Wall
Street Journal* Interview," *Politico*, August 1, 2017.

8. Trump, "Address on Immigration."

9. Robert Kaufman and Barbara Stallings, "The Political Economy of Latin
American Populism," in *The Macroeconomics of Populism in Latin America*,
ed. Rudiger Dornbusch and Sebastian Edwards (University of Chicago
Press, 1991), 15–43.

10. "Trump: Address on Immigration."

11. See Danielle Kurtzleben, "Rural Voters Played a Big Part in Helping
Trump Defeat Clinton," *National Public Radio*, November 14, 2016.

12. On college education and mobility, see John Bound and Harry Holzer,
"Demand Shifts, Population Adjustments, and Labor Market Outcomes
During the 1980s," *Journal of Labor Economics* 18 (2000): 20–54.

13. Thus, authors such as Katherine Cramer and J. D. Vance spoke of "rural
consciousness" and "rural resentment" of being left behind economically
and socially in explaining these voting patterns. See Katherine Cramer,
*The Politics of Resentment: Rural Consciousness in Wisconsin and the Rise of
Scott Walker* (University of Chicago Press, 2016), and J. D. Vance,
Hillbilly Elegy: A Memoir of a Family and Culture in Crisis (Harper, 2016).

14. See David Autor, David Dorn, Gordon Hanson, and Kaveh Majlesi, "A
Note on the Effect of Rising Trade Exposure on the 2016 Presidential

Election," unpublished manuscript, Massachusetts Institute of
Technology, March 2017.

15. See Arthur Miller, "'Will It Play in Peoria?' Public Opinion in Regional
and National Politics," in *The American Midwest: An Interpretative
Encyclopedia*, ed. Andrew Cayton, Richard Sisson, and Christian Zacher
(Indiana University Press, 2007), 1707–1709. Other statements in this
paragraph are based on this same source.

16. These calculations are based on U.S. Energy Information Administration,
Annual Energy Review (EIA, 2012), tab. 7.7.

17. Strikingly, the areas in question were not disproportionately in the
Midwest, where the swing from Romney to Trump was greatest. David
Autor and his coauthors rank metropolitan regions by the intensity of
Chinese competition in 2000–2007. Only two of their top ten metro
regions, Chicago and Milwaukee, are in the Midwest, and neither was
exactly a bastion of support for Trump. The remaining top ten
metropolitan areas (or more precisely commuter zones) on their list, with
the sole exception of Dallas, are all on the Atlantic and Pacific Coasts.
The authors consider the forty largest commuter zones for purposes of
this enumeration. David Autor, David Dorn, and Gordon Hanson, "The
China Syndrome: Local Labor Market Effects of Import Competition in
the United States," *American Economic Review* 103 (2013): 2121–2168.

18. Patrick Kline and Enrico Moretti, "Local Economic Development,
Agglomeration Economies, and the Big Push: 100 Years of Evidence from
the Tennessee Valley Authority," *Quarterly Journal of Economics* 129 (2013):
275–331. A review of the evidence more generally is David Neumark and
Helen Simpson, "Place-Based Policies," in *Handbook of Regional and
Urban Economics*, ed. Gilles Duranton, Vernon Henderson, and William
Strange (Elsevier, 2015), 5:1197–1287. These studies also find that
proximity to a college or university helps regional adjustment and
growth, although transplanting a vibrant institution of higher learning to
a depressed community is easier said than done.

19. See, for example, Dean Baker, "The Necessity of a Lower Dollar and the
Route There," Center for Economic and Policy Research, February 2012,
tab. 2, on attempts to estimate how manufacturing employment would
be affected by a weaker dollar.

20. On the role of unions, see Cihan Bilginsoy, "The Hazards of Training:
Attrition and Retention in Construction Industry Apprenticeship
Programs," *Industrial and Labor Relations Review* 57 (2003): 54–67. In the
United States one can see hints of this in construction, where unions are
relatively strong and help to diffuse new techniques, but not elsewhere.
See Susan Helper, "Supply Chains and Equitable Growth," Washington
Center for Equitable Growth, October 31, 2016.

21. Peter Navarro, Trump's trade policy advisor, controversially argued
otherwise in early 2017. See Shawn Donnan, "Trump's Top Trade

Adviser Accuses Germany of Currency Exploitation," *Financial Times*, January 31, 2017.

22. For discussion, see David Deming, "The Growing Importance of Social Skills in the Labor Market," *Quarterly Journal of Economics* 132 (2017): 1593–1640. A source of evidence is Per-Anders Edin, Peter Fredriksson, Martin Nybom, and Björn Öckert, "The Rising Return to Non-Cognitive Skill," IZA Discussion Paper no. 10914, Institute of Labor Economics, Bonn, July 2017.

23. Knightscope website, http://knightscope.com' (accessed on January 31, 2017).

24. See Sandra Mathers, Naomi Eisenstadt, Kathy Sylva, Elena Soukakou, and Katharina Ereky-Stevens, "Sound Foundations: A Review of the Research Evidence on the Quality of Early Childhood Education and Care for Children Under Three: Implications for Policy and Practice," University of Oxford and Suttton Trust, 2014.

Chapter 10

1. The image appeared, unfortunately for Farage, on the same day that Jo Cox, member of Parliament for Batley and Spen, was fatally shot and stabbed by a fifty-two-year-old mentally disturbed constituent who reportedly shouted, "This is for Britain—Britain will always come first." The Dusseldorf bomb plot refers to a foiled attempt by ten conspirators traveling from Syria to carry out suicide bombings and shootings in Germany in 2016.

2. Farage is quoted in Heather Stewart and Rowena Mason, "Nigel Farage's Anti-Migrant Poster Reported to Police," *Guardian*, June 16, 2016.

3. The advertisement can be seen at http://static1.businessinsider.com/image /575eb4e3dd0895ea098b463d-1200/leave.eu.jpg (accessed February 6, 2017).

4. These rules were a reform, or a "democratization," of traditional Conservative Party procedures where the leader was elected by MPs. Labour Party procedures had traditionally been broadly similar, assigning voting power in the Electoral College to MPs, the constituency Labour Parties, and the trade unions, but were reformed in 2014 to reduce the agenda-setting power of such groups by moving to a one-member-one-vote primary system open to all registered party supporters and affiliated members, lowering the barrier to renegade candidates. See Agnès Alexandre-Collier and Emmanuelle Avril, "The Use of Primaries in the UK Conservative and Labour Parties: Formal Rules and Ideological Changes," Université Sorbonne Nouvelle Paris 3 and Université de Bourgogne, April 2017.

5. The long-term legacy of 1930s protectionism in suppressing competition is described in Chapter 6. Evidence that EU membership, by freeing up trade, intensified competition and stimulated organizational and

technological upgrading is in Nicholas Crafts, "British Relative Economic Decline Revisited: The Role of Competition," *Explorations in Economic History* 49 (2012): 17–29, and Crafts, "The Impact of EU Membership on UK Economic Performance," *Political Quarterly* 87 (2016): 262–268.

6. An assessment of Thatcher's contribution is Roger Middleton, "'There Is No Alternative,' or Was There? Benchmarking the Thatcher Years," School of Humanities, University of Bristol, March 2008.

7. The extent of the improvement shouldn't be overstated. In part, Britain became leader of the pack because growth in the other three big European economies decelerated. Still, that it decelerated by less in Britain suggests that EU membership and Thatcher-era reforms had positive effects. See Nauro Campos, Fabrizio Coricelli, and Luigi Moretti, "Economic Growth and Political Integration: Estimating the Benefits from Membership in the European Union Using the Synthetic Counterfactuals Method," CEPR Discussion Paper no. 9968, Centre for Economic Policy Research, May 2014.

8. Among Thatcher-era legislation affecting the unions were a 1982 act exposing them to legal liability and subjecting their funds to fines for contempt and sequestration, a 1984 act exposing unions to civil action if they failed to hold a ballot before undertaking industrial action, and a second 1984 act tightening the conditions under which unions could establish a political fund. See Sandra Fredman, "The New Rights: Labour Law and Ideology in the Thatcher Years," *Oxford Journal of Legal Studies* 12 (1992): 22–44.

9. The problem with Thatcher-era sales of council housing was that purchasers, disproportionately households whose heads enjoyed stable employment, received substantial discounts, leaving local councils less rental income and fewer resources with which to provide housing and other services to poor tenants. See Andy Beckett, *Promised You a Miracle: Why 1980–82 Made Modern Britain* (Penguin, 2015).

10. This stability from the early 1990s to the financial crisis is evident in both the Gini coefficient and the relative incomes of the 90th and 10th percentiles of the income distribution. Both measures then fell after the crisis, reflecting lower asset returns for high earners. Juxtaposed against this was some increase in inequality at the top, with the top 1 percent of earners receiving a higher share of all income between the early 1990s and the crisis. See Anthony Atkinson, *Inequality: What Can Be Done?* (Harvard University Press, 2015).

11. Dirk Pilat, Agnès Cimper, Karsten Bjerring Olsen, and Colin Webb, "The Changing Nature of Manufacturing in OECD Countries," OECD Science, Technology and Industry Working Paper 2006/09, provide the accounting.

12. This was as of 2013.

13. "A Divided Britain? Inequality Within and Between the Regions," Regional Inequality Briefing Note, Equality Trust, London, n.d.

14. Philip Bunn and May Rostom, "Household Debt and Spending," *Bank of England Quarterly Bulletin* 54 (2015): 304–315.

15. "How the United Kingdom Voted on Thursday...and Why," Lord Ashcroft Polls, June 24, 2016.

16. Only about a third of voters, according to the poll, expressed aversion to multiculturalism and social liberalism. Ibid.

17. Similar conclusions flow from the survey reported in Miranda Phillips, Eleanor Attar Taylor, and Ian Simpson, "Britain Wants Less Nanny State, More Attentive Parent," *British Social Attitudes* 34 (August 2017).

18. Jil Matheson and Carol Summerfield, eds., *Social Trends* 31 (UK Government, 2001), 36–37.

19. The strategy, known as the "Third Way," was that Labour should govern from the center, rather than positioning itself on the left or ceding the right, as the best way of successfully implementing its reformist agenda. It owed much to Anthony Giddens, *The Third Way: The Renewal of Social Democracy* (Polity Press, 1998).

20. Erica Consterdine, "Managed Migration Under Labour: Organised Public, Party Ideology and Policy Change," *Journal of Ethnic and Migration Studies* 41 (2015): 1433–1452.

21. Christian Dustmann, Maria Casanova, Michael Fertig, Ian Preston, and Christoph Schmidt, "The Impact of EU Enlargement on Migration Flows," Report Commissioned by the Immigration and Nationality Directorate of the UK Home Office, 2001.

22. David Cameron, "A Contract Between the Conservative Party and You," April 30, 2010, https://www.facebook.com/conservatives/posts/118872268131511.

23. See Martin Ruhs and Carlos Vargas-Silva, "The Labor Market Effects of Immigration," Migration Observatory of the University of Oxford, May 22, 2016, and the discussion in Chapter 8.

24. The statement applies to English and Welsh regions, Scotland and Northern Ireland being special cases.

25. Matthew Goodwin, *Right Response: Understanding and Countering Populist Extremism in Europe: A Chatham House Report* (Chatham House, 2011).

26. Ibid., 9.

27. Jens Rydgren, "Immigration Sceptics, Xenophobes or Racists? Radical Right-Wing Voting in Six West European Countries," *European Journal of Political Research* 47 (2008): 737–765. See also Elisabeth Ivarsflaten, "What Unites Right-Wing Populists in Western Europe? Re-Examining Grievance Mobilization Models in Seven Successful Cases," *Comparative Political Studies* 41 (2008): 3–23.

28. This refers to these countries' most recent elections as of 2016. Data on inequality, as measured by the Gini coefficient, are for 2013 from the OECD.

29. This hostility toward Muslims is surpassed only by hostility toward Roma. Comparisons in this paragraph are based on European Social Survey, "Attitudes Towards Immigration and Their Antecedents," *ESS Topline Results Series* 7 (November 2016), figs. 2–4.

30. See W. R. Böhning, "Estimating the Propensity of Guestworkers to Leave," *Monthly Labor Review* 104 (1981): 37–40. On the *Rotationprinzip*, see Amelie Constant and Douglas Massey, "Return Migration by German Guestworkers: Neoclassical Versus New Economic Theories," *International Migration* 40 (2002): 5–38.

31. See Werner Smolny and Alexander Rieber, "Labor Market Integration of Immigrants—Evidence for German Guest Workers," Beiträge zur Jahrestagung des Vereins für Socialpolitik 2016: Demographischer Wandel, no. D22 C1, May 2016.

32. Panos Tsakloglou and Ioannis Cholezas, "The Economic Impact of Immigration in Greece: Taking Stock of the Existing Evidence," IZA Discussion Paper no. 3754, Institute for the Study of Labor, Bonn, October 2008.

33. See Gregory Wegner, "The Legacy of Nazism and the History Curriculum in the East German Secondary Schools," *History Teacher* 25 (1992): 471–487.

34. This is as of the summer of 2015, according to a poll conducted by the Institute for New Social Answers for Focus Online: http://www.focus.de/politik/deutschland/umfrage-fuer-focus-online-zeigt-fluechtlingspolitik-merkel-hat-die-mehrheit-der-deutschen-gegen-sich_id_4966591.html.

35. Difficult is not the same as impossible. Only members of the Schengen Area, which is not coterminous with the EU, allow border-control-free movements of people, and even the Schengen Agreement has emergency exemptions and escape clauses. The Single Market, in contrast, merely limits the ability of member states to restrict the movement of workers, not also their families and nonworking individuals.

36. Those penalties would be imposed by the European Court of Justice. An additional infringement procedure was launched in the summer of 2017 against the Czech, Hungarian, and Polish governments for failing to comply with the 2015 EU agreement on harboring refugees.

37. This was essentially the conclusion of the so-called five presidents (the presidents of the European Commission, European Council, Eurogroup, European Central Bank, and European Parliament). See Jean-Claude Juncker, in close cooperation with Donald Tusk, Jeroen Dijsselbloem, Mario Draghi, and Martin Schulz, *Completing Europe's Economic and Monetary Union* (European Commission, June 2015).

38. Nicolas Demorand, "Thomas Piketty: 'Fillon et Macron ont commis les même erreurs,' " *Franceinter*, February 12, 2017. These ideas are discussed and critiqued in Chapter 12.

39. An example of this third, hopeful (some would say unrealistically hopeful) approach is Henrik Enderlein et al., *Repair and Prepare: Growth and the Euro After Brexit* (Bertelsmann Foundation and Jacques Delors Institute, 2016). The origins of disagreement on how best to foster economic growth are the subject of Marcus Brunnermeier, Harold James, and Jean-Pierre Landau, *The Euro and the Battle of Ideas* (Princeton University Press, 2016).

Chapter 11

1. Timothy Bresnahan and Pai-Ling Yin, "Adoption of New Information and Communications Technologies in the Workplace Today," in *Innovation Policy and the Economy*, ed. Shane Greenstein, Josh Lerner, and Scott Stern (National Bureau of Economic Research, 2017), 95–124.

2. The case is made by Lee Branstetter and Daniel Sichel, "The Case for an American Productivity Revival," Policy Brief 17-26, Peterson Institute for International Economics, June 2017.

3. On capital's share, see Olivier Blanchard, "The Medium Run," *Brookings Papers on Economic Activity* 2 (1997): 89–158, and Michael Elsby, Bart Hobijn, and Ayşegül Şahin, "The Decline of the U.S. Labor Share," *Brookings Papers on Economic Activity* 2 (2013): 1–63. To the extent that the fall in labor's share is most dramatic in industries and sectors with rising levels of concentration, where so-called superstar firms dominate, another way of addressing the problem is by using competition policy more aggressively to limit their market share and power. See David Autor, David Dorn, Lawrence Katz, Christina Patterson, and John Van Reenen, "The Fall of the Labor Share and the Rise of Superstar Firms," NBER Working Paper no. 23396, National Bureau of Economic Research, May 2017.

4. See Anthony Atkinson, *Inequality: What Can Be Done?* (Harvard University Press, 2015).

5. Brigitte Madrian and Dennis Shea, "The Power of Suggestion: Inertia in 401(k) Participation and Savings Behavior," *Quarterly Journal of Economics* 116 (2001): 1149–1187. Here too we saw the United States moving in the opposite direction in 2017, when Congress overrode an Obama administration order authorizing states to impose opt-out requirements on public employees and other workers.

6. Dodd-Frank's Section 951 included a so-called say-on-pay provision. In 2011 the Securities and Exchange Commission then amended its corporate disclosure rules to mandate such advisory votes at least once every three years.

7. Oliver Denk, "Financial Sector Pay and Labour Income Inequality: Evidence from Europe," OECD Economics Department Working Paper no. 1225, June 2015.

8. Michael Carr and Emily Wiemers, "The Decline in Lifetime Earnings Mobility in the U.S.: Evidence from Survey-Linked Administrative Data," Working Paper 2016-05, Washington Center for Equitable Growth, September 2016.

9. Technically, this is for those in the 50th to 90th percentiles. Persistence is even higher at the very top. These estimates are from Pablo Mitnik and David Grusky, "Economic Mobility in the United States," Pew Charitable Trusts, July 2015.

10. Raj Chetty, Nathaniel Hendren, Patrick Kline, and Emmanuel Saez, "Where Is the Land of Opportunity? The Geography of Intergenerational Mobility in the United States," *Quarterly Journal of Economics* 129 (2014): 1553–1623. See also Raj Chetty and Nathaniel Hendren, "The Impacts of Neighborhoods on Intergenerational Mobility," unpublished manuscript, Harvard University, May 2015. On public policy impacts and responses, see Jonathan Rothwell and Douglas Massey, "Density Zoning and Class Segregation in U.S. Metropolitan Areas," *Social Science Quarterly* 91 (2010): 1123–1143.

11. And the same argument can now be made with respect to the advent of distance learning.

12. Raj Chetty, John Friedman, Emmanuel Saez, Nicholas Turner, and Danny Yagan, "Mobility Report Cards: The Role of Colleges in Intergenerational Mobility," NBER Working Paper no. 23618, National Bureau of Economic Research, July 2017.

13. High-income parents, it should be acknowledged, have other ways of giving their kids a leg up on the admissions process. Still more ambitious proposals taking this observation into account require top institutions to admit qualified applicants by lottery, neutralizing the ability of wealthier families to give their children curricular and extracurricular advantages.

14. Here the authors' measure of earnings mobility is bottom quintile to top quintile, not to top 1 percent.

15. The other key elements of the Affordable Health Care Act of 2010, along with the subsidies, were taxes on so-called Cadillac policies to provide funding, an individual mandate to obtain insurance, and state-run insurance exchanges.

16. The RTAA empowered the president to negotiate bilateral tariff reductions with foreign (mainly Latin American) countries. On its significance, see Kenneth Dam, "Cordell Hull, the Reciprocal Trade Agreements Act, and the WTO," unpublished manuscript, Brookings Institution, 2004.

17. See C. Michael Aho and Thomas Bayard, "Costs and Benefits of Trade Adjustment Assistance," in *The Structure and Evolution of Recent U.S.*

Trade Policy, ed. Robert Baldwin and Anne Krueger (University of Chicago Press, 1984), 153–194.

18. In addition, there would have been an allowance of 625 francs per child.

19. In the United States the idea has gained the support of conservative politicians who see it as a way of block-granting and ultimately replacing other government programs for the poor.

20. If robots were taking over a growing share of jobs where labor productivity was low, then remaining workers would have increasingly high productivity. But productivity growth has been slowing, not accelerating. And if employers thought that robots were more attractive than humans, they would be ramping up their investment in information technology and high-tech capital equipment, where in fact these parts of the capital stock are now growing more slowly than before. Things may change in the future; in other words, this may be the calm before the productivity storm, as noted at the beginning of this chapter. Or not, to repeat what is said there.

21. Target groups include disabled and unemployed veterans, members of needy families that have been on public assistance, certain food stamp recipients, and the long-term unemployed. The Work Opportunity Tax Credit has advantages relative to the Earned Income Tax Credit. Under the latter, workers pay taxes or receive a credit only once a year, whereas the Work Opportunity Tax Credit subsidizes employment continuously. In addition, with a wage subsidy workers effectively receive more total benefits when they work more hours, whereas with an income tax credit they receive less as they work more hours and family income rises. And unlike higher minimum wages, wage subsidies would not induce employers to shift toward more skilled workers. See Employment Policies Institute, *The Case for a Targeted Living Wage Subsidy* (EPI, 2001), and Edmund Phelps, "Low-Wage Employment Subsidies Versus the Welfare State," *American Economic Review Papers and Proceedings* 84 (1994): 54–58.

22. The idea was also raised by Mady Delvaux, a member of the European Parliament, in a draft report in May 2016, and by Benoît Hamon, the Socialist candidate in France's 2017 presidential election. In mid-2017 the South Korean government of Moon Jae-in proposed a modest step in this direction, reducing the tax deduction for enterprises that invest in automated equipment (while keeping the deduction for other forms of investment unchanged).

23. "Overall" is a reminder of those pesky but important distributional considerations. It is also a reminder that the difficulty of directly compensating the losers in practice—the problem to which I turn next—is why some people are prepared to contemplate indirect and costly alternatives such as taxing robots.

24. Durkheim developed these concepts of mechanical and organic solidarity in his doctoral dissertation, published as Emile Durkheim, *The Division of Labour in Society* (*De la division du travail social* [Félix Alcan, 1893]).

25. For evidence, see Eric Gould and Alexander Hijzen, "Growing Apart, Losing Trust? The Impact of Inequality on Social Capital," IMF Working Paper no.16/176, International Monetary Fund, August 2016.

26. These ideas are from Emmanuel Saez and Gabriel Zucman, "A Blueprint for a Californian Tax Reform," unpublished manuscript, University of California, Berkeley, March 2017.

27. Caitlin MacNeal, "Mulvaney: If Your State Doesn't Mandate Maternity Care, Change Your State," *Talking Points Memo*, March 24, 2017.

28. James Coleman, *Foundations of Social Theory* (Belknap Press of Harvard University Press, 1994).

29. Klaus Desmet, Joseph Gomes, and Ignacio Ortuño-Ortin, "The Geography of Linguistic Diversity and the Provision of Public Goods," CESifo Working Paper no. 6238, CESifo, Munich, January 2017.

30. There is more behind observed income differentials than simple selectivity (that is, more than the fact that unusually talented and motivated individuals migrate). See Michael Clemens, Claudio Montenegro, and Lant Pritchett, "The Place Premium: Wage Differences for Identical Workers Across the U.S. Border," Working Paper, Kennedy School of Government, Harvard University, 2009.

31. See, for example, Ethan Lewis and Giovanni Peri, "Immigration and the Economy of Cities and Regions," in *Handbook of Regional and Urban Economics*, ed. Gilles Duranton, Vernon Henderson, and William Strange (Elsevier, 2015), 5:625–685.

32. Christian Dustmann and Tommaso Frattini, "The Fiscal Effects of Immigration to the UK," *Economic Journal* 124 (2014): F593–F643; Organization for Economic Cooperation and Development, "The Fiscal Impact of Immigration in OECD Countries," *International Migration Outlook 2013* (OECD, 2013), 125–189.

33. There is also the fact that migration is less from the poorest countries, since poor people generally lack the resources to finance a move, so a bit of economic development can increase emigration. To be clear, the arguments in the text are not arguments against foreign aid, only arguments against viewing it as an alternative to immigration.

34. George Borjas, "Immigration and Globalization: A Review Essay," *Journal of Economic Literature* 53 (2015): 961–976.

35. Michael Clemens and Lant Pritchett, "The New Economic Case for Migration Restrictions: An Assessment," Working Paper no. 423, Center for Global Development, February 2016. The available evidence, from comparisons across U.S. states for example, generally suggests that the productivity of natives is higher where the share of immigrants is larger.

See Giovanni Peri, "The Effect of Immigration on Productivity: Evidence from U.S. States," *Review of Economics and Statistics* 94 (2012): 348–358.

36. Again, that is the implication of the balance of the evidence, like that cited in the previous note.

37. A recent assessment is Francine Blau and Christopher Mackie, eds., *The Economic and Fiscal Consequences of Immigration* (National Academies Press, 2017), which finds evidence of such effects for native-born high school dropouts in the United States but concludes that they are relatively small.

38. We saw this in Chapter 8.

39. The case is made by Eric Uslaner, "Does Diversity Drive Down Trust?," Nota di Lavoro No. 69.2006, Fondazione Eni Enrico Mattei, 2006.

40. Dani Rodrik, "Feasible Globalizations," in *Globalization: What's New?*, ed. Michael Weinstein (Columbia University Press, 2005), 196–213, and Javier Hidalgo, "An Argument for Guest Worker Programs," *Public Affairs Quarterly* 24 (2010): 21–38.

41. Relevant to this argument is the observation that the United Farm Workers union achieved significant advances only after the Bracero Program was abolished.

42. There is the possibility of an interstate compact under which states holding the majority (270) of electoral votes agree to cast them for the candidate winning the national popular vote. But smaller states disproportionately represented in the Electoral College would not be inclined to agree. There is also the question of whether this compact would violate the Constitution provision that "no state shall, without the consent of Congress, enter into any agreement or compact with another state."

43. Following the first round of the 2017 French presidential election, the *Economist* noted that had the same votes been cast under an American-style electoral college system, where France's eighteen regions were treated as states, Le Pen's heavily rural vote could have carried her to victory. "How Marine Could Have Trumped," *Economist*, April 29, 2017.

Chapter 12

1. See Ian Hurd, "Legitimacy and Authority in International Politics," *International Organization* 53 (1999): 379–408, and for the European context Fritz Scharpf, "Economic Integration, Democracy and the Welfare State," *Journal of European Public Policy* 4 (1997): 18–36.

2. Government of Hungary, "Prime Minister Viktor Orbán's State of the Nation Address," Budapest, February 10, 2017.

3. Hellenic Republic, "Prime Minister Alexis Tsipras's Speech to the Economist's Annual Financial Event in Athens," May 16, 2015.

4. ECB president Mario Draghi made occasional appearances before the parliaments of large euro-area members, but also stated that he was "not normally" accountable to national parliaments.

5. European Commission, Directorate-General for Communication, "European Citizenship," *Standard Eurobarometer* 83 (Spring 2015).

6. Dijsselbloem's remarks were especially charged because he was head of the Eurogroup, the group of finance ministers of countries that have adopted the euro. Maria Tadeo and Corina Ruhe, "'Women and Drink' Remark Prompts Call for Eurogroup Head to Quit," *Bloomberg*, March 22, 2017.

7. Again, this is documented by Eurobarometer surveys, where respondents are asked, "What does the EU mean to you personally?" The choices include "peace," "stronger say in the world," and "economic prosperity," and they more frequently respond with the first and second answers than the third.

8. See Maria-Grazia Attinasi, Magdalena Lalik, and Igor Vetlov, "Fiscal Spillovers in the Euro Area: A Model-Based Analysis," European Central Bank Working Paper no. 2040, March 2017.

9. These connections are highlighted by Tamim Bayoumi, *Unfinished Business: The Unexplored Causes of the Financial Crisis and the Lessons Yet to Be Learned* (Yale University Press, 2017).

10. Compounding the problem, government bonds were also exempt from concentration rules that limit the share of a bank's asset portfolio that can be invested in a single asset class.

11. Consistent with this observation, the most detailed proposal for how to disconnect the banks from the sovereign debt market (by imposing exposure limits and loss-absorption requirements) comes from the German Council of Economic Advisors, *Annual Report 2015/16: Focus on Future Viability*, 2015.

12. This is Article 125 of the Treaty on the Functioning of the European Union, as amended in Lisbon in 2009, which states that "the Union shall not be liable for the commitments of central governments, regional, local or other pubic authorities, other bodies governed by public law, or public undertakings of any Member State."

13. Quotes here are translations from the Hungarian, courtesy of Sean Lambert, "Notable Quotes: Prime Minister Viktor Orbán," *The Orange Files*, https://theorangefiles.hu/notable-quotes-prime-minister-viktor-orban-by-subject.

14. In addition, there was no change to the Dublin system and only limited help for front-line states.

15. As described in Karl Lamers and Wolfgang Schäuble, "More Integration Is Still the Right Goal for Europe," *Financial Times*, August 31, 2014.

16. For the Google Ngram graph, see https://books.google.com/ngrams/graph?content=flexible+integration&year_start=1970&year_end=2008&corpus=15&smoothing=0&share=&direct_url=t1%3B%2Cflexible%20integration%3B%2Cc0. There was then a secondary peak in references to the term in 2006, around the time eight Eastern Europe and Baltic countries were admitted to the EU.

17. This is known for self-evident reasons as the "consultation procedure." There is also a "co-decision" or "ordinary" procedure under which the Parliament must approve the legislative initiatives of the Commission, but it applies only in certain areas.

18. At present the European Parliament has only the nuclear option of forcing the Commission as a whole to resign by adopting a motion of censure.

19. Stéphanie Hennette, Thomas Piketty, Guillaume Sacriste, and Antoine Vauchez, *Pour un traité de démocratization de l'Europe* (Seuil, 2017). Emmanuel Macron proposed something similar in his 2017 French presidential campaign.

20. See note 7 and the surrounding discussion.

21. An official fiftieth-anniversary history of the European Parliament acknowledged these shortcomings with unusual candor. "A second more serious problem derived from the amount of time that MEPs could spend on EP activities, given that their overriding commitment was to voters in their own country. In this regard, the objections raised had more to do with the merits than the principle. How could the legitimacy of an institution depend on the presence of members—regardless of the level of representativeness of their respective electorates—when at times their commitment was limited or even non-existent? Without direct elections, the Parliament was seen as distant even by those European citizens who knew of its existence, while others were utterly oblivious of it. Some were not even aware that their national MPs held this second office." Yves Mény et al., *Building Parliament: 50 Years of European Parliamentary History 1958–2008* (European Communities, 2009), 36.

22. There is also the problem that, by the standards of national parliaments, representation in the European Parliament is more uneven—voting-age population per representative varies more, since small countries such as Malta, Cyprus, and Luxembourg are vastly overrepresented. Enhancing the legitimacy of the European Parliament would therefore require some rebalancing across countries to reduce this inequality, although the experience of national parliaments does not suggest that it is necessary to go all the way to equalizing population per representative. Some observers recommend a lower chamber where states are strictly represented according to population and an upper chamber in which smaller states are overrepresented (as in the United States). But this would add an additional layer of complexity and institutional duplication, where less complexity rather than more is required.

23. The president must then put forth his team of commissioners, who are voted up or down as a group.

24. Related objections are that no candidate would command a majority, while a minority president would lack legitimacy, and that popular election could provide an opening for an anti-EU populist renegade. This

points to the need for a French-style election, where only the two leading candidates proceed to the second round, or for some other suitable electoral arrangement.

Chapter 13

1. On assuming the presidency, Trump appointed a secretary of state and director of central intelligence who similarly acknowledged the impact of Rand's writings on their world views. James Stewart, "As a Guru, Ayn Rand May Have Limits. Ask Travis Kalanick," *New York Times*, July 13, 2017. The last quote in this paragraph, from Rand's 1964 *Playboy* interview, is also taken from Stewart.

2. Ayn Rand, "What Is Capitalism?," in Ayn Rand with Nathaniel Branden, Alan Greenspan, and Robert Hessen, *Capitalism: The Unknown Ideal* (New American Library, 1966), 18.

3. William Julius Wilson, *When Work Disappears: The World of the New Urban Poor* (Knopf, 1996), 193. Elsewhere (159) Wilson describes how the American predilection for individualism extends to individualistic as opposed to structural explanations for poverty and unemployment, further undercutting public support for social programs.

4. This definition is taken from Julia Bläsius, Tobias Gombert, Christian Krell, and Martin Timpe, *Foundations of Social Democracy* (Friedrich Ebert Stiftung, 2009). All such definitions are contested, of course; see the introduction to Michael Keating and David McCrone, eds., *The Crisis of Social Democracy in Europe* (Edinburgh University Press, 2013).

5. The German Christian Democratic Party descended from the Center Party, described in Chapter 4.

6. See Karsten Grabow, ed., *Christian Democracy: Principles and Policy-Making* (Konrad-Adenauer Stiftung, 2011).

7. This is documented by Dani Rodrik, "Why Do More Open Economies Have Bigger Governments?," *Journal of Political Economy* 106 (1998): 997–1032, and Alberto Alesina and Romain Wacziarg, "Openness, Country Size and the Government," *Journal of Public Economics* 69 (1998): 305–321.

8. See Sabina Avdagic, Martin Rhodes, and Jelle Visser, *Social Pacts in Europe: Emergence, Evolution and Institutionalization* (Oxford University Press, 2011), and Martin Rhodes, "The Political Economy of Social Pacts: 'Competitive Corporatism' and European Welfare Reform," in *New Politics of the Welfare State*, ed. Paul Pierson (Oxford University Press, 2001), 165–194. The need for cooperation in small open economies, with a focus on Europe, is the emphasis of Peter Katzenstein's classic analysis, *Small States in World Markets: Industrial Policy in Europe* (Cornell University Press, 1985).

9. Even the Polder Model, it can be argued, has material roots, having grown out of the historical need for communities to cooperate in

building the dikes that hold back the sea (a *polder* being a tract of reclaimed land).

10.   This difference is sometimes attributed to an early history of unionism, giving rise eventually to the Labour Party, and to the limited traction of revolutionary Marxism, in response to which social democratic parties developed in other European countries. Graham Johnson, "Social Democracy and Labour Politics in Britain, 1892–1911," *History* 85 (2002): 67–87.

11.   The categorization of political parties as populist follows Ronald Inglehart and Pippa Norris, "Trump, Brexit and the Rise of Populism: Economic Have-Nots and Cultural Backlash," Faculty Research Working Paper no. 16-026, Kennedy School of Government, Harvard University, August 2016. A full analysis is in Christian Dustmann, Barry Eichengreen, Sebastian Otten, André Sapir, Guido Tabellini, and Gylfi Zoega, *Europe's Trust Deficit: Sources and Remedies* (Centre for Economic Policy Research, 2017).

12.   Alasdair Sanford, "What Are Marine Le Pen's Policies?," *Euronews*, September 2, 2017, http://www.euronews.com/2017/02/09/what-do-we-know-about-marine-le-pen-s-policies.

13.   "Les 144 engagements présidentiels," Front National, 2017, http://www.frontnational.com/le-projet-de-marine-le-pen.

INDEX

235